LOOKING CLOSER
CRITICAL WRITINGS
ON GRAPHIC DESIGN

EDITED BY
Michael Bierut, William Drenttel,
Steven Heller & DK Holland

INTRODUCTION BY
Steven Heller

ASSOCIATE EDITORS
Elinor Pettit, Theodore Gachot

Allworth Press, New York
Copublished with the American Institute of Graphic Arts

Published by Allworth Press, an imprint of Allworth Communications, Inc.
10 East 23rd Street, New York, NY 10010.

Distributor to the trade in the United States and Canada:
Consortium Book Sales & Distribution, Inc.
1045 Westgate Drive, Saint Paul, MN 55114-0165.

Cover and book design by Michael Bierut, Pentagram Design.

Typography by Sharp Designs, Holt, MI.

ISBN: 1-880559-15-3

Library of Congress Catalog Card Number: 93-71922

The publishers are grateful for the sponsorship of both
ALDUS CORPORATION *and*
CHAMPION INTERNATIONAL CORPORATION

Aldus Corporation creates computer software solutions
that help people throughout the world effectively communicate
information and ideas.

Aldus Corporation has provided generous support for the production
of this book, which is typeset in PageMaker 5.0 software.

Champion International Corporation manufactures fine printing,
writing, and publication papers, and has been an
active supporter of graphic design for over sixty years.

Champion International Corporation donated the paper and cover stock
on which *Looking Closer* is printed.

CONTENTS

ACKNOWLEDGEMENTS

The editors of *Looking Closer* are indebted to Elinor Pettit, our chief researcher and loyal collaborator—without her this book would have been impossible to compile and produce. Thanks also to Ted Gachot, our editor, without whom this book would be an undisciplined mass of type; and to Esther Bridavsky for her design and production help. Last but certainly not least, our deepest gratitude goes to Tad Crawford; without his total commitment this project would never have happened.

The authors are grateful for the cooperation of the following editors and publishers: Rick Poynor, editor of *Eye* published by Wordsearch, London; Rudy VanderLans, editor and publisher of *Emigre;* Martin Fox, editor of *Print* magazine; Rob Dewey, publications director of The American Center for Design; Caroline Hightower, director of the American Institute of Graphic Arts; Chee Pearlman, editor of *I.D.* magazine; Patrick Coyne, editor and publisher of *Communication Arts* magazine.

INTRODUCTION
LOOKING CLOSER AT
DESIGN CRITICISM
by
Steven Heller

The assumption that little has been written about graphic design worth preserving and rereading is non- sense. The past ten years of graphic design publishing have been bountiful, not only for uncritical annuals, how-tos, and monographs, but for serious new analyses of design and designers. *Looking Closer* is the first, and one hopes not the last, anthology of such critical writing. This diverse collection of articles and essays demonstrates that contemporary design writing is not a patchwork of disparate ideas but a discipline with fundamental concerns that include ethics, social responsibility, linguistics, education, and style. Over 200 articles from a dozen publications were originally considered, and under 50 were selected for inclusion in this book. While the quality of writing differs, these essays reveal an intellectual rigor that has been absent in graphic design literature since the 1920s (when the Moderns issued manifestos attacking antiquated practices). Yet this generous sampling represents only the early stage of a newly formed discipline. Rough edges have not been smoothed out. Forums for critical writing are still developing, and the writers are attempting to find potent voices to discuss viable themes. In this sense *Looking Closer* is a status report on contemporary design as well as a keen look at contemporary design criticism.

Whoever said that "criticism is easy, art is difficult" echoed the lament of many artists bruised by judgmental reviewers who pontificate from the sidelines. Yet true criticism is endemic to any public endeavor where the quality of ideas and execution requires scrutiny. "Criticism is the chandeliers of art," wrote the critic George Jean Nathan, "it illuminates the enveloping darkness in which art might otherwise rest only vaguely discernible and perhaps altogether unseen." Graphic design is indeed vaguely discernible; seen but not understood, consumed but not appreciated as part of a larger social, commercial, and cultural context. At least that is the complaint of those practitioners who view themselves and their work as more culturally significant than the world (or their clients) give them credit for. This has prompted the clamor for a body of criticism that will help legitimize the graphic design profession—in the way it did for architecture and industrial design. In turn, some editors and writers have rejected the conventional celebratory "journalism" in the trade press for critical analysis.

Yet the critical response to criticism has been mixed. Some veteran designers, who for years have been sheltered from criticism, have referred to it as name-calling. Younger designers insist that they want a cold eye, but in fact prefer a warm hand. Celebrating success and ignoring failure has been the prevailing editorial policy of most graphic design magazines. Substituting intellectual rigor, no matter how positive the outcome, does not compensate for uncompromisingly flattering profiles used as design firm self-promotion. This ambivalence has forced most design magazines to continue to showcase good work as primary content, and since relatively few outlets are available, intelligent criticism is developing slowly. Although the quality of design writing has generally improved as journalism replaced cronyism, contemporary writers are grappling with the basic problem of how to develop a critical vocabulary; a few are adapting existing models, such as semiotics and French linguistic theory, others are following less academic forms.

This leads to the curious conclusion that there is both too much *and* too little graphic design criticism today: too much undisciplined rhetoric and too little rigorous analysis. Yet for a profession that until a decade ago had a dearth of critical discourse, save for the tacit disapproval that comes with rejection from annual competitions, it could also be argued that a little graphic design criticism is better than none. But the parameters of graphic design criticism have yet to be adequately defined. Is it academic or journalistic? Who is qualified to practice? What are the rules of the game? And what and who is fair game for critical investigation? Without answers to these questions graphic design criticism is merely an amateur sport.

Most writers of graphic design criticism are capable amateurs with little training in historical or critical analysis. Most are self-taught, and engage in critical writing as a sideline to their design or teaching practices. While practitioner/critics are vital to the discourse, graphic design also deserves qualified professional journalists like those who are paid to write about art, architecture, and industrial design, and who, by virtue of their "professional" status, are afforded credibility outside their fields. Although it might be argued that—like amateur verses professional athletics—salary, not competency, is the only real factor in distinguishing the amateur from the professional critic. But the ability to earn money is nonetheless key to the development of healthy criticism. A profession that cannot support even a few professional critics is in danger of noodling its own navel.

So where do we begin? Critical discourse in literature and art is initially played out in the academic arena, and often as an adjunct to graduate education. This process exposes students to the importance and acceptance of criticism outside of the academic environment as well. Yet with its emphasis on formalism, academic criticism is not generally a viable means of investigating the bulk of commercial graphic design. Unlike fine art, which is essentially about form (even intent, function, and context are viewed through a formal lens), graphic design must be analyzed, in addition to formal considerations, through a wide angle lens of commerce.

Thus, formal issues are but one part of the equation. Graphic design criticism also needs to address the problem of values: What does graphic design mean in terms of the evolution of culture and our ability to confront our environmental and sociological dilemmas? Compared to architecture criticism, which is naturally concerned with the function of a building in its environment and its relationship to people, there has not been a compelling need—particularly given the criteria of beauty pageant shows—to analyze graphic design in other than aesthetic (usually superficial) terms.

One of the stumbling blocks in developing acceptance for design criticism is that designers expect that design criticism should merely report on their role as problem solvers.

"The critic doesn't understand what went into my work," is a common complaint among designers who are placed in the spotlight and feel wronged by the misinformed critic, usually defined as one who either failed to understand the *intention* of a work or did not discuss it directly with its creator. While understanding the goal of the project and intention of the designer is sometimes useful, it is not essential to the development of an informed analysis. Criticism should not need any kind of validation from the person who produced the work. The job of the critic is not to report on what the person who made it thinks, but to explain what the work does.

The critic is an interpreter; sometimes an ally of the creator, other times a pariah. On one hand, a critic might try to get inside the mind of the creator. On the other, the critic attempts to take the position of the audience. Criticism moves between the two. When you only talk about the cultural meaning or function you lose *design*. Conversely, you can reduce the practice into something that's pure style and gesture by not talking about culture.

The client is another mitigating factor. Should the critic focus on problem solving and downplay cultural nuance? Or should graphic design criticism transcend the specific business issues to focus on more formal issues? In the related field of advertising, critics almost exclusively focus on function at the expense of form and aesthetics. While advertising is a melange of typography, imagery, and concept, the component parts are less important than how the problem was solved and its success or failure, particularly in terms of marketplace sales. Graphic design is harder to quantify in terms of results. A poster or brochure may stimulate awareness, and a direct mail campaign may generate sales, but these are softer, less powerful media than those employed by advertising. Still, the client does have needs and demands that govern how a graphic design project develops. Therefore, it is incumbent on the critic to somehow deal with these factors of commercial intent and effectiveness.

With such baggage, is graphic design criticism viable outside of our tiny business or academic worlds? In this early stage, even the best graphic design critics are not writing for a general audience. In the mainstream press, the few articles on graphic design are usually about quaint stylistic phenomena by general reporters who know little about the field.

Graphic design criticism will continue to be directed inward as long as its main audience is designers. But this does not mean that graphic design criticism is in a holding pattern. Indeed, the editors of *Looking Closer* were surprised to find as much good material in the trade and professional periodicals. Yet critical writings were often squirreled away in the back-of-the-book columns, as if to suggest that critical reading is hard work too. If accessible criticism is the goal, it must be brought into the main feature sections and accepted by practitioners and the public as a common approach to design analysis.

MODERNISM
AND ITS
MALCONTENTS

A NATURAL HISTORY
OF TYPOGRAPHY

by

J. Abbott Miller and Ellen Lupton

In the mid-nineteenth century, Charles Darwin broke with earlier approaches to natural history by asserting that there is no ordered progress governing the evolution of organisms. Instead, individuals with particular genetic traits survive and bear offspring, while their ill-equipped siblings tend to perish. Darwin's theory erased the comforting image of a rational, paternal law regulating the life and death of species; Darwin also upset the humanistic belief that "Man" is a finished biological entity with a tidy origin and a guaranteed future.

Is the history of typography a logical evolution toward perfect forms, or is it a string of responses to random catastrophes in the philosophy and technology of design? This essay charts a shift away from an understanding of printed letters as stable reflections of handwriting or an ideal classical past towards a view of typography as the endless manipulation of abstract relationships. A canon of ideally proportioned letterforms has yielded to a flexible genetic code capable of breeding an infinity of new species.[1]

Printed letters were invented in the fifteenth century by Johannes Gutenberg, who cast individual blocks out of lead, each bearing a raised letter. In Gutenberg's system, thousands of metal characters are stored in gridded wooden cases and assembled by hand into fields of text. The printer inks the raised surfaces of the letters and passes the type and paper through a press. After the job is printed, the metal letters are returned to their cases, ready to be composed into new texts.[2]

Almost unchanged, Gutenberg's system flourished for nearly four centuries. In 1884 the Linotype machine combined into one process the casting of letters out of metal and their composition into lines of text. The operator of the Linotype machine strikes a keyboard, which is connected to a matrix of molds; when the series of molds has fallen into sequence, the machine fills them with molten lead and assembles the lines of type into pages of text. After the job is printed, the lead is melted down into new letters. Subsequent technologies have further dematerialized the making of type, replacing hot metal with a photographic negative and then a digital signal. Today, a desktop computer can store a vast library of typefaces, each capable of being stretched, condensed, or slanted into new configurations.

In the epoch between Gutenberg's invention and the Linotype machine, the philosophy behind the design of printed letters evolved in response to smaller technological and cultural shifts. Whereas Gutenberg based his type on the characters found in handwritten manuscripts, some of his contemporaries turned back to Roman inscriptions as the classical ancestors of typography.[3] This essay looks at the disappearance of printed letters' sacred origins in handwriting and classical proportions, and examines the reconception of the alphabet as a system of infinitely changeable relationships between elements.

The Darwin of linguistics was Ferdinand de Saussure (1857-1913), who destroyed the ordinary assumption that language exists to represent ideas.[4] While language is commonly understood as a collection of names assigned to pre-existing concepts, Saussure argued that without language, there *are* no concepts. For Saussure, the most troublesome feature of the linguistic sign was its arbitrariness: there is no resemblance between a sound such as "horse" and the concept of "domesticated quadruped." No natural link binds the material, phonic aspect of the sign (the signifier) to the mental concept (the signified): only a social agreement appears to hold the two sides together.

While Darwin challenged the centrality of "Man" to the natural world, Saussure challenged the centrality of "ideas" to the realm of communication. According to Saussure, both thought and sound are shapeless masses before the acquisition of speech. Without language, the realm of potential human sounds is just a continuum of noises; the plane of concepts is equally unformed, consisting of a vague nebula of emotions and perceptions rather than distinct ideas. Language links these two layers together and cuts them up into discrete, repeatable segments, or *signs*. Thus "ideas" do not precede language, but emerge only when both of these formless slabs are sliced into distinct units.

If the connection between the signifier and signified, the sound and the concept, is arbitrary, what, then, binds the two together? If there is no iconic, natural relationship between the sound "horse" and the concept it invokes, why is the link between them so dependable, so persistent? To explain this link, Saussure introduced the principle of linguistic *value*. The identity of a sign rests not in the sign itself, but solely in its relation to other signs. The sound *horse* is recognizable only in opposition to other sounds used in the language: *horse* is distinct from *morse, force, bourse, house, hearse,* etc. Likewise the concept "horse" has identity only in opposition to other concepts, such as "cow," "antelope," and "pony." The "meaning" of a sign does not belong to the individual sign, but is generated by the surrounding system. The sign taken by itself is empty.

Saussure's theory of the linguistic sign infused many currents of twentieth century thought, including Claude Levi-Strauss's anthropology, Roland Barthes's social mythology, and Jacques Derrida's philosophy of writing. These writers have looked at human phenomena—from soap bubbles to the unconscious—in terms of systems of opposition, patterns or *structures* of difference that generate meaning.

THE CRYSTAL GOBLET

What sort of semiotic system is typography? What are its signifiers, and what are its signifieds? Typography is one aspect of the broader practice of writing, which Saussure described as a sign system separate from speech itself. He saw speech as the original, natural medium of language, while writing is an external system of signs (for example, the alphabet) whose sole purpose is to represent speech. Writing is thus a language depicting another language, a set of signs for representing signs. Typography, then, is removed one step further: it is a medium whose signified is not words themselves, but rather the *alphabet*. The critic Beatrice Warde claimed that a page of type should transparently reveal its verbal text like the gleaming bowl of a crystal goblet.[5] But is it possible for typography to ever passively contain a pre-existing, "content" or signified? Westerners revere the alphabet as the most rational and transparent of all writing systems, the clearest of vessels for containing the words of speech. Unlike ideograms or hieroglyphs, the alphabet depicts only the material surface of language, rather than its ideas. The alphabet is a mechanical device, a short string of characters capable of converting an infinity of spoken words into script.

This alphabetic goblet is, however, clouded with imperfections. Take for example, the word "horse" and the series of other English words whose sound it can be contrasted against: *morse, force, bourse, house, hose, hearse,* etc. If one were to examine the spoken, verbal sign in isolation from writing, one would find simple phonetic differences. But written English inconsistently employs the alphabet to represent these sounds: a single sound is variously written *-orse, -orce,* and *-ourse.*

The opacity and inconsistency of writing infuriated Saussure, who felt that the alphabet had violated the innocence of the original, oral word with a monstrous perversion; writing had diverted the natural evolution of speech and had contaminated its crystal purity. The philosopher Jacques Derrida has confronted a contradiction in Saussure's theory: while Saussure celebrated the fact that verbal signs do not transparently reflect ideas, he could not tolerate the same situation in writing.[6] Saussure was outraged by the alphabet's refusal to patiently reflect its spoken referent, yet he had discovered that in writing, as in language, the realm of the signifier generates meaning apart from a pre-existing signified. And the same is true for typography's relationship to the alphabet.

STRUCTURALIST TYPOGRAPHY

In what ways has typography responded to its alphabetic signified? While Gutenberg's fonts naturalistically simulate the variety and aura of handwriting, humanist designers at the turn of the sixteenth century distanced the letter from calligraphy by constructing Roman alphabets with the tools of geometry. The letterform was no longer thought of as a sequence of manual pen strokes, but as a conceptual ideal bound to no particular technology. This Platonic structure became typography's new signified. A committee established by Louis XIV in 1692 further ldealized the alphabet. Embracing the current passion for scientific method, the *Roman du Roi* imposed an orthogonal grid over the organic forms of traditional lettering. Italic forms were generated by shifting the grid; a procedure divorced from calligraphy and prophetic of the mechanical distortions enabled by nineteenth- and twentieth-century technologies. For the King's committee, the grid was an objective filter though which to glimpse the ideal alphabet, figured as clearly as the image cast on the gridded glass of a camera obscura.

Typographic historians commonly see the fonts of Bodoni and Didot as completing a logical development away from calligraphy; called "modern," these faces polarized letterforms into extremes of thick and thin and reduced serifs to wafer-thin slabs.[7] There is a difference, however, between the idealism of the "modern" faces and the idealism of the older rational letter designs. Renaissance theorists had hoped to discover absolute proportions legislating the alphabet; the *Roman du Roi* pursued a norm grounded in scientific and governmental legality. Bodoni and Didot signalled an idealization of a different sort: in place of a Platonic model or a bureaucratic standard, these fonts reconceived the alphabet as an arbitrary system of elements whose existence hinges on its material expression. In Saussure's terms, the *signifier* now took precedence over the *signified*. The fonts of Bodoni and Didot reduced the alphabet to a system of polar oppositions—thick and thin, vertical and horizontal, serif and stem. Typographic form was no longer compelled to refer to an ideal canon of proportions: instead, the alphabet was understood as a collection of linguistic elements open to manipulation. Modern typography replaced *idealism* with *relativism*. The notion of a direct ancestral bond between the typography of the present and a divine classical past was displaced by a model of the alphabet as a code of relationships that could yield an infinity of variations. The alphabet understood as a collection of individual organisms gave way to a genetic code that could spawn offspring of endless diversity. The alphabet had lost its center: operating in its place was a new mode of design which we call *structuralist* typography.

SIGNS OF NOVELTY

The break initiated by Didot and Bodoni helped trigger a population explosion in nineteenth-century commercial typography, spawning bizarre new specimens which rejected classical norms in favor of the incessant pursuit of novelty. Technology encouraged the proliferation of new fonts. The introduction of the combined pantograph and router in 1834 revolutionized wood-type manufacture. The pantograph is a tracing device which, when linked to a router for carving letters out of wood or metal, allows different sizes and styles of a font to be generated from a single parent drawing, eliminating the painstaking task of cutting individual punches by hand. This automated approach to type design led the historian Daniel Berkeley Updike to later denounce the pantograph for its tendency to "mechanize the design of types."

The programmatic shifts in scale enabled by the pantograph encouraged an understanding of the alphabet as a flexible system, susceptible to systematic variations divorced from a calligraphic origin. The swelling population in the nineteenth-century of typographic mutants—compressed, expanded, outline, inline, shadowed, extruded, faceted, floriated, perspective, bowed—signals a shift in the "signified" of typography. The notion of letterforms as essential, archetypal structures gave way to a recognition of letters as units within a larger system of formal features (weight, stress, cross-bars, serifs, angles, curves, ascenders, descenders, etc.). The relationships *between* letters within a font became more important than the identity of individual characters. The variety of nineteenth-century display faces suggested that the "alphabet" is a flexible system of differences, not a pedigreed line of fixed, self-contained symbols.[8]

The proliferation of typefaces available for use in books and advertising led the American Type Founders Company (ATF) to organize fonts into "type families" in the early twentieth century. Each family consists of variations of a single parent design—book, italic, bold, condensed, etc. This system—still in use today—aimed to encourage printers and their clients to use genetically related characters rather than combining fonts of mixed heritage. The use of type families, claimed the 1923 ATF catalogue, had "added dignity and distinction ... to commercial printing." It also reflected the structuralist view of a typeface as a set of genetic traits that could be mechanically translated across a series of siblings.

MODERNISM

Avant-garde designers produced fonts in the early twentieth century which tested the structural limits of the alphabet. Theo van Doesburg's 1919 font and Bart van der Leck's 1941 design for *Het Vlas* are typefaces built out of the principles of De Stijl painting. The stencil construction of Josef Alber's 1925 stencil typeface generates an alphabetic ensemble out of a restricted repertoire of elementary shapes. Similarly, Herbert Bayer's 1925 "universal," designed at the Bauhaus, relies upon interchangeable geometric parts to produce a self-consciously rational font. An even more radical reduction is Wladystav Strzeminski's 1931 font, which generates letterforms out of right angles and the arcs of a single circle.

The experimentation which we call "structuralist typography" was inaugurated by Bodoni and Didot and was continued by advertising display faces; in the twentieth century, Modernism invested this mode of formal manipulation with ideological significance. Structuralist typography rejects the ideal of an essential, core letterform. By shifting the emphasis from the individual letter to the overall series of characters, structuralist typography exchanges the fixed identity of the letter for the relational system of the font.

The format parameters of these avant-garde typefaces suppress the individuality of letters by forcing attention to the system—the discrete figures in Strzeminski's radically geometric font, for example, are indecipherable apart from the surrounding code. These fonts are a typographic analogue for structuralist philosophy and linguistics, which seeks to find, as Derrida has written, "a form or function organized according to an internal legality in which elements have meaning only in the solidarity of their correlation or opposition."[9]

The Modernism of De Stijl, Dada, Futurism, Constructivism, and the Bauhaus aimed to "defamiliarize" writing. Defamiliarization, as theorized by the Russian formalist critic Victor Shklovsky in the 1910s, held that the everyday world is invisible until we are forced to see it differently, and that art is a primary means for "making strange" the already-seen and already-known. Cinematic shock techniques, the "New Vision" of photography, and typographic experimentation were facets of the Modernist attack on the familiar.

NEO-MODERNISM

Designers today continue to invent typefaces which manipulate the formal system of the alphabet, and attempt to defamiliarize the experience of reading. Zuzana Licko's font Emperor, 1985, embraces the limits of coarse-resolution output. Jeffery Keedy's 1989 font Neo Theo is an homage to Modernism. The reduced template of angles which generates Max Kisman's 1988 Zwartvet is akin to the minimal geometric vocabulary used in Albers's 1925 stencil letters. The emphatic constructedness of Licko's 1988 Variex family shares the fascination with system and geometry found in Bayer's 1925 "universal."

These neo-avant-garde fonts do not, however, take the structuralist principle to the extremes approached by the historical avant-gardes. Licko's 1989 Lunatix, for example, conserves the conventional relationships of the alphabet, while in contrast, Strzeminski's elliptical font expresses a vast range of functional roles with a minimal set of elements.

Like the fonts of the avant-gardes, many of these neo-modern typefaces look to technology for aesthetic cues, rather than imitating traditional typography. In the 1920s

Bayer saw industry as the potential foundation for a universal and democratic society. A similar technological optimism appears to inform many neo-modern typefaces; these are produced, however, in a changed, post-industrial world in which technology can no longer be seen as a benign source of liberation.

The exuberance of nineteenth-century display typography is distinct from the avant-garde experimentation of the twentieth century. Modernism brought a self-consciously ideological attitude to typographic design, displacing the solicitous novelty of advertising display faces with the vanguardist assault of defamiliarization. Echoing the historical avant-gardes, neo-modernism implicitly defines itself against the commercial mainstream, which has included such "novel" fonts as Milton Glaser's Baby Teeth and Herb Lubalin's Lubalin Graph. While the typefaces of the neo-avant-garde initially projected a mystique of removal from mainstream culture, however, they were rapidly absorbed into the graphics of advertising, mass-circulation magazines, and department stores.

POST-STRUCTURALISM

Post-structuralist theory builds upon and revises Saussure's ideas by questioning the generation of "meaning" by the speaking—rather than the *writing*—subject. Saussure had faulted writing for not being a transparent sign system or "crystal goblet" for conveying speech; Derrida has challenged this devaluation of writing, seeing it as another instance of Western philosophy's characterization of writing as a faulty reflection of speech, an artificial by-product of the otherwise natural workings of the mind. In response, Derrida has foregrounded the typographic and rhetorical force of writing. Post-structuralism has provoked suspicion of coherent "master-codes" such as Marxism, which grounds meaning in a single totalizing structure. This destabilizing, (de-structuring, deconstructing) move corresponds to a philosophical shift which has been termed *post-structuralism*.

In typography there has been a shift between the approach we have described as structuralist and the attitude seen in fonts such as Jeffery Keedy's 1990 Manuscript, and Barry Deck's 1990 Canicopulus Script and Template Gothic. While these faces participate in the structuralist displacement of the archetypal letter in favor of the alphabetic structure, they modify that tradition by setting up systems which are not consistent or univocal, which fail to obey consistent master codes. Deck's Canicopulus Script, for example, engages in a conspicuously "bi-fontual" cross breeding. It does not, in the tradition of classical typography, attempt to synthesize the best features of two fonts; instead, it is a schizophrenic hybrid. Keedy's Manuscript is an anti-heroic amalgam of Modernist geometry and grade-school penmanship, recalling the naive yet normative scenario of learning to write—its forms suggest the plodding of the pencil rather than the precision of the Machine Age. Deck's Template Gothic similarly mixes the hand-made and machine-made. While Albers's stencil font foregrounds its means of production and celebrates industrial standardization, Deck's "template" is an imperfect matrix yielding irregular yet mechanically mediated characters.

These fonts which we call post-structuralist are involved with issues of represen-tation: Deck's Template Gothic implies an inexact, degraded form of mechanical repro-duction, while Keedy's Manuscript recalls elementary school exercises—"reproduction" is shown to result not only from external technologies but from the disciplinary socialization of the individual. These post-structuralist fonts have a figurative, narrative character that is distinct from the hermetic abstraction of structuralist typography. They suggest a typographic practice that participates in the broader cultural re-evaluation of Modernism; while the avant garde and its afterlife in the neo-avant-garde have institutionalized the "shock of the new," Post-modernism has replaced this faith in renewal with parody, quotation, pastiche, and an uneasy alliance with technology.

Originally published in: A Natural History of Typography, *J. Abbott Miller ed. Design Writing Research, New York and The Jersey City Museum, Jersey City, NJ 1992.*

Endnotes

1. In natural history a *type specimen* is the one example of an organism that is used to describe it. In printing a *type specimen* refers to display of typography, collected in books or presented on *specimen sheets.*
2. *Dead-matter* refers to metal type that has been composed, but is no longer in use. It is stored in *dead-matter cabinets.*
3. Geofroy Tory's *Champ Fleury,* published in 1529, advocated the design of letters based on the proportions of the body.
4. For a comparison of Darwin and Saussure, see Jonathan Culler, *Ferdinand de Saussure* (Ithaca: Cornell University Press, 1976, 1986).
5. "You have two goblets before you. One is of solid gold, wrought in the most exquisite patterns. The other is of crystal-clear glass, thin as a bubble, and as transparent ... [an] amateur of fine vintages ... will choose the crystal, because everything about it is calculated to reveal rather than to hide the beautiful thing which it was meant to contain.... the virtues of the perfect wine glass also have a parallel in typography." Beatrice Warde, *The Crystal Goblet,* 1932.
6. Jacques Derrida, *Of Grammatology* (Baltimore: Johns Hopkins University Press, 1976).
7. Frank Denman, *The Shaping of Our Alphabet* (New York: Alfred Knopf, 1955).
8. In the early twentieth century, reform-minded designers and typographers dismissed the genetic experiments of the nineteenth century as evidence of deteriorating standards and typographic decadence. Edward Johnston published diagrams of "essential" letterforms based on inscriptions from Roman monuments. While he derided the structural aberrations found in commercial display faces, Johnston accepted similar devices used in manuscript initials, reflecting the Arts-and-Crafts tolerance for all things medieval. Edward Johnston, *Writing & Illuminating & Lettering* (London: Sir Issac Pitman & Sons, 1932).
9. Jacques Derrida, *Writing and Difference* (London: Routledge and Kegan Paul, 1978).

GOOD HISTORY/BAD HISTORY[1]

by

Tibor Kalman, J. Abbott Miller, and Karrie Jacobs [2,3]

It's been over a year since the end of the eighties. This gives us some distance, some perspective. The eighties are now, officially, history.

The eighties were a decade of comebacks: suspenders, mini-skirts, Roy Orbison, Sugar Ray Leonard.... But the really big comeback was history. We got rid of history in the sixties; saw what the world looked like without it in the seventies; and begged it to come back in the eighties.

And it did; it came back with a vengeance.

In design, history came back as well. Suddenly, there were countless books—big, glossy, oversize volumes—and starchy[4] little[5] journals[6] devoted to the history of design. Careers were constructed around this fascination. Conferences, too.

And there's nothing wrong with studying the history of design. In fact, it's healthy and smart, especially for design professionals. At the same time, the indiscriminate use of history has produced some really bad, unhealthy design. History in itself isn't bad, but its influence can be.

There are two problems with design history. The first is how design history is written, for how history is written affects how the past is seen and understood. How history is written also affects how the past is used. And that's the second problem: Most design history is not written, it's shown. There's a lot to look at, but not much to think about. Maybe this is because designers don't read. That particular cliché (which, like most clichés, has a basis in truth) provides a good excuse for a lot of hack work in publishing: collections of trademarks, matchbooks, labels, cigar boxes, you name it—volumes and volumes of historical stuff with no historical context. And since these artifacts are mostly in the public domain, unprotected by copyright, such books are a bargain for the publishers and a godsend to designers who are starving for "inspiration."

We seem to be locked into a self-fulfilling prophecy: Designers don't read, so design writers don't write.[7] Let's amend that: They write captions. Sometimes they write really long captions, thousands of words that do nothing but describe the pictures.

Books of design history that are packaged for a supposedly illiterate audience only engender further illiteracy. Visual literacy is important, but it isn't everything. It doesn't teach you how to think. And an enormous amount of graphic design is made by people who look at pictures but don't know how to think about them.

The study of design history is a way of filtering the past; it's a way of selecting what's important to remember, shaping it and classifying it. It's also a way of selecting what's important to forget.[8] In a way, historians are inventors. They find a design movement, a school, an era, and if it doesn't already have a name, they make one up: Depression Modern, The American Design Ethic, Populuxe.

Design historians construct a lens through which they view design—and we view design. This lens is selective: It zooms in on a subject and blocks our peripheral vision. What we see is a narrow segment of design history: one period, one class of designers within that period. What we don't see is the context, both within the design profession and within social history.[9]

Design history provides us with terminology, a shorthand for thinking about the design of an era. We come across phrases like the "New York School," under which Philip Meggs, in his *History of Graphic Design*, groups innovators like Paul Rand, Bradbury Thompson, Saul Bass, Otto Storch, Herb Lubalin, Lou Dorfsman, and George Lois. The New York School is made up of designers about whom we've reached a consensus: Most of us believe they were the great designers of the fifties and sixties. Even so, looking at their work gives us a very stilted, narrow view of those decades. If we remember the fifties and sixties, then we know that most things did not look as if they were designed by Bradbury Thompson or Herb Lubalin. We know how elite the design represented by the term "New York School" is. And we know first-hand how selectively design history remembers.

The historical lens is both a way of seeing (or including) and a way of not seeing (or excluding). When we look back at eras that are beyond personal experience and memory, we become more dependent on what we see through the lens. What we don't see, in effect, didn't exist.

Meggs uses another term, "Pictorial Modernism," to describe graphics of the tens, twenties, and thirties that were inspired by certain movements in Modern painting—Cubism, for instance—but that did not depart altogether from the conventions of representation. We look through the lens of Pictorial Modernism and we see work by Lucian Bernhard or A. M. Cassandre, design we now think of as great. What we don't see is the angry, frightening graphics of a tumultuous era. We see a Modernism that's deceptively cool, deceptively pretty. Even Ludwig Hohlwein's posters for the Nazis are neutralized by a lens that isolates only aesthetic qualities.[10, 11]

Through this lens, we see Western European design, and design that was used primarily for selling expensive but tasteful luxury products—design that can be put to those same uses today. What we see through this lens becomes the design we know, and remember, and admire.[12]

Our ideas about what we see through the lens shape our ideas about contemporary design. A restricted view of the past creates an equally restricted view of the present. If we see the past as a series of artifacts, then we see our own work the same way.[13]

Graphic design isn't so easily defined or limited. (At least, it shouldn't be.) Graphic design is the use of words and images on more or less everything, more or less everywhere. Japanese erotic engravings from the fourteenth century are graphic design, as are twentieth-century American publications like *Hooters* and *Wild Vixens.* Hallmark has as much to do with graphic design as Esprit does. Probably more. The Charter paperback edition of *Eden's Gate* is as much a part of graphic design history as Neville Brody's book.

Graphic design isn't so rarefied or so special. It isn't a profession, it's a medium. It's a mode of address, a means of communication. It's used throughout culture at varying levels of complexity and with varying degrees of success. That's what's important about graphic design. That's what makes it interesting. And it is at work every place where there are words and images.

But design history doesn't work that way; it operates with a restrictive definition. Graphic design, says history, is a professional practice with roots in the Modernist avant-garde. Design history creates boundaries: On this side is high design; on that side is low design. Over here is the professional and over there is the amateur. This is what's mainstream, that is what's marginal. Preserve this, discard that.

For design history to be worth anything, it has to have a more inclusive definition of graphic design and a more inclusive way of looking at graphic design. Graphic design has artistic and formal qualities, and much of what's written about design focuses on these qualities. Design history becomes a history of aesthetics, of taste, of style. But there is another, more important history; it is the history of graphic design and its audience. It tells how political images have been crafted, how corporations have manipulated public perceptions, how myths have been created by advertising. This other history is the history of design as a medium and as a multiplicity of languages speaking to a multiplicity of people.

In focusing on its artistic and formal qualities, history has neglected graphic design's role as a medium. It has presented design as a parade of artifacts, each with a date, a designer, and a place within a school or movement. But each artifact marks more than a place in the progression of artistic sensibility. Each also speaks eloquently of its social history. All you have to do is learn the language.

Don't misunderstand. The formal evaluation of objects is okay, but it's tricky to evaluate objects from another era intelligently. Our aesthetic standards are different from those of the past. What looks cool to us today may have been embarrassing, regressive, offensive, or just run-of-the-mill in its own day. To look at artifacts without knowing what they were in their own time is to look into a vacuum.

We try to use contemporary language and standards to talk about design from the past. But do we mean the same thing by "modern" as designers did in the first half of the century? What was modernity in the nineteenth century? What did the Museum of "Modern" Art mean by the phrase "good design" in the 1950s? When and where did the term "white space" come into use? Did they have it in the Renaissance? Did it mean the same thing?

The lack of critical commentary in design and design history has produced an ambivalence toward language. Writing about design sometimes seems pointless or suspect, and design as the expression of the written language has been seen as a less-than"artistic" pursuit. Design becomes the composition of purely pictorial elements rather than the manipulation of both image and language. Design becomes mute. Anyone who has tried to design with dummy copy knows that hypothetical situations don't inspire brilliant work. Some of the best designers—Paul Rand, Herb Lubalin, Saul Bass, Alvin Lustig—are those who consistently engaged the editorial and textual dimensions of design.

The key word in bad design history is de-contextualization. A history of design artifacts is only interested in constructing an evolutionary chain of progressive design styles. In order to do this, the object must be extracted and abstracted from its context. The abstraction occurs because stylistic features are discussed apart from the content of a given work.

One symptom of this tendency has been the production of graphic design in which style is a detachable attribute, a veneer rather than an expression of content. This is nowhere clearer than in the so-called historicist and eclectic work which has strip-mined the history of design for ready-made style. And this brings us to the second part of the problem: the use and abuse of history.

Designers abuse history when they use it as a shortcut, a way of giving instant legitimacy to their work and making it commercially successful. In the eighties and even today, in the nineties, historical reference and outright copying have been cheap and dependable substitutes for a lack of ideas. Well-executed historicism in design is nearly always seductive. The work looks good and it's hard not to like it. This isn't surprising: nostalgia is a sure bet; familiarity is infinitely comforting.

So this criticism has nothing to do with whether the execution is good or bad, but with the question of use and abuse. It is possible to compare works that fall under the heading of "Modernism" (recognizable, well-known works by Modernist designers), and works directly influenced by these (well-known works by contemporary designers) which represent "jive modernism."[14]

There's a lot of confusion about Modernism these days, mostly engendered by the use and abuse of the term "Post-modernism." Jive modernism is not Post-modernism. In a way, it's the opposite. In architecture, Post-modernism has come to mean the habit of affixing pre-modernist stuff—classical ornament—to the facades of otherwise Modernist buildings. In graphics, the term has been used to mean just about anything, at least anything that departs from the most austere, Swiss-born, corporate-bred Modernism.

Jive Modernism is not a departure from Modernism. It's a revival, a way of treating Modernism as if it were something that was thought up by the ancient Romans, something dead from long ago. And in reviving Modernism, jive modernism is a denial of the essential point of Modernism, its faith in the power of the present, and the potential of the future. Modernism was an attempt to jettison the confining aspects of history. It replaced the nineteenth century's deep infatuation with the past with a twentieth-century optimism about the present and the future. Our infatuation with Modernism—jive modernism—is now an infatuation with the past.

The Modernists invented new formal languages that changed not just how things looked, but how people saw. Modernism was a heartfelt attempt at using design to change the world.[15] It succeeded. And it failed.

Modernism was optimistic about the role of design. Even the pissiest Modernists, the Dadaists and Futurists, believed that design has a responsibility to carry a new message. Modernism believed in itself, in its contemporaneity: It believed in the present.

Clearly, the aesthetic part of the new message was carried forward successfully. And that is Modernism's failure. We've learned the esthetics of Modernism by rote, and we repeat these lessons as faithfully and with as little thought as a schoolchild repeating the Pledge of Allegiance.[16] Modernism failed because the spirit of it, the optimism, was lost. Modernism without the spirit is Trump Tower. It's a fake Cassandre poster advertising Teacher's Scotch.

Contemporary work of that sort has a parasitic relationship to the past. Modernism is the host organism and jive modernism is the parasite that feeds off it. The relationship is one-sided and opportunistic. Like a real parasite, jive modernism doesn't care about what the host organism thinks. It doesn't care about Modernism's politics or philosophy or anything that might be below the surface of the look.

Jive modernism[17] gains—prestige, instant style, clients, awards—while real Modernism loses. Jive modernism has invoked Modernism as nostalgia. It's pessimistic about the present, which it rejects in favor of the past. Jive modernism is very useful in graphic design, in politics, in advertising, in fashion, in films. It feeds into a prevailing Reaganesque conservatism in America, which seeks solace in images whose familiarity is comforting. Modernism, which was once radical, is now safe and reassuring. And the amazing thing about jive modernism is, unlike other, sloppier, more sentimental forms of nostalgia, such as Art Nouveau, you can use it and still seem hip.

Jive modernism succeeds to the extent that it does because our conception of the bygone era it invokes is based on a stock of fuzzy, out-of-context imagery. We think of the twenties as the Jazz Age and the thirties as the Streamlined Decade. We know what we know mostly from Hollywood movies, television, and selected graphics. The vernacular, the eccentric, the marginal, and the minority have been filtered out of our collective memory.

Jive modernism turns up in some odd places, places where it shouldn't even be: Ralph Lauren advertising, for example. These ads generally involve a cast of characters who seem to have successfully colonized some third world nation and have now turned their attention to lawn tennis. But here they use what Meggs calls Pictorial Modernism. The look is an amalgam of Ludwig Hohlwein, Lucian Bernhard, and Joseph Leyendecker, mixed with some nonspecific heroic realism. It's not even very Modern (except when compared with most of Lauren's graphics). Mostly, it's jive.

But let's just suppose that a box designed for Ralph Lauren in the late 1980s with an illustration of a golfer in twenties dress, an early prop plane overhead, rendered in high-contrast style, really is an historical object: What kinds of questions should we ask if it were designed in 1927, and what should the questions be if it were designed in 1987? For starters, we should ask: *Who played golf in 1927, and what did it signify as a social activity?*

Upper-class white men being exclusive.

And then we should ask:

Who played golf in 1987, and what did it signify as a social activity?

Middle- and upper-class white people, including a growing number of female executives, being exclusive.[18]

What did the artist of 1927 intend by rendering the image in this high-contrast style?

Here we can answer that, in 1927, it was a progressive, state-of-the-art style. It was also a way of incorporating color and the look of photography without the expense of photography.

What did the artist of 1987 intend by rendering the image in this high-contrast style?

Here we can answer that it was a way of achieving a retro look by referring to what was once a progressive, state-of-the-art style. The decision not to use a color photograph carries with it certain anti-technological associations. These associations are useful because they support the sense of Ralph Lauren products as hand-crafted rather than machine-made.

What did the image of the airplane signify in 1927?

Progress.

What did the image of the airplane signify in the late 1980s?

Quaintness.

Jive modernism thrives on our collective memories of the past. The Ralph Lauren design works because it plugs into an existing network of personal associations and recollections. It's effective. It's also a cheap shot.

Is this a problem? Well, if jive history is so successful that it replaces both the past and the present, then future historicist design will be double-jive-history, twice removed from the original reference.

We'll be living in hyper-jive.

Bad historicism reduces history to style. We learn no more about the historical forms being used than we learn about music from a lounge musician playing note-for-note reproductions of the hits. Bad historicism reduces Cassandre, Lissitzky, Mondrian, Schlemmer, and Matter into names to be dropped or designer labels to be conspicuously displayed. The history of design becomes a marketplace where we shop for style—the proverbial marketplace of ideas. We pull a style off the rack, we try it on. If it fits, we take it.

Now, the point of this article is not to argue against the appropriation of ideas. And it's certainly not to argue against influence. Designers can borrow ideas from other media, contemporary ideas or historical ideas, and transform them into good design ("transform" is the key word here).[19] Cross-pollination is an important and legitimate aspect of how culture works.

What we're arguing against is design that cashes in on history. We object to contemporary designers who take ideas that might have been radical seventy years ago but have since become legitimate—more than that, endearing and very, very safe—and reuse those ideas without even reinterpreting them. We're not opposed to historical reference: Just as there is good history and bad history, there is good historical reference and bad historical reference. Reference means just that: You refer to something. It gives you an idea. You create something new.

Real Modernism is filled with historical reference and allusion. And in some of the best design today,[20] historical references are used very eloquently. But those examples were produced with an interest in re-contextualizing sources rather than de-contextualizing them.[21]

There's an important difference between making an allusion and doing a knock-off. Good historicism is not a lounge act. It's an investigation of the strategies, procedures, methods, routes, theories, tactics, schemes, and modes through which people have worked creatively. If we have any monuments in the history of design, they should be the basis for critical evaluation.

We need to learn from and interrogate our past, not endlessly repeat its recipes. What we can learn from Constructivism is not type placed at forty-five degree angles and the reduction of colors to red, white, and black, but freedom with word order and the lack of strict hierarchies in the typographical message. We need to look not at the stylistic tics of Modernism but at its varied strategies. We should focus not on its' stylistic iterations but on its ideas.

How can we change bad history into good history? How can we change bad historical reference into good historical reference? We need fewer coffee table books and more ambitious design writing. We need as much time spent on the editorial conception of books as is spent on sexy layouts and glossy photography. We need to ask the right questions. After all, good history is a matter of asking good questions.

While we have access to the individuals who have been influential in graphic design, we should ask the questions that can't be answered by the work alone, questions that can't be addressed directly or empirically, but are elusive and genuinely historical. They are questions such as: What is it about this piece of design that we can't understand because we are not part of the culture in which it was produced? What did the style of this image communicate to its audience? What was the relationship of the designer to his or her client? If this object is an example of good design at the time, what was considered bad, or banal, or mediocre? What aspects of the image have become transparent to the eyes of a contemporary viewer?

Good design history is interested in the finished product not as a point of perfection bound for the Museum of Modern Art but as the culmination of a process. Because of this, good design history pays attention to the fringes of design as well as the mainstream, and to the rejects and failures as well as the award-winning examples.

We need design history that does not see itself in the role of a service to the design profession, but as a history of ideas. Such a design history would tell us not only who produced something when and for whom, but would situate the object in a historical moment and would reveal something about the way design works on its audience.

A good history of design isn't a history of design at all. It's a history of ideas and therefore of culture. It uses the work of designers not just as bright spots on the page but as examples of the social, political, and economic climate of a given time and place. This isn't really much of a stretch. Good history in general presents ideas in context in a way that teaches us more than how things once looked. It is not just a roster of names, dates, and battles, but the history of how we have come to believe what we believe about the world. Likewise, good design history is not just a roster of names, dates, and objects; it is the history of how we have come to believe what we believe about design.

The biggest difference is this: Bad design history offers us an alternative to having ideas. Bad design history says, here, this is nice, use it. Good design history acts as a catalyst for our own ideas. Good design history says, this is how designers thought about their work then, and this is how that work fits into the culture. Now, what can *you* do?

Originally published in Print *magazine, March/April 1991.*

Endnotes

1. The title should tip readers off to the fact that this is a polemic: more concerned with *having* an argument than with *making* an argument. In keeping with this strategy, the authors exploit appealingly succinct, unqualified pronouncements that are the hallmark of devil-may-care glibness. JAM

2. This speech was written by Tibor Kalman and J. Abbott Miller. It was then rewritten by Karrie Jacobs. The finished product, the speech given by Kalman at the "Modernism & Eclecticism" symposium (sponsored by the School of Visual Arts in New York City in February 1990), was full of highly debatable points. But since Tibor delivered the speech, he took the flack. The rest of us were able to sink down in our seats and watch from a safe distance. Now all of our names are attached, so we are doing the only prudent thing. We are qualifying and modifying. We are writing footnotes. KJ

3. After Kalman's presentation, some members of the audience felt left out in the cold from the rough draft that filled the room. The version of the talk published here is no less rough, yet it includes annotations which clarify, modify, qualify, deny, reiterate, and eliminate aspects of the original. JAM

4. This little word seemed to cause consternation during the discussion period following the presentation. Perhaps this is the perfect moment to check [Webster's] dictionary.
   Starch *n.* (15c) 1: a white odorless tasteless granular or powdery complex carbohydrate $(C_6H_{10}O_5)_x$ that is the chief storage form of carbohydrate in plants, is an important foodstuff, and is used also in adhesives and sizes, in laundering, and in pharmacy and medicine 2: a stiff formal manner: FORMALITY 3: resolute vigor TK

5. *Journal of Decorative and Propaganda Art* (circulation: 5000, trim size: 7¼" by 10"); *Design Issues* (circulation: 1500, trim size: 7" by 10"); *The Journal of Design History* (circulation: 750, trim size: 6" by 8½"); *TV Guide* (circulation: 15,800,000, trim size: 5" by 7⅜").
   Well, maybe this could be understood as a negative reference. It's not intended that way. If the journals were less starchy, they might not provide the kind of pure academic study that's actually needed in this area. If they were physically larger, chances are they'd only get glossier with bigger and better-reproduced artwork, which isn't the point, either. If the circulations were larger, these journals would be taking ads, worrying about their "reader profiles," and probably lowering their standards. None of this is desirable. In short, we think these journals are pretty good, and we like them. TK

6. One man's starch is another man's complex carbohydrate. The journals designated by Kalman as "starchy" are not part of the same commercial enterprise as "big, glossy, oversize volumes." Academic journals—particularly *Design Issues*—represent, in fact, alternative models to the kind of history writing criticized here.
   In its first year of publication (1984), *Design Issues* published Clive Dilnot's two-part essay "The State of Design History," which laid out many of the crucial problems facing the development of design history. Specifically, Dilnot called attention to the narrow focus on professional design activity, the emphasis on solitary genius-creators, and the fetishization of design as a "value" expressed through style.
   Apart from the forum such journals provide to designers, writers, and academics, they are a means through which design and design history may be recognized by other disciplines as a worthwhile arena of study. The status of design in relation to other established disciplines matters if one hopes to affect the institutional structure of design education and design within general education. JAM

7. There are, of course, exceptions. KJ

8. It's arguable that the influential texts on graphic design history (Meggs *A History of Graphic Design,* Remington and Hodik's *Nine Pioneers of Graphic Design,* Muller-Brockmann's *A History of Visual Communication*) have focused on the sunnier side of the street. The persistent forgetting of (refusal to notice?) the "shady" side of the street (advertising, propaganda, forced obsolescence, the designation of "vernacular" forms, the relationship between designers and the client class they serve) needs to be viewed critically, and in relation to the way in which the expanding bank of design history is being put to use. JAM

9. The line of argumentation throughout this essay finds its "low sodium/high carbohydrate" antecedent in Clive Dilnot's statement that "the essential field of design's meaning and import … is *not* the internal world of the design profession, but the wider social world that produces the determining circumstances that lead to the emergence of designers." (Dilnot, "The State of Design History," *Design Issues* [Spring 1984]:14) In our presentation, we tried to bring this theoretical point home through specific examples of graphic design and references to what we think are familiar texts on design. JAM

10. These references to Hohlwein seem to have gotten Phil Meggs, author of *A History of Graphic Design,* into a nettle. You'll no doubt be reading his spirited response in a forthcoming issue of *Print.* However, the authors stand by this analysis and suggest a re-reading of the aforementioned tome's pages 299–300 (including captions) to better enable the reader to decide which analysis is correct. Perhaps future editions of Meggs' book might be revised to include a broader discussion of not only Hohlwein's pro-Nazi views, but the development of the most powerful logo ever: the swastika, which was apparently designed (presumably for a big fee) by a local corporate identity firm. TK

11. Philip Meggs considers Ludwig Hohlwein's career (including his involvement with Nazi propaganda) within the over-arching framework of "Pictorial Modernism." The question remains: Are stylistic features an adequate means to describe the role of design in society? Or is Hohlwein and the style of graphics he helped to establish better understood as an especially important part of a historically evolving relationship between images of power and governmental sponsorship of such images. What about the recurrence and resonance of this style in American mass media then and now? JAM

12. Between all these lines we are asking: What about all the other design? The newspapers, the ads for hemorrhoid products, retail handbills, License plates, signs, diplomas—all the stuff people saw everyday. Where is that history? TK

13. In fact, this is exactly the way we look at out own work, as artifacts out of context, reproduced in annuals. KJ

14. Examples of jive modernism:
   Compare a Herbert Matter poster from 1934 promoting Swiss tourism, and an ad designed by Paula Scher for Swatch watches in 1986. Scher's Swatch image self-consciously mimics the Herbert Matter poster, not merely uses it as a point of departure. This is a familiar strategy (see Duchamp's Mona Lisa). However, the contextual displacement effected from Swiss tourism to Swatch watches is not particularly thought-provoking.
   Possible explanations why a Paul Renner poster (*Bayerns,* 1928) was swiped for the cover of James Joyce's *Ulysses* (Carin Goldberg, book cover for Vintage Books, 1985) include: 1) Joyce wrote parts of *Ulysses* in Zurich and even died there; 2) Joyce employed

mimicry and parody in his writing; 3) "Bayerns" and "Ulysses" each have seven letters; 4) the letters "B" and "U" each have both straight and curved forms; 4) things look good when they're tilted.

Charles Spencer Anderson reworked a matchbook cover by an unknown designer in the 1930s into a promotion for French Paper (1989). Might there be a connection between the extent of twenties and thirties nostalgia in graphic design and the fact that works produced before 1941 are considered in the public domain?

An A. M. Cassandre poster for a steamship line (1931) and Fernand Léger's painting *The Syphon* appropriated in an ad for Teacher's Scotch (Agency: Eisaman, Johns & Laws, 1990): This is only fair since Cassandre himself strip-mined Léger so frequently, and since Léger's *Syphon* is itself based on a small advertisement for Campari that appeared in the French newspaper *Le Matin*.

A poster for a 1929 Soviet film called *Living Corpse,* based on a play by Leo Tolstoy (Design: Grigory Borisov and Pytor Zhukov) and a record cover for Jerry Harrison, *The Red and the Black* by M&Co., 1982. *The Red and the Black* is the title of an 1831 novel by Stendhal. Jerry Harrison is an American musician. None of this explains the connection between revolutionary Soviet film posters and Romantic French literature. Perhaps Warner Records has a subversive, left-wing agenda? JAM

What's going on here? Theft? Cheap shots? Parody? Appropriation? Why do designers do this? Is it because the designers don't have new ideas? Is it glorification of the good old days of design? Is it a way to create a sense of old-time quality in a new-fangled product? Are the designers being lazy, just ripping off an idea to save time and make for an easier client sell?

I can only speak for the last example. It was designed by M&Co. in 1982; and in this case the answer to the questions above is yes. This is a mistake we've all made. Students of art and design are taught to copy as a way of understanding a process so they can better understand the way to evolve their own styles. But you're *supposed* to outgrow this. This is included by way of purging our own guilt about a cheap-shot copy. TK

Think about how much graphic design relies on quotation. Not just the lifting of historic styles, but also the lifting of contemporary styles. In fact, this may be how period revivals happen. One person mines and everyone else swipes.

If we were being better historians, we wouldn't just discuss Renner and Goldberg or the original charming graphic and the Anderson charming graphic; we'd also discuss the imitations of the imitations, the faux Goldbergs and Andersons. If we were being good historians, we would really show you bad history. KJ

15. This remarkably general discussion of "Modernism" rhetorically lumps an actually divergent set of ideas and practices, not all of which are so utopian. Not all Modernists were (and are) of the Howard Roark variety (see Gary Cooper as Howard Roark as Frank Lloyd Wright in King Vidor's version of Ayn Rand's *The Fountainhead*). Other facets of Modernism were melancholic, dystopian, and deeply pessimistic. Yet this pessimism still reserved a role for art and design as a mode of criticism. For a discussion of different aspects of Modernism's critical potential, see Peter Burger's *Theory of the Avant-Garde* (Minneapolis: University of Minnesota Press, 1984). JAM

16. Actually, I think it's more complicated than this. I think there are several layers of historicism. On one hand, there is a self-conscious use of Modernist style, and on the other, there is a use of Modernism that occurs almost naturally because Modernist style has been incorporated into the generic language of design. KJ

17. And every other nostalgic device. KJ

18. People play golf for many reasons, yet the decision to market clothing by associating it with golf highlights the popular understanding of golf as a country-club activity. JAM

19. "Transform" is the key word on any side of a debate about the use of historical sources. The argument rests on opinions about how effectively, creatively, or cleverly historical sources are "transformed" by the designer. The very same set of comparisons we've used here to make our point about the abuse of history could, in the hands of someone else, be used to argue the vitality of contemporary designer's use of historical sources. This essay attempts to distinguish different varieties of and motivations for using historical sources: It argues for self-consciousness about what it means to transform. JAM

20. e.g., by Tom Bonauro, Rick Valicenti, the photographers Geof Kern and Bruce Weber, *Spy* Magazine, etc. TK

21. There is an almost automatic sense of indignation when a vanguardist, political form of art, design, or language is used in a different context and for different (typically commercial) ends. The indignation arises from the fact that the original meaning gets lost, subsumed, or sugar-coated under the pressure of the new context. In architecture, preservation councils protect buildings considered significant so that new construction and planning do not violate the buildings' original contexts. We don't have such things in graphic design: Trademarks and packages are updated without regard for their status as icons of our consumer landscape. This is partly why there is so much nostalgia in design and design history.

But the anxiety about style as a detachable attribute—the uneasy feeling that in much design, form is cleanly separable from content—relates to the fundamentally ephemeral status of graphic design as a sign system. Graphic design is a medium enabled by the possibility of making new signs out of existing verbal and visual elements. Thus, recontextualization and decontextualization are at the heart of the enterprise. Design functions because signs of any sort (colors, textures, typefaces, etc.) do *not* retain meaning across contexts, but are adaptable, mutable, unstable, and vulnerable. JAM

THE TIME MACHINE
by
Steven Heller

Nostalgia. It sounds like an ailment, doesn't it? Neuritis, neuralgia, nostalgia. Take a bromo and call me in the morning. In fact, the word was coined in the seventeenth century to describe a severe illness brought about by homesickness afflicting soldiers during the Thirty Years' War. In addition to fits of melancholia induced by battle, protracted absences from hearth and home caused these warriors to experience intense stomach pains and nausea. By the nineteenth century, the word had come to signify a romantic memory of, or dreamlike return to, a more sublime time and place in history.

In the original usage, such yearnings were based entirely on personal experience. No matter that the memories were often idealized, those stricken longed to return to *their* homes and *their* families in *their* time. The later usage, however, implied returning not to a recent or subjective past, but to a distant, objective epoch that could be anywhere from decades to centuries earlier. Other psychological terms have replaced nostalgia, the disease, but the word as a social experience has become synonymous with a desire for things that are old-fashioned or ante-modern.

Despite these negative connotations, we have all felt nostalgic for something. During episodes of stress, one longs for a time when life was easier. Many of us also inhabit nostalgic environments replete with the clothes and furnishings of bygone eras. One might even argue that such preferences are not always based on a desire to return to the past, but on an inherent interest in a certain form or style. I have a Thonet chair, for example, not because I feel nostalgic for the 1930s—two decades before my birth—but because the chair has beautiful and classic form and is comfortable, too.

Yet there are those who find nostalgia inexcusable in any form. One vociferous cultural critic argues that "nostalgia is a desperate clinging to the past because people are unwilling to face their present yet are quite content to surrender their claims to the future." Its manifestations, he continues, are like opiates that dull mass thinking. And there is justification for this criticism. Nostalgic references and images are accepted codes that marketers, propagandists, and both fine and applied artists use to market their wares, probably so that they won't have to challenge the limits of audience acceptance or perception. In the past couple of years, two new nostalgia magazines, *Good Old Days* and *Memories,* hit the newsstands, and a number of mainstream products, such as 20 Mule Team Borax, Quaker Oats, Maypo, and Coca-Cola, have reissued their early packages in "limited collectors' editions" of millions. The reason behind this rejection of the old "new and improved" marketing strategy is apparently to attract a consumer longing for homespun values by trading on a product's venerable history. John Clive, a historian who is interested in the ethical dimension of history and its impact on contemporary society, writes that "nothing works better to further a cause—good or bad—than to lend it legitimacy by supplying it with a long heritage." And so one might ask about those handsomely designed Crabtree & Evelyn packages: "Isn't all that faux Victorian and Ye Olde English imagery based on the assumption that the public has an insatiable appetite for the antiquated and picturesque?"

Maybe. But like any fashion, trends in nostalgia are cyclical. Not all nostalgia is rooted in a sentimental preference for Gilded Age quaintness. If László Moholy-Nagy were alive, he would be shocked to find that the material evidence of his efforts to replace bourgeois sentimentalism with machine-age rationalism is being used nostalgically by some contemporary graphic designers who have mined historical resources for usable styles. Indeed, Piet Mondrian, Theo Van Doesburg, El Lissitzky, and Alexander Rodchenko, all masters of the Modern and proponents of the timeless, would have been dumbstruck by some of the appropriations that are currently in vogue. Despite Moholy's advocacy of a universal visual language, he would have been the first to recognize that new social contexts alter the content and use of graphic design. I think he probably would have railed against mimicry of any kind. Moholy said that art should be of its time.

This statement is central to a debate going on today between those who argue that culture is a "big closet" (as Tom Wolfe termed it) from which graphic designers can freely select old and new styles, and those who admonish designers to find their own ideas—to ignore the past and address the present. In February 1990, the issue was posed by Tibor Kalman in a critical lecture titled "Good History/Bad History" given before the third annual design-history symposium sponsored by the School of Visual Arts in New York. Kalman asserts that contemporary design historians, and those like myself who edit design books, discourage original thinking by providing a cornucopia of "decontextualized" scrap on which designers parasitically feed. This argument implies that if history serves only as style-fodder, it cannot nourish, which leaves the designer hungry for more style. If historical reference is decontextualized, then the result is unabashed nostalgia. Though the worst-case scenario is correct, Kalman's argument is nevertheless myopic.

Some critics call the 1980s the "decade of appropriation," but artists and especially graphic designers have been appropriating form and style certainly since the nineteenth century—if not before—and often for good reasons. Leon Trotsky wrote in *Literature and Revolution* that "artistic creation is always a complicated turning inside out of old forms, under the influence of new stimuli which originate outside of art." Appropriate historical use is not the recycling of hackneyed techniques but the application of new ideas.

Here are some examples: In the 1890s, William Morris, the Victorian prophet and socialist thinker, returned to the medieval workshop tradition not simply as a reactionary stand against the ugliness of industrialization, but as a gateway to new social awareness. He believed that medievalism represented a more humanist philosophy. In the 1920s, the respected advertising designers T. M. Cleland and Walter Dorwin Teague borrowed rococo mannerisms from eighteenth-century French book design to enhance advertising art (specifically for automobile advertising) as a means of reconciling the fast pace of progress with traditional values. They were probably also reacting to the newly adopted concept of forced obsolescence, and used classical design forms as a code to offset any recognition that products were not being made to last. Also during the 1920s, the Dadaists and Surrealists used nineteenth-century printers' cuts to suggest the ad hoc nature of their messages. In the forties, Lester Beall drew inspiration from Dada and Surrealism and borrowed some of their graphic and photographic elements, yet developed a distinctly American approach that reflected changes in art and media. In the 1950s, in part as a rejection of the spartan International Style, New York's Push Pin Studios, whose principals Milton Glaser and Seymour Chwast were interested in reviving drawing as an integral element of the design process, invested the early twentieth-century styles of Art Nouveau and Art Deco with new energy and thus invented their own distinctive period style. In the early 1960s, a reappreciation of nineteenth-century Victorian woodtypes, by Otto Storch, Ed Benguiat, Herb Lubalin, Phil Gips, and later Bea Feitler, offered an eclectic alternative to orthodox Modernism yet did not slavishly imitate the original models. In the early 1980s, David King (in England) and Paula Scher (in America) reintroduced Russian Constructivism to the design vocabulary and so unlocked another treasure chest of forms unknown to an entire generation of young designers. And in the mid-1980s, with his manipulation of 1930s advertising cuts, Charles Spencer Anderson brought design back full circle to its nascent period when we were lowly commercial artists. Although Anderson's approach has ignited acrimonious responses among orthodox Moderns, who argue that this is the kind of stuff they fought so hard to eliminate forty years ago, I tend to be more generous in viewing the work as a form of satire that comments on a bygone age. An astute friend of mine put this so-called retro phase into clearer focus, asserting that we all borrow from the past but that designers are invariably limited in what they do by their knowledge. "My bookshelf," she said, "has many more books going further back in time than does Anderson's."

Which raises the issue of cultural Alzheimer's (or cultural illiteracy). I was startled to read in a recent study of New York high school students that only thirty-two percent could place the American Civil War in the correct half-century. I'll bet that a similar level of ignorance would be exposed if graphic designers were asked to take a design history test. In fact, I met an AIGA member from Florida in her mid- to late thirties who had never heard of Paul Rand. That Chuck Anderson may be better known than Paul Rand is astonishing. And this explains why certain historical styles have become trivialized: Too many young designers—and some vets, too—are simply ignorant of original or even secondary contexts.

If ignorance is not excusable under the law, then why is it rewarded by so many graphic design shows and publications? While I allow that Anderson's graphic style is appealing because it is humorous, and am fairly sure that it will evolve into something else, I was disturbed that *Print* magazine, with which I am closely associated, chose to recognize an Anderson lookalike recently in its Mini-Portfolio section. Why do we celebrate clones of clones? Yet for balance, we must look back to when the Modern approach was funneled into the mainstream through style books and typographic specimen sheets. The results were varied; but today, some of the imitators are celebrated for expanding the boundaries of design. Indeed, some imitators did build upon the methods of the avant-garde with intelligence, making their approach more commercially accessible.

Given the absence of a codified graphic design history (until Philip Meggs's *A History of Graphic Design* was published in 1983), reapplications provide a kind of ad hoc history course for designers unaware that graphic design even has a history. John Clive writes that "the mere fact that someone uses the past for purposes not strictly or exclusively historical ... does not necessarily mean that the result cannot constitute a major contribution to historiography." Some clip-art books, which preceded the current crop of in-depth analyses and histories, are indeed showcases of historical material. Without Clarence Hornung's compendia of nineteenth-century commercial engravings (published by Dover Books in the 1950s), it probably would have taken much longer to become aware of some lost and important graphic forms. Without Leslie Cabarga's German trademark books and Eric Baker and Tyler Blik's compilations of vintage logos and trademarks, our collective knowledge, I think, would be lessened. While these books are invariably used by many as a reservoir of ideas and forms—and the images are so frequently clipped that they sometimes become nostalgic clichés—they are nonetheless records of design archeology.

Borrowing from the past is an evolutionary stage in virtually every designer's and illustrator's life, akin to the venerable practice of drawing from plaster casts. Milton Glaser once told me that "every generation has to make its own discoveries even if they are old discoveries." Sometimes the results are unique and unforeseen. Brad Holland has often copied the styles, though not the ideas, of his admired masters as a bridge between influence and originality. After Paul Davis discovered naive American art, he combined it with elements of René Magritte's Surrealism, resulting in a uniquely personal vision. Paula Scher's eclectic education, as evidenced in some, but certainly not all, of her work, is a guided tour of Victorian, Modern, and modernistic styles. Each historical application is not an exact reprise but an homage or parody translated through her wit. Tibor Kalman has intentionally given a portion of his work the ad hoc look of the untutored sign painter or printer, as both a celebration of the naive and a wry commentary on the state of contemporary professional design.

Intentionality as opposed to sentimentality is an important distinction here. Used as a logical reference point or subject of parody, historical reference is valid and necessary. But as Oscar Wilde wrote, "A sentimentalist is simply one who desires to have the luxury of an emotion without paying for it." And this is the essential difference between the user and abuser of history. When nostalgia is an end in itself, the result is often sentimental. Using Constructivism just for its colors and shapes, or Social Realism just for its heroic façade, is cultural vandalism. Using these styles to randomly convey ideas and products without any relation to their original context is stupid.

History provides paradigms, and paradigms change over time. Rand's own half-century of work is evidence of how this happens. For example, he owes a lot to an understanding of the various methods and ideas developed before he even became a graphic designer. He admired designers such as Lucian Bernhard, Gustav Jensen, and Otto Arpke, but with the exception of a few very early pieces, his work bears no overt resemblance to theirs. The formal ideas embodied in Constructivism, De Stijl, and the Bauhaus philosophically contributed to what is undeniably Rand's original approach. But just look at his work. No one can accuse it of being Bauhausian or, to coin a term, De Stijlian. Rand's work is about communication through economy and often wit. It is of the moment, yet timeless. If we didn't see or know some of the dates, an accurate chronology would be impossible. In transcending ephemeral style, Rand's design is classic.

Yet it must also be noted that style is a necessary signpost. The design critic Misha Black wrote, "It is impossible for man to produce objects without reflecting the society of which he is a part and the moment in history when the product concept developed in his mind. In this sense everything produced by man has style." We must expect designers to work in the ambient or vernacular language of their eras. Answering a question about the distinctive period look of the 1984 Summer Olympics graphics system, Deborah Sussman once told me, "Many of the great things that we love in the environment, from monuments to public buildings, from cathedrals to temples, are of *their* time. Most art is."

And so we ought to turn to the designs of Bernhard, Cassandre, Garretto not for imitation but inspiration. Although they aren't cathedrals or temples, they are monuments of a sort. They vividly represent the broader style of their era. True, by today's measure, these styles are now locked in time. But their makers were not prisoners of time.

Originally published in Print *magazine, March/April 1991.*

MORALITY AND MYTH: THE BAUHAUS REASSESSED
by
Dietmar R. Winkler

Designers have been nourished by the Bauhaus' teachings and wearied by its doctrines. Since its close in 1933, the Bauhaus legend has exerted profound impact on late Modern graphic design. The author believes that in recent years these repeated myths have obscured many truths about the Bauhaus' failure to cope with real world issues. In spite of its utopian promises, the Bauhaus never really succeeded at working for the public good.

The exalted status that the Bauhaus has assumed in the history of the design profession, a status fostered and enhanced by publications and exhibitions, some sponsored even by governments of East and West Germany, has had the unique luxury not to be scrutinized or held accountable for its behavior and ideology. Little has been published on its moral and ethical positions, and most assumptions rest on the closing of the Bauhaus by the authoritarian fascist government as an indicator of the school's moral positions. Indeed, prevailing assumptions portray an educational institution of integrity and high moral fiber: open-minded, anti-fascistic, cross-culturally responsive, and universally astute. But are those assumptions correct, in part or at all? Or is the super-heroic mystique only a shadow of human traits which, besides great accomplishments, include some severe shortcomings?

Why worry about it now? Maybe for the reason that the professional design field has matured and is looking at its information base to establish guidance for future endeavors? Maybe because design mirrors its attitudes in either selfish opportunism or ethical responsibility? Maybe because it's important to clear the whole house to be able to examine present behavior in the design community?

What is most surprising is the set of very naive attitudes that the Bauhaus represented. It did not hold deep or discriminating opinions about the social content of its ideas or about the purpose and impact of its design philosophy on artifacts and, through these, on the lives of consumers and audiences. Its ideology was gleaned mostly from the cultural and social concerns of Ruskin and Morris, whose benign British socialism was to alter the social conditions of the largely working-class population. This romantic socialism envisioned beautiful but practical and functioning images and objects borne out of socially responsible design philosophies. The time was right for the integration of the social concerns, and German socialists, Marxists, and internationalists tried to find support for unions and working-class needs, while the Bauhaus took advantage of existing credos but did little in refining or redirecting the missions.

As an emerging school, with an interest in being quickly recognized, the Bauhaus took an opposing stance to nearly anything resembling a previous order. It condemned the intellectual components of academic education in the arts, and indirectly barred intellectual discourse of social, political, and philosophical nature, allowing only intellectual activities that concerned themselves with the development of the language of form, color and image, and object construction. The Bauhaus staff and students were surprisingly ill-informed on the politics of their epoch, and critically ignorant and behind the times in their knowledge of the then-current movements in literature, philosophy, and behavioral and social sciences. Contemporary events like Hitler's putsch of 1923 or the central fascistic uprising made little impression on staff and students, borne of a social-ethical attitude that had nothing to do with politics. Writings of Kafka, Brecht, Benn, and Buber were unknown to most, and their warnings and premonitions were left unheeded. The narrow studio concentration of the Bauhaus made it possible to avoid intellectual and ethical confrontation.

While surrounded by the ideologists of the new Republic, whose national assembly was housed in Weimar, the Bauhaus found it more important to isolate itself from even the new and positive influences on the German political horizon. On one hand, the Bauhaus responded with great enthusiasm to the vast and energetic American life, especially the vitality of the larger cities and the corresponding skyscraper architecture, which it revered. But it found little in American ideology to transfer to the German social condition. Instead it steadfastly adhered to the traditional German class consciousness, making clear separations between working classes and those strata of the educated and financially affluent. Although the rhetoric proclaimed better goods or living conditions, the intended consumers, the public, had little chance to influence or shape Bauhaus ideology. The public became a misunderstood and mostly unwilling participant, blamed for its lack of worldly perspective and aesthetic-value discrimination.

This social separation, isolation from the public, and lack of understanding of its daily events and cultural experiences, gave impetus to the design of products that were equally remote from the public's perception and contributed to a continuously growing lack of interest and an abundance of critical, and mostly wrong, responses. The truth lies in the fact that the disparate cultural experiences of Bauhaus members and the small-town public, coupled with the absence of an adjudicating language, allowed the Bauhaus to emerge as an alarming irritant to the cultural traditions of the various class systems. Since all public opinion finds its way into local and regional politics, it is the Bauhaus and its political naïveté that is surprising.

The greatest paradox lies in the discrepancy between the education received by the Bauhaus staff and the education it provided for its students. Gropius and several of his staff were educated in the most aristocratic and classical manner in a system open mostly to the privileged or the unusually gifted and intelligent. While they received the classical liberal and high-quality education with emphasis on literateness in the humanities, they nevertheless imposed an anti-intellectual bias on the studio education, thereby handicapping and restricting design education for the future. Because of the adoption of their methods in most design schools even today, the narrow vision of the Bauhaus takes its toll.

The Bauhaus faculty assumed themselves capable of furnishing all necessary information. However, much of what was shaped into Bauhaus publications depended heavily on loose and unpublished bits of information from other sources. Much of it was spawned at the other schools or originated in Constructivist, Suprematist, Futurist, De Stijl, and Dada ideologies as well as in the early definitions of visual languages or the principles of form, color, and construction. There was little acknowledgment of the contributions by others. By assembling the publications, the Bauhaus received credibility and as holder of these new truths was easily identified, but wrongly so, as the originator.

The Bauhaus open-mindedness was in reality only skin deep. To protect its interests, it resisted any challenge or interference from other evolving or competing dogmas. A wonderful experiment when it started, it coagulated only after a short time span into dogmatic rigidity. The period of unhampered experimentation changed into a posture of public relations, whereby exhibition-quality work interfered with the process of searching. The famous Bauhaus exhibitions were in true contradiction to all of its pervious pedagogical statements. The public relations efforts accelerated to such an extent that when Hannes Meyer replaced Gropius as director of the school, his critical assessment was that its reputation outstripped manifold the quality of the work produced. He attributed this to the unparalleled public relations effort.

Although the Bauhaus is considered an important originator of product design, it must be understood that the functionalist label applied only to the primarily technological area. Functionalism at the Bauhaus assumed standardized cultural experiences. It did not concern itself with the value systems of people and the cultural obstacles that bar an object or image from cultural integration. It also made little effort to respond to traditions, languages, and customs. Its typography shows a deep ignorance, not only of the evolution of letterforms, but also of the mechanics of reading, legibility, and perception. The belief that one approach could satisfy many problems is a lapse between the reality and a wish to have all segments of culture function in the same mode and within the same value system.

This lack of cultural perception and the restricted model of design, although it never really blossomed, was imported by the U.S. The impediments which restricted its integration into the German public were the same for the American.

The Bauhaus faculty that settled in the U.S. held misperceptions about the American culture. They came with distinct prejudices and, like Thomas Mann, thought of Americans as uneducated and boorish. They had a hard time understanding that the U.S. Constitution offers not just a single but multiple and utopian futures, unlimited by social or economic position and not guided by class restrictions. In the periods of cultural shifts from agrarian to industrial society and to world power, the dreams of true success or leisure pursuit were fostered by the film and print media and allowed each American, unlike the German, to have realistic expectations that his dreams could become reality.

The failure of the Bauhaus model has helped designers recognize the need for cultural data. Unlike the parameters of the sciences, the boundaries of the sociological information base, which is helpful for sound design decisions, are transient and dynamic. The field of import shifts according to interpretation of the philosophies and world views and the corresponding social processes of evaluation. Individual and social behaviors do not respond in predictable, repeatable or consistent cycles. Although the Bauhaus was searching for sets of binding principles of high dependability, it succeeded in finding those in areas of visual perception, but even there, only within the framework of very restricted visual languages. The fact is that no matter how scientifically or empirically sound bits of information may be, people will align with them or defer from them for reasons other than empirical truth. Any culture's behavior is based on perceptions of the environment. They are not proof of a reality of truth, but interpretations which responded to all social dynamics, including territorializing status, the development of symbols, and the making of meaningful, but subjective reality.

The bright light of the Bauhaus might dim even further through a look at its political morality. It is true that times were difficult and positions against the political mainstream dangerous. However, although the school held a place in the forefront of world opinion, it took a very neutral and a political stance. It had become accustomed to play by the rules of the legislators. It had gotten its monies first from the post-World War I remnant, imperial government; then from officials of the Weimar Republic; and finally from the representatives of the Hitler regime. Like all members of state-run institutions, they were in touch with the legislators who forged the conditions of the time. But Gropius and van der Rohe had used their organizations (*November Gruppe, Arbeitsrat für Kunst*) to influence the government. They could not have been so naive as not to see the conflicts between their educational rhetoric and the rhetoric and propaganda of their government. There is a strong suspicion that Hannes Meyer was sacrificed to appease the right wing's demand for censorship of his Swiss socialism. Granted that conditions were perilous, the last statement by van der Rohe—that he closed the school for fiscal reasons only—and his willingness to sacrifice both Hilberseimer and Kandinsky are very disturbing. "We would have agreed to these conditions, but the economic conditions do not allow for a continuation of the Institute." The conditions were: Ludwig Hilberseimer and Wassily Kandinsky are no longer permitted to teach; the curriculum has to satisfy the requirements of the civil service examination.

The Bauhaus history is an important tool for gauging the progress of the design profession. Has the field taken the same stance of political aloofness in terms of the moral issues of present times? What is the design morality or the design responsibility of the professional? Is it still possible to have no discriminatory opinions about the contents, purpose, and impact of communication messages on users and consumers? Can the designer be allowed to be politically neutral and not take a position on human rights, world politics, questions of ecology and natural resource survival, consumption of resources? Is it possible to be so uninvolved as to design a political campaign for a conservative movement one year, a moderate the next, and a left-liberal the following year without stretching integrity and credibility?

Designers must determine if information in itself is neutral and supportable by a design effort. Not all design missions pursued are desirable from a cultural perspective. A number of them are neither honorable, responsible, nor of benefit.

Can the field of practitioners continue to ignore large segments of society and, through the choice of abstract and culturally foreign iconography, bar them from access to information or services and participation in the governing process of this very complex ecosystem of multicultures and races?

The design practice must reassess the statements on which it founded its success. The slogan of good design as cost-efficient or selling surely deserves scrutiny. Is it reflected in the design of a six-color poster, with flat and glossy varnishes, for which expenditures for design and printing far outdistance the return of the box office (the rental of the hall, the hiring of the performers, and their conductor)? Does it not matter that the recruitment brochure suggests an idyllic campus located at a lakeside, which in reality is barely within driving distance? Is there not something wrong when publications show minorities as if in active control when in reality that is not true? Is not Yves St. Laurent's designer cigarette a moral blow to the whole essence of the design function? Can we sit by and not aggressively reject his contribution to the increase of cancer in women?

Unfortunately, designers are mimicking architects who have been spending time designing uncomfortable furniture and pretentious dinnerware, and who are proudly presenting their utopian or non-implementable ideas in drawing or model forms in galleries and museums. Designers develop posters for which there is no practical purpose. There is no designated space in which they might function and therefore they become an interior decorator's opportunity to solve a home-environmental beautification problem. Designers have discovered that being closer to corporate management is being closer to power and that this power provides status in the design community. Bigger is better, larger budgets more desirable and more opportune for posturing. Design is seen as an end, not a means to an end of facilitating access to information and opportunities. For example, the government proudly recognizes the prestigious sign and mapping projects for the leisure-oriented needs of the Park Service, but it seldom focuses attention on the quality of communication design in more complex areas like the social services. It is here where the affluent value systems of designers clash with those of the illiterate, the unprivileged, and alienated.

It is right to celebrate the Bauhaus' successes, but it is also prudent to use its failures as warnings. Designers have become accustomed to dogmatic credos, mottos, and manifestos: ornament is crime; less is more; form follows function. It is not acceptable to embrace these statements without responding to the relevant causal circumstances. The substantiation must include responsibility to the social environment and honest appraisals of the real worth of the design efforts.

If the anti-intellectualism of design schools could be changed, we might expect that our information base, and its interaction with the rest of the national intelligentsia, would result in a better system of critique of professional behavior and lead to the responsibility that the public deserves.

Originally published in the AIGA Journal of Graphic Design, *vol. 7, no. 4, 1990.*

SOME THOUGHTS ON MODERNISM: PAST, PRESENT AND FUTURE

by

Milton Glaser, Ivan Chermayeff, Rudolf deHarak

Milton Glaser

Growing up in the thirties and forties one could not be immune to Modernism. It was the pervasive *zeitgeist*, the spirit of the time. It was the beginning of post-Bauhaus thought, the International School of architecture, the idea that beauty is the inevitable consequence of appropriate form. We were products of a Modernist age without ever thinking about it. We ingested the philosophy of Modernism and accepted the idea of reducing everything to its most expressive form. There was really very little to counter it as a proposition.

Yet I have never felt that there was any "single" truth. Modernism offered me a set of conventions to work with or against, because in the absence of beliefs (even temporary beliefs), it is just much harder to act. Anyway, I tend to view all philosophical notions as sometimes useful and sometimes not.

My own training was not very doctrinaire. I went to the High School of Music and Art in New York where I received one body of instruction, and then on to Cooper Union where I got another, then to the Art Students League for yet another. I had a variety of educational experiences before I ever realized that design existed as a profession.

When I was growing up, there was a real struggle between notions of what was called "abstraction" and "reality." The question of how to view the world and represent it most convincingly is art's oldest question. More than any other artist in history, Picasso demonstrated clearly that you could, in fact, represent the world from innumerable vantage points, all of which turn out to be equally compelling. Understanding that I could change my vantage point was one of the instructive lessons of my life. It meant that I did not have to be loyal to a single belief.

There is a certain arrogance in the idea that one can develop a universal methodology that works in every case for every person. It does not make any sense. I have never been able to simply subscribe to the idea that any one principle, such as simplicity or reductiveness, can be universally applied to every problem. Life and people are too complicated. I must admit to one belief about design: first, you have to accomplish your intended task. Then, if you are lucky and talented, you may also create something extraordinary that goes beyond the objective task.

The responsibility of reflecting our time is another idea inherent in Modernist thought. The truth is that people with talent do good things which last, and people without talent, no matter how much they follow the rules, do work that is discarded by history. There is no way to avoid being in your time. I do not think that anybody should worry about being timeless but rather be concerned about doing the job at hand.

I wonder if one had to define Modern graphic design for the last twenty years as opposed to the previous twenty years whether we would find much difference. Much of contemporary graphic design is a reiteration of fifties design thinking in terms of its appearance and vocabulary of form. Along these lines, one of the things that binds a lot of designers to a certain way of working is the fact that they cannot draw. As a result, they are limited in terms of their ability to create form. One way to deal with this limitation is to rely on geometric forms or existing materials.

Drawing was discouraged during the Modernist era, and this impulse still continues. Imagine, that designers should not be able to represent form through drawing. What stupidity! This is an example of ideology gone crazy. It is the aesthetic equivalent of eating yogurt, tofu, and wheat germ for life. The result of this constraint results in a specific working method—collage. Finding things, cutting them out, and assembling them in new combinations is the basic design methodology of our time. It is a way of working that had its parallels in the fifties.

The Modernist idea was not to imitate anything that existed in reality. Talk about limitation. It seems to me that the power of visual work is transmitted through the metaphors and recreation of existing imagery. The idea that you cannot use the visible world as a subject is like saying you can only eat brown rice. Undernourishment comes from eating only one thing; you can become undernourished from having only one aspect of the visual world as a diet.

It is true that you can take a very narrow piece of the world and produce extraordinary things. The collage method can produce remarkable imagery. A whole generation of people are basically working off that idea. Drawing skills are technically significant and help in the understanding that occurs when you attempt to represent the world in some way. You cannot reject the body's form or the swell of a breast or thigh. Life is erotic, and the only thing that is missing from most Modernist work is eroticism. You really want to feel that a work has passion and sexuality. Why give it up? This has to do with the idea of purity. The idea that Modernism refuses to use the symbols and archetypes of history is its greatest limitation.

It is therefore understandable why Modernism became a useful tool for corporate representation. Corporations do not want to deal with issues of individuals, or eroticism, or the messy side of life. So Modernism became a wonderful way of detoxifying dirty people and dirty ideas. A corporation can represent itself through the vehicle of Modernism as being progressive and above the human squabble without ever having to deal with human sweat. If we look at history, it is not surprising that the utopian ideals of Modernism would be captured by people who want to use it for their own purposes. With all of that, the extraordinary unity of vision that Modernism provided us with is beginning to erode. Its all-encompassing principles are being questioned. Post-modernism has been officially announced but has not quite found its philosophical base. At the moment, it is addressing questions of style and fashion. Conversely, Modernism is powerful and pervasive. Although I've had my own problems with Modernism, I believe our world view is still a Modernist view.

Modernism is about progress, the endless frontier, and ceaseless development. Modernism is essentially utopian. Its origins are in the idea of good coming from boundless technology. Despite its contradictions and the erosion of its strength, the announcement of its death is premature.

Ivan Chermayeff

I was brought up in a world in which Modern was taken for granted rather than discovered. Modern was at my doorstep as a way of contemplating and dealing with the visual and tactile world. My father, Serge Chermayeff, was involved in the Modern movement almost by default. Although he was not trained as an architect or designer, he worked his way into these professions. I was taught that Modern art, design and architecture are presentations of expression that is clean and simple.

For the past several years, however, there has been a betrayal of Modern in the form of endless rationalizations about decoration, coupled with complaints about the coldness of Modern design. Post-modern is a desire to return to the appearance of things, rejecting the idea of Modern as a background for whatever else is going on. Modern is not an end in itself, but rather a framework in which to accomplish something else.

For example, I work in a completely white room. It was bequeathed to me and was once Marcel Breuer's office. But if it hadn't been white, I would have painted it white right away. The room is merely a canvas in which other things happen. It is not an end in itself. If it were, I'd have to take all the art off the walls and anything else that gives it focus. I would have to remove myself as well.

Painting and sculpture have had a tremendous influence on the way I look at design. I grew up with the usual gang of classic Modern painters—Klee, Miró, Picasso, Léger and Mondrian. The explorations that they made generally lead one away from a sense of coldness, repetition and sterility, which can exist in Modern art. As a young boy, Miró was my favorite painter, but later as a young man, I went through a long period of thinking how wrong I had been. A decade later I came back to feeling that Miro had tremendous, original qualities—comic, fresh, vibrant, immediate. I understand his visual language and feel once again that he is one of the great painters of the Modern era to whom I owe a great deal. That made it easier to intuitively understand the artists who came later: de Kooning, Tomlin, Brooks, Kline. With all their rawness and immediacy, the Abstract Expressionists still had the same predecessors. Modern art and design grows in a logical way. And that is the Modern's virtue; it changes and expands, becoming endlessly redefined and forward moving. It is an attitude that invites reconsideration and shifting according to time, yet holds on to the best of what has been accomplished.

All my thinking about the process of design in the development of graphic tone and composition comes more from painters than from any other source. The strength of painters like Léger or Stuart Davis comes from the simple directness in their development of forms and flat colors; the whole, a bridge between symbol and picture, and a change from illustration to symbol-making. I would not say that I made the same explorations, but nevertheless, contemporary graphic design deals with similar problems, like eliminating unnecessary elements.

I do not have the belief that there is a proper way to do things. What makes graphic design so interesting is that there are few real rules. However, having said that, there are nevertheless purposes. I am not sympathetic to purposelessness in design. What is called

"New Wave" is a revisionist return to bygone periods, arbitrary and incredibly boring. Art Deco and Art Nouveau are important to be aware of as styles. The Bauhaus and Pop Art are important as ideas, which are greatly reduced in value when distilled into style alone. To bring any style out of the drawer unrelated to the subject matter at hand is depressing. If there is a single rule, it is that there should be some logic in the application of the past to current communication needs. And this logic has to be based on more than predilections of taste.

If one is drawn to anything in a positive way, it is because one immediately grasps the reason for its being. Then one can analyze how successful or how original it is. If it works, it looks good after a while, like the original Volkswagen. Nowadays there is an enormous volume of graphic design work that is at a high level of professionalism. There is more good work around than ever before. But the amount that is really refreshing, in a purposeful way, is not greater at all.

What has happened to Modern design is that its horizons have expanded. Some people have abandoned it because it seems not to be there anymore. But in fact there is more opportunity for varied attitudes to coexist than when Modernists were more doctrinaire.

An excellent example of a new Modern spirit can be found in the work of Grapus, a group of Parisian graphic designers who lend their talents to politically significant causes. They go to great lengths to make their work appear immediate. Their posters always look as though they were done in ten seconds flat. One knows perfectly well that they aren't, yet their process demands and produces a level of freshness that the others rarely reach so consistently. They believe that something which appears "hot-off-the-press" demands attention. This is a Modern thought.

The Grapus philosophy differs significantly, for example, from the theories about typography design emanating from Basel. The Swiss have too many stylistic tenets that have to do with spacing, weight, and color. The Basel approach appears to spread like wildfire because it is recognizable, consistent, and therefore, teachable. It is too easy and repetitive, and the levels of boredom attached to it are high. The essential difference between the Modern tradition and the Basel Style is that the latter abandons function altogether. This does not mean that Modern design is void of style or artistry. On the contrary, Modern design can include anything, including "New Wave" graphic styles.

The refuge of the untalented is to make more of things, never less. Modern graphic design of the thirties did not. That does not make it less modern, but rather evolutionary.

The bulk of graphic design today is done without designers. Most houses are designed without architects. In architecture, for example, despite the Modern legacy, the building that goes on in the name of capricious fashion is more notorious than any other kind. It is successful because it demands a lot of conversation and gains high rents for its developers.

Similar practice occurs in graphic design. There are those who rest on their fashionable accomplishments, while a few others attempt to push boundaries.

Rudolph deHarak

In the late forties as a beginning commercial artist in Los Angeles, I attended two lectures which introduced me to Modernism and had a profound effect on my life. The first was a lecture by Will Burtin entitled "Integration, The New Discipline in Design." Burtin not only spoke about design and communications, but also presented an exhibition of his work, which guided the viewer through a series of experiences which were described as the four principal realities of visual communications. They were the reality of man, as measure and measurer; the reality of light, color, and texture; the reality of space, motion, and time; and the reality of science. He was the first person I had heard use the term "visual communications."

A short time later, I heard Gyorgy Kepes speak. At the time I didn't fully understand everything he was saying, yet I knew that his words were very important to me. I recall my excitement, as I was able to draw parallels between what he was saying about the plastic arts and what Will Burtin had said concerning the realities of visual communications.

It was the beginning of my realization that it was possible to communicate visual information which transcended common conventions and could become art. I discovered the possibility of having a viable vocation and at the same time to be able to experience deep fulfillment. These lectures were so important that they inspired me to leave my job as a mechanical artist and commit myself totally to design.

As I became more involved with this profession, I realized that my deepest concerns with design were centered on what I felt were the mysteries of form—discovering new forms and using them to construct creative and meaningful solutions to design problems.

I attempted to evolve forms that covered the entire emotional spectrum and were also impeccable in their sense of order. This to me was the essence of Modernism, and toward that end, I wanted to create constellations so rich that they could communicate content. I was searching for what I called "the hidden order"; trying to find some common principle or scheme inherent in all things that would answer questions that maybe I hadn't yet asked.

The Bauhaus was perhaps the most profound example of Modernism in their break with the rigid ideologies of "grand manner" art education. Dedicated to research and instruction, their objective was a social reconditioning through a synthetic curriculum. Simultaneously, all of the arts were examined in the light of contemporary conditions.

Modernism is also exemplified in the International Style of design that developed following World War II. Its mostly Swiss contributors included such notable designers as Max Bill, Josef Muller-Brockmann, Armin Hofmann, Max Huber, Richard Lohse, Hans Neuberg, Siegfried Odermatt, Emil Ruder, and Carlo Vivarelli. These Modernists breathed new life into design, cutting away all unnecessary graphic appendages and leaving only the essentials. Their work, which manifested itself in this timeless style, was thoughtful and systematic. The work was beautiful, thoroughly crafted, and communicated complex information quickly and simply. Like the Bauhaus, it was an essential development and a strong reflection of its time.

In the forties and fifties, I believed that Modern design was a means to precipitate reactions and new actions. At that time, there was a sense of urgency—a design revolution that was alive that aimed at developing openness to what many considered radical forms of communication. The goal was to create a platform for design from which could be communicated bold, new graphic ideas. I think that platform today is firmly rooted, thus, expanding the possibility of producing intensely creative, dynamic and even bizarre ideas. There is now much more awareness and acceptance of good design.

As times changed, so did my design philosophies. Now I am more interested in the process of problem-solving. This is not to say I don't want my design to be beautiful. But in the past I was preoccupied with finding something profound and revealing within a form. Today I am much more concerned with the clear, direct communication of an idea.

Twenty-five years ago I said in a lecture, "The attitudes that forms communicate dictate the ultimate validity of a design. Form is necessary and vital to the expression of ideas. Without it, content is barren. So in an effort to effect a solution to any visual problem, the designer relies on his abilities to create new forms or use existing forms in unique concepts, and manipulate them."

Just a few years ago at another lecture I made quite a different statement. "Design is a problem-solving process, but for many of us it is much more than that. It is also a very personal process of searching for and developing new concepts that serve to clarify and extend ideas. Herein lies the creativity in design.

"The climate that the designer works within is very complex, and as in all creative fields, at times painful and frustrating. The designer's work must satisfy the tastes and opinions of the client, but most important, it must successfully reach and communicate to the audiences for which the work is intended. Even though the design work should also be self-rewarding, it is frequent that personal preferences have little meaning in the solving of design problems."

The differences in these two statements, made more than twenty years apart, are apparent. Yet, because my fundamental belief in Modernism has not changed, I believe that they mostly represent a shift in emphasis and priorities.

Before I became fully aware of the International Style, and the Swiss pioneers in particular, my design inclinations moved in a somewhat similar direction. Before we had Helvetica in the United States, I primarily used sans-serif typefaces such as Futura, News Gothic, and Franklin Gothic. When Helvetica was first introduced, I specified it almost exclusively because it had a purity and uniformity that signaled no-nonsense information without embellishment. It is the way I feel about the old Remington typewriter face—beautiful, direct, and systematized. Typography is a profound issue, and when I started in this field, I felt that developing an understanding of all typefaces would be an extraordinary, time-consuming challenge.

It was preferable for me to work with just a few typefaces on a consistent basis, thereby developing a more intimate understanding of the letterforms. The challenge and ideal solution to a book design, for example, would be to set the entire book—titles, subtitles, text and folios—in one style and size, establishing priorities of information through position and spatial relationships.

I am not implying that this approach was better than others, but it gave me a more disciplined position in which to understand type and to achieve viable solutions. Moreover, in designing a record cover on the music of Mozart, I was never interested in using a typeface that would be representative of the eighteenth century. Personally, I can no more identify Mozart with Caslon than with Futura. If I were to follow this design philosophy to its conclusion, it would be logical to put flames on the word "fire" or ice-caps on the word "cool." I believed the problem-solving process requires intelligent selection of a typeface that functions most appropriately for an overall design concept.

Changes in style, or new preferences in typefaces or color, have little to do with the basic responsibilities of problem-solving in visual communications. The designer making a poster today has the same responsibilities to communicate clearly as El Lissitzky, Rodchenko, or Cassandre had decades ago.

I don't believe in change for the sake of change. Change comes about through a natural process of development or because something needs improving. Modernism suggests movement which is ahead of its time. If we do something that has been done before, we are not being creative; we are being redundant. Creativity, which is what Modernism is all about, is a constant searching process that promises a greater chance for failure than it does for success.

Originally published in the AIGA Journal of Graphic Design, vol. 5, no. 2, 1987.

RETHINKING MODERNISM, REVISING FUNCTIONALISM
by
Katherine McCoy

When I think of the undercurrents that shape my graphic design, I think of ideas about language and form. Ideas about coding and reading visual form, about challenging the viewer to construct individual interpretations, about layers of form and layers of meaning. These are at the forefront of my mind, but behind that lie other deeper and older concerns that go back to my earliest years of design. Perhaps these are what could be called a philosophy or an ethic, a personal set of values and criteria, a thread that winds through the lifetime of work and sustains its rigor, the continuity in the cycles of change.

Undergraduate school in industrial design was a very idealistic time. The strong emphasis on problem-solving and a *form follows function*alism struck a resonance with my personal approach toward the opportunities and problems of daily life. As a college junior, I enthusiastically embraced the rationalism of the Museum of Modern Art's Permanent Design Collection, abandoning the ambiguously intuitive territory of fine art. This somewhat vague midwestern American Modernist ethic had its roots in the Bauhaus, and our group of students gained a dim understanding of its application by the Ulm School of Germany. Added to this was a reverence for the insights of George Nelson, Marshall McLuhan, and Buckminster Fuller. In hindsight I continue to appreciate the foundation built by those years of industrial design training. At that time, in the middle 1960s, even the best American education in graphic design would not have gone much further than an intuitive *"ah ha"* method of conceptualizing design solutions and an emulation of the design masters of the moment.

This faith in rational functionalism (and not a polished portfolio) found me my first job, at Unimark International, then the American missionary for European Modernism, the graphic heir of the Bauhaus. There I had the opportunity to learn graphic design from "real" Swiss and to have my junior design work critiqued by Massimo Vignelli, the greatest missionary of them all, the master of Helvetica and the grid. Our ethic then was one of discipline, clarity, and cleanliness. The highest praise for a piece of graphic design was: *"This is really clean."* We saw ourselves as sweeping away the clutter and confusion of American advertising design with a professional rationality and objectivity that would define a new American design. This approach was fairly foreign to American clients and in 1968 it was remarkably difficult to convince corporate clients that a grid-ordered page with only two weights of Helvetica was appropriate to their needs. Now, of course, one can hardly persuade them to give up their hold on "Swiss," so completely has the corporate world embraced rationalist Modernism in graphic design.

But after a few years of striving to design as "purely" as possible, employing a minimalist typographic vocabulary, strongly gridded page structures and contrast in scale for visual interest, I came to view this desire for "cleanliness" as not much more than housekeeping. A number of us, mainly graphic designers in the "Swiss" method, began to search for a more expressive design, paralleling a similar movement in architecture now known as Post-modernism. Eventually what came to be called "New Wave," for lack of a better term, emerged in the 1970s as a new operating mode of graphic design. This included a new permission to employ historical and vernacular elements, something prohibited by "Swiss" Modernism. Then in the mid-1980s at Cranbrook we found a new interest in verbal language in graphic design, as well as fine art. Text can be animated with voices and images can be read, as well as seen, with an emphasis on audience interpretation and participation in the construction of meaning. But now, as the cycles of change continue, Modernism may be re-emerging somewhat, a renewed minimalism that is calming down the visual outburst of activity of the past fifteen years.

Through these years of continual change and new possibilities, where does the ethic lie? Does not the idea of ethic imply some sort of unshakable bedrock impervious to the winds of change? For me, there seems to be a habit of functionalism that shapes my process at the beginning of every design project, the rational analysis of the message and the audience, the objective structuring of the text. Each cycle of change during the passing years seems to have added another visual or conceptual layer laid upon that foundation of functionalism, but inside of every project it is always there. Although this emphasis on rationalism would seem to be at odds with recent experimentation at Cranbrook, in fact it has been the provocation to question accepted norms in graphic design, stimulating the search for new communications theories and visual languages. I have never lost my faith in rational functionalism, in spite of appearances to the contrary. The only thing lost was an absolute dedication to minimalist form, which is a completely different issue from rationalist process.

Part of this ethic is a strong conviction and enthusiasm that design is important, that it matters in life, not just mine, but in the lives of our audiences and users of designed communications. Graphic design can be a contribution to our audiences. It can enrich as it informs and communicates. And there is a faith in not only the possibility, but the necessity for advancement and growth in our field, an imperative for change. That only through change can we continue to push ahead in knowledge and expertise, theory and expression, continually building our collective knowledge of the process of communication. These convictions were formed early and sustain me today.

Originally published as "How I Lost My Faith in Rational Functionalism" in the AIGA Journal of Graphic Design, *vol. 9, no. 4, 1990.*

LONG LIVE MODERNISM!
by
Massimo Vignelli

I was raised to believe that an architect should be able to design everything from a spoon to a city. At the root of this belief is a commitment to improve the design of everything that can be made—to make it better. To make it better not only from a functional or mechanical point of view, but to design it to reflect cultural and ethical values, ethical integrity. Integrity of purpose, materials, and the manufacturing process.

Integrity of purpose implies a severe analysis of what the problem is; its meaning, what the possibilities for a range of solutions are: solutions which have to be sifted through to determine the most appropriate for the specific problem—not just alternatives I may like, but one that answers all of the questions posed by the problem. The solutions to a problem are in the problem itself. To solve all the questions posed by the problem, however, is not enough. The solutions should reflect the approach taken, and by virtue of its configuration, stimulate cultural reactions in the viewer, rather than emotional titillations. In this process, nothing is taken for granted, no dogmas are accepted, no preconceived ideas are assumed or adopted without questioning them in the context of the project.

I was raised to believe that, as a designer, I have the responsibility to improve the world around us, to make it a better place to live, to fight and oppose trivia, kitsch, and all forms of subculture which are visually polluting our world. The ethics of Modernism, or I should say the ideology of Modernism, was an ideology of the fight, the ongoing battle to combat all the wrongs developed by industrialization during the last century. Modernism was a commitment against greed, commercialization, exploitation, vulgarization, cheapness. Modernism was and still is the search for truth, the search for integrity, the search for cultural stimulation and enrichment of the mind. Modernism was never a style, but an attitude. This is often misunderstood by those designers who dwell on revivals of the form rather than on the content of Modernism. From the beginning, Modernism had the urgency of utopianism: to make a world better by design. Today we know better. It takes more than design to change things. But the cultural thrust of the Modernist belief is still valid, because we still have too much trash around us, not only material trash, but intellectual trash as well. In that respect, I value, endorse, and promote the continued relevance of the Modern movement as the cultural mainstream of our century.

The cultural events of the last twenty years have expanded and deepened the issues and values promoted by the Modern movement. The revision of many of the Modernist issues have enriched our perception and have contributed to improving the quality of work. The increased number of architects and designers with good training has had a positive effect on our society and our environment. Much still has to be done to convince industry and government that design is an integral part of the production process and not a last-minute embellishment.

The cultural energy of the Modern movement is still burning, fueling intellects against shallow trends, transitory values, superficial titillations brought forward by the media, whose very existence depends on ephemera. Many of the current modes are created, supported, and discarded by the very media that generates that change and documents it to survive. It is a vicious circle. It has always been, only now it is bigger than ever.

As seen in a broad historical perspective, Modernism's ascetic, spartan look still has a towering position of strength and dignity. Modernism's inherent notion of timeless values as opposed to transient values still greatly appeals to my intellectual being.

The best architects in the world today are all Modernists at the core, and so are the best designers. The followers of the Post-modernist fad are gone, reduced to caricatures of the recent past. Post-modernism should be regarded at best as a critical evaluation of the issues of Modernism. In that perspective, it has been extremely helpful to correct, expand, improve the issues of Modernism. None of us would be the same without it. However, the lack of a profound ideology eventually brought Post-modernism to its terminal stage. In the cultural confusion provided by pluralism and its eclectic manifestations, Modernism finds its *raison d'être* in its commitment to the original issues of its ideology and its energy to change the world into a better place in which to live.

Long live the Modern movement!

Originally published in the AIGA Journal of Graphic Design, *vol. 9, no. 2, 1991.*

LIFE, STYLE, AND ADVOCACY
by
Dan Friedman

At first, I was reluctant to talk about life-style. I thought it would be superficial. But then I realized it would be at the very heart of my larger agenda. I was given just ten minutes to talk about the way I live. But it was necessary for me to begin with some observations about design and culture in general, and our profession in particular, because these things very much affect the way I have chosen to live. I also showed images which indicate how our homes express our lifestyles; how they reflect our disposition, creativity, knowledge, taste, wealth, and view of ourselves in relationship to the rest of the world.

We exist in a culture which generates all kinds of recipes for how we should look.

Like changing channels on TV, we are shown that everyone can aspire to various lifestyles, from the look of Ralph Lauren to the look of Guns n' Roses. Our consumer society classifies all of us by style.

So it seems only natural that designers would also fall into this business of creating style even while maintaining to each other that we possess keener sensibilities and that we are above such things previously described as fashion. To the contrary, we seem to admire most the work that packages a message in a new look even if we can't always tell what that message is. We see this development everywhere from Los Angeles to New York and from Michigan to Texas. Even one of our foremost architects, Philip Johnson, has gotten into this game. Six years ago, his office made their first proposal for a project in Times Square in the "Post-modern" style when it was at the height of its popularity. Recently the same firm made a new proposal for the same project which indicates that a "deconstructivist" style is now better. It is no surprise to me that the biggest contribution designers seem to be making these days is in promoting styles.

What we don't seem to realize is that, culturally, much of society has moved way ahead of the designer. There was a time when things were the other way around! Designers and artists were visionaries leading society. I think we should aspire to do that again. The early Modernist movement still provides a noble message about the role of design in effecting culture and lifestyle. The spirit of early pioneers such as Ruskin, Gropius, Wright, Schwitters, or Le Corbusier was that design—like art—would be a service and inspiration to humanity. And designers would reflect this spirit in every aspect of their work, their lives, and their ethics.

I was lucky early in my career to get to know other pioneers such as Armin Hofmann, Paul Rand, and George Nelson. I admired them mainly because of their passion, their dedication, and for the manner in which their work was an inseparable part of their lifestyles. I too developed this idea that my lifestyle and design style would be effortlessly integrated. Each would be unified within the other. I saw graphic design as something integral to larger environmental and social issues so it seemed only logical to me that our homes and personal style would likewise express the same criteria. This was the foundation of Modernism which I have always embraced.

But I don't think that the first pioneers of Modernism would have anticipated how our profession, and even the lifestyles of its practitioners, would have become so thoroughly dominated by purely economic and corporate values. For example, I learned in the mid-1970s, during an association with a New York design firm, how my idea of integrity somehow mutated from service to the public good into service to the corporation. In my opinion, this is a process in which designers eventually become willing to look and act as bland and predictable as the work they create. I always point out that Modernism forfeited any claim to a moral authority when designers sold it away as corporate style. If you want to discuss dangerous ideas, I would say, despite indications of change, that this practice has now dominated our profession for more than twenty years and is celebrated every year at the AIGA Communication Graphics Show.

If consumer society has brought us to one end of a spectrum, excess of style with limited substance, then corporate society has brought us to the other extreme, blandness of spirit at the expense of personal value.

In the late 1970s, my personal, domestic landscape became my primary source of experimentation and a laboratory for studying issues of design. I expected this expression of my lifestyle would lead me into some new design profession; I certainly no longer wanted my profession to define my lifestyle as I did earlier in my career. For me, my home is like a diary. It is always changing, it makes references to the world around me, and it provides a very private way of trying design ideas. Since there are always more ideas than space, I accept complexity as a necessity. I create an extreme caricature of the beautiful modern American home in order to bring into question our notion of what is a beautiful modern American home. There is something very satisfying about applying my design skill to things where you actually live everyday rather than those bits of corporate paper that end up in the garbage. And the more I make it look like something no one else in their right mind would want to achieve, the more visits I seem to get from journalists, art collectors, and even architects from around the world who take it very seriously. My home has become the ideal place to re-examine the relationships between design, art, nature, culture, technology, and modern urban living. It helps me focus my pursuit of an art which has meaning and function and a design that has poetry and value.

This activity all comes together into a kind of grand assemblage; it seems a result of some primordial explosion of energy, radiating with intense color and complexity. I have created elegant mutations of a hyper-Modernist world which deconstructed in my imagination into a wild ritualistic playground. You can walk in my door and find the coherent, integrated world of Modernism brought to its wildest extreme. I choose to celebrate progressive optimism, fantasy, and playful exuberance. I reject solutions which revert to excessive historicism and nostalgia. This is not an easy route when most of our culture has moved in the opposite direction. Therefore, I see myself as a radical Modernist, one who still believes in an idealism bound to a moral imperative, even if it might take some sort of apocalyptic process for it to happen. The objects I live with do more than function; they express ideas and tell stories. My goal has been to signal a realignment with the spirit of primal societies—the spirit through which one is surrounded not by art or design, but by objects which are artfully conceived, culturally significant, useful in daily rituals, related to human scale, and energized by magic.

So is this the work of some crazy schizophrenic lost in his personal metaphorical space, or is there really insight from one man's lifestyle which other designers can use? Like all of you, we have moments when we ask ourselves: How do I fit into the grand scheme of things? What do I want to do professionally? What kind of lifestyle do I desire? And of course, how much money do I need to make? But there are other questions which I think I only fully resolved in the midst of my odd domestic experimentation, and I gather they will be questions you too may be asking:

How can I make my profession an expression of my lifestyle rather than the other way around?

Why are there so few graphic designers whose lifestyle I truly want to emulate?

Why do good designers have a relatively minor impact on our overall environment or on our popular culture?

What happened to our sense of humor?

Why must a bottom line mentality tend to squeeze out artistic and humanistic concerns?

Are very personal forms of expression inappropriate to impose on jobs for clients, or are these expressions better left at home?

Why have designers allowed themselves to become servants to increasing overheads, careerism, and predominantly corporate goals?

As someone who has successfully spent most of the last decade in both the worlds of art and design, I now believe our most pressing issue in the next decade is not about art versus design but is about reinvesting both with a moral authority and a higher vision. It has always been my goal to inspire my peers to perform with a sense of quality, exuberance, freshness, danger, responsibility, and optimism. I now dream of designers becoming advocates. I'm not talking about the few attempts some of us make which we refer to as *pro bono* work, but truly a change of mind set which reorients us away from purely aesthetic or narrow corporate values toward educational, technological, cultural, informational, environmental, social, and even domestic values. I think this would really be the way to enhance our lifestyles and to work us out of the corner in which the profession finds itself. If it's our priority, I expect in the 1990s that this endeavor could be leveraged into an industry and could even be profitable.

Originally published in the AIGA Journal of Graphic Design, *vol. 7, no. 4, 1990.*

ON OVERCOMING MODERNISM
by
Lorraine Wild

To those who wish to respond to the new art,
we say that it is not enough to stare at it with one's eyes;
one's whole head must be turned in a different direction.
—El Lissitzky

What were you doing the day the newspapers featured that picture of the flag coming down all over what was the Soviet Union? I was on the phone going over type changes with an editor on the other side of the continent, for a book that was being printed on the other side of the globe. Had I done this project justice? Will someone in the future be able to look at this work and see all the effort and desire that went into it? Who can possibly answer these questions, as enmeshed as we are in the speed of communication, the technology, the information overload, the conflicting ethics and values of our present condition?

To what degree are each of us futurists? To what degree are each of us hopelessly mired in the day-to-day?

We know, intuitively, that our personal struggle with idealism and pragmatism is affected by the values we bring to our work and the context in which we create it. The uncertainty of values in contemporary graphic design practice and the discourse that surrounds it now (and probably will through the nineties), has led to a notion that there has been a loss of consensus as to what constitutes "good" design. The shifting nature and context of our activity as graphic designers is now often described in terms of loss. What we have definitely lost is the ability to lean on the principles of Modernism to regain that consensus. This presents a conceptual challenge to graphic designers, because the ideals of Modernism, especially those having to do with universality, objectivity, timelessness, "problem-solving," and social values, have been the wobbly base upon which the professional identity of the graphic design community has traditionally rested.

A sense of confusion and rancor has crept into discussions about contemporary graphic design practice, questioning the meaning of graphic design that does not conform to the rules that embody the myths of Modernism. These discussions often split along generational lines, with an old guard (those who believe in the Modernist credo, even if they do not actually practice it) often demanding an allegiance to Modernist ideals and forms. The frequent reference to a unified Modernist past and its subsequent dissolution is important because those terms may well end up delineating how the new guard will be able to think through this confusing present to find the future of design.

AGE OF DISCONTENT

In the world of graphic design there is still abundant sentiment that nothing is inherently wrong with contemporary design that a little economic upturn wouldn't cure; and if only our clients would cooperate, we designers could return to the production of the same kinds of "problem solving" we have been engaged in since 1950. The trouble with that attitude is that the entire backdrop against which we solve our problems has radically shifted, and a lot of designers either haven't noticed the change, or they harbor fantasies of being able to fend it off.

In recent years universality has collapsed into multiculturalism, focus groups, zip-code clusters, etc.; objectivity has collapsed into subjectivity, at the same time as the author and the subject, or both, have been declared dead in some quarters; and the optimistic march of progress has been canceled. The linear is harder to detect and the simultaneous has become habitual.

All of these conditions are symptoms of what is called Post-modernity. But this term has not been very appealing to graphic designers; the "post" part of it seems to imply exhaustion, decline or missed opportunities. There is also the lingering confusion of Post-modernism with a conservative, historically allusive style that characterized much architecture and graphic design of the 1980s. Some still confuse nostalgia with the sum total of Post-modernism, because a few earlier interpretations of Post-modern theory (such as Charles Jencks' use of semiotics to elevate the stylistically eclectic work of Robert A. M. Stern) were used to support the growing conservatism of the 1980s.

Another characteristic of Post-modernity is the intellectual acknowledgement of the existence of many Modernisms—a range of strategies, from the merely aesthetic to the attainment of social reform (or complete revolution). Some Modernists, such as Heartfield, were extremely temporal, and posed direct challenges to the political status quo; other Modernists, such as Mies van der Rohe, searched for an aesthetic absolute that would transcend the particulars of context and politics. Some other Modernists, such as El Lissitzky or van Doesburg, did both. But recent attempts by graphic designers to declare the definition of Modernism as a *successful* search for either aesthetic absolutes or social reform are symptomatic of the alienation of those who want to avoid the complexity of both the past and the present.

The influence of Modernism on American graphic designers may have originated in the work of the European Futurists or the Constructivists or the designers of the Bauhaus, but the social utopianism of the aesthetic that accompanied early Modernism never reached the United States. Indulging in sloppy thinking, fake history and romance, we attribute a fantasy of ethical accomplishment to Modernism as a reaction against the uncomfortable unknowns of Post-modernism. Some design fields have recognized this, but not graphic design. "Design is communication." "Design is problem solving." One hears these clichés repeated endlessly, the mantra of the graphic designers stuck in the denial and anger phases of mourning for a time when we thought that the values by which we lived and defined ourselves made sense in the larger world.

Despite those who would attribute functionalism solely to Modernism, functionalism can be seen as inherent in the definition of design itself; a series of actions taken to produce a desired effect. It may be time to detach the notion of function from the failed ideology of Modernism in order that function might regain its simplicity and clarity as a design value. Weren't pre-Modernists such as Gutenberg or Diderot or Benjamin Franklin rational functionalists? Recent design historians have clarified that under Modernism, function (or simply the imagery of function) was more often dedicated to the production or distribution of an artifact than to function dedicated to the object itself. Yet graphic designers persist in talking about function as our invention, a gift we generously grant to our audiences.

Another aspect of Modernism some would like to retain (even if it is deeply misunderstood or misinterpreted by those yearning for the old days) is a defined visual style. The aesthetic security of the International Style is now missed by many of those who functioned well within it. They are attempting to revive Modernist conviction now that so many other aspects of design practice affecting form have been destabilized.

First and perhaps foremost, the complete rethinking of the production of printed materials wrought by digital technology has thrown graphic design's identity as Modern into question. The computer has affected all design practices; CAD programs are now commonly used in architecture and industrial design. The professional identity of graphic design developed at a time when the conceptual processes of layout and form were separated from the setting of type and print production, but current technology reunites those activities, and what should be merely convenient or even liberating turns out to be traumatic.

UNDERSTANDING MODERNISM'S MYSTIQUE

It is now possible for anyone with a word-processing program and a layout program to become a graphic designer. The mystery of making is gone, and while optimists predict that this will increase the public interest in graphic design, pessimists observe that the prosaic projects that used to occupy designers are now gone for good precisely when more graduates are pouring into the graphic design field than ever. The technology has challenged many of the precepts of graphic design education, which is based on Modernist interpretation of form and technique, and educators must struggle to rethink curricula because of it. Technology has irrevocably changed the way younger designers enter the field, the way projects are managed and offices are run and ultimately, the way design is consumed.

The computer has also had a greater effect on the quality of the products of graphic design than on the products of the other design fields; for example, computer-aided renderings of buildings look "different" than hand drawings, but buildings in their built form remain largely unaffected. But the evolving technology of electronic typesetting has taken its toll on the quality of typesetting, and a set of standards inherited from metal typesetting (which were already altered significantly during the change to "cold" type) have been shaken.

But in the midst of this perceived decline, new developments in digital typography have brought about an explosion of font design, and the energy coming from small font publishers and distributors has enlivened typographic design. Those who are not terrified by the new typographic technologies are using them in all sorts of ways, as an opportunity to reinvent type aesthetics in response to the technology itself. Unfamiliar forms of work produced in response to major changes in technology are often classified as "ugly" because of their formal strangeness, and interpreted as evidence of aesthetic malfeasance, the obliteration of standards and practices of craft. It is a functional Modernist impulse to submit aesthetics to the demands of the machine, but in this case the subject of the technology is dematerialized, infinitely variable; the resulting aesthetic mirrors those same qualities, and the Modernists are confused!

WEIRD SCIENCE

There are a few members of the old guard who are knowledgeable enough about typographic history to recognize our present condition as similar to other moments of great creativity brought on by technological revolution. Yet, it is neither possible to valorize all of the products of our current typographic mania, nor is it desirable, since the designers working in this field are not seeking the timeless or classic by any stretch of the imagination. But the refusal by so many of our Modernist diehards to see this historical moment is ironic in light of the fact that the technology of computers has brought us closer to one of the great old fantasies of machine-driven design, the "electro-library" of El Lissitzky, the extension of the Modernist technological reverie taken to its logical Post-modern conclusion.

Berkeley architecture professor Mark Treib has pointed out that the essential difference in the professional status and relative levels of security between architects and graphic designers can be traced to the existence of regulated contracts in architecture and the contrasting free-for-all of graphic design practice. Architects, notes Treib, are contractually bound to be the representative of their clients in relation to the contractor or builder. Treib suggests that the lack of craft attached to function in graphic design (printing being simpler than construction) has always contributed to a more tenuous relationship between graphic designers and their clients. If Treib is right, that tenuousness would have to be on the verge of obliteration since the production-related reasons for any client to hire a graphic design consultant are decreasing steadily. Obviously, fear of unemployment is driving graphic designers crazy.

During the eighties we had to endure such inanities as Michael Peters' declaration that only big offices could offer legitimate design services; small offices were primitive and doomed to fail. At the same time, design educators suffered a barrage of criticism for not preparing students as entry-level employees for big offices. Criticism of the commercial abuse of design is always problematic: if it comes from Stuart Ewen, it's rejected because he's an academic; if it comes from Neville Brody, it doesn't count because he's English; if it comes from Tibor Kalman, it's invalid because he is somehow tainted by his own commercial practice; if it comes from Dan Friedman, well "doesn't he design furniture now?"; if it comes from someone like me, it is written off because my practice is not commercial enough.

Our current recession grants us all a moment to reconsider our positions in light of history and the inexorable present. Speaking for myself, trained in vestigially Modern ways but practicing during this period of great flux, exposure to the current level of quandary and challenge in the design office and the classroom is, I believe, enough to drive anyone back into pipe dreams of old Dessau. To accept that design is complicit in our real environment is to reject the myth of the designer as disinterested genius or moralist or super-hero. As difficult as it is, we must keep questioning preconceived notions of what good design is. This does not mean that we must reject what history we have, or that we must decline the pleasures of formal innovation. It does mean that we must become honest about the work we choose to do, the forms that we give to it, the circumstances under which we produce and how our work actually functions in the world.

The inability to describe a set of universal formal guidelines for "good" graphic design should not be seen as a handicap (even if it often feels like one). This condition offers us a "window of opportunity" in which we may be able to address some of those other issues that so many educators and practitioners pay lip service to but are still so easy to ignore as long as we can be distracted by the more immediate gratifications of form. This is not to denigrate form. If the audience has changed and the production has changed and the messages might change, wouldn't common sense (dare we call it functionalism?) suggest that the notion of form might evolve too? There is no doubt that aesthetics are a tough call. As the educator Jacques Girard states about critiquing work in the classroom these days, "Someone who refers to a design as beautiful, ugly, good or bad is not talking as much about the object as about himself." Appropriateness cannot be held up as a value in and of itself without looking closely at the situations to which we pledge our obedience. And, under the current terms of our existence, there may only be particularly appropriate formal solutions instead of general ones.

For a few years now some designers have been using the metaphors of language to describe the workings of design. Actually this is not new, as some members of the old guard are always quick to point out. Yes, they taught semiotics at Ulm. But their understanding of semiotics was still affected by late Modernist design theory that trained them to look for universal signs; the interpretation of semiotic theory is significantly different now. Another linguistic theory that may lead to the development of new paradigms for graphic design is the use of rhetorical concepts as a framework for design analysis. Again, this is not a new idea in design studies, but timing is everything. In the past, academic problems in graphic design studies that used rhetoric as an analytical tool were often contradicted by the combination of expressive linguistic analysis with "objective" Modernist typography. You didn't know what you were looking at. The revival of interest in rhetoric now comes at a time when we may be less concerned by the split between expression and objectivity.

Reception theory, another Post-modern construct, is a revision of Modernist notions of function, use and meaning. The prospect of graphic designers starting to think about meaning as a result of situations of use is a challenging one. Graphic designers have not had to live with marketing the way industrial designers have, and market testing or legibility testing are often seen as pernicious activities that only reinforce the obvious. So how do you build alternative understandings of use or performance in graphic design? I doubt that the practice will ever be quantifiable in any way, but I'm sure that any understanding that evolves will be particular and local.

The pressure on the young designer today is not to become a star, a master or mistress of the universal, but to become a participant in communication process, a co-conspirator, a co-author, maybe even an author/designer. This is why the development of the personal voice or agenda has emerged as an important new aspect in the training of young designers today. Their educational experiences should equip them with this expanded, much more accountable role that will be demanded of them if they are to retain any validity in a new context.

But what about the old folks, the old guard, or those of us who straddle the two guards? We are the ones who, in the last fifteen years, have complained that graphic design had an inadequate body of theory and history to guide its own development; but ironically, as more theoretical and historically informed ways of thinking about graphic design have evolved, our heroic Modernist dreams have gone to hell in a handbasket. We're not sure what to believe anymore. We're distressed, we're unhappy, we're in pain! What should we do?

CALLING DR. FREUD

In her influential book, *The Drama of the Gifted Child,* psychoanalyst Alice Miller posits that children who are consistently forced to subjugate their desires to the demand and wills of their parents will experience a kind of stunting of their own personalities, leading to depression (based on never really being able to feel securely loved) or what Miller calls "grandiosity," the tendency to repeat behavior that gains approval (in lieu of love) over and over, no matter how emotionally unfulfilling. The grandiose are literally trapped in their own success, and miserable because of it.

When I encountered Miller's thesis, I thought that I had stumbled upon a good psychoanalytic paradigm to explain the inability of graphic designers, particularly American ones, to withstand the vicissitudes of history and theory in our collective unconscious. Our old guard fought battles for us dedicated to the ideology of Modernism; the audience, in the role of parents, didn't buy the story (for their own neurotic reasons) but they rewarded many designers by using them up, ignoring their ideals, paying them for their style very, very well ... but still never granting those designers the same level of status and glorification reserved for artists (even much more mediocre ones). Thus in our old guard we frequently encounter bitterness despite lifetimes of success, a lack of generosity toward new work or new designers, defensiveness, the desire for control, and worst of all, the attempt to dictate the intellectually pathetic idea of a singular history. Consider the recent spectacle of several of the most highly regarded names in graphic design excoriating the Walker Art Center for daring to assemble an exhibition titled "A History of Graphic Design" (note: not "The History"), which, they thought, failed to pay suitable homage to their accomplish-ments.

When graphic designers complain that their parents don't understand what they do, it used to sound like an innocent little joke, repeated to reinforce group identity; now it takes on a sinister tone, like a symptom of disease, grounds for professional counseling. Remember, admitting that there is a problem is the first step to the road to recovery.

Originally published in I.D. *magazine, September/October 1992.*

ON WHITE SPACE/
WHEN LESS IS MORE
by
Keith Robertson

White space is nothing. White space is the absence of content. Yet white space is the ultimate value in graphic design. How could something so minimal be ascribed with so much value?

If we were to draw a continuum of taste from trashy to quality there is one graphic design variable that would constantly grow with the increase in quality—white space. Quality design has developed an association (a code) with white space as its principle variable (or sign). The presence of white space is a symbol of smart, of class, of simplicity, of the essence of refinement. The absence of white space is a symbol of vulgarity, of crassness, of schlock, of bad taste. These values are something we all take years to learn at design schools and for most of us as practicing designers, it is an opinion which rules the rest of our working lives. Because white space is the supreme symbol of class, it is difficult to disentangle it from our other art values, because to do so, makes you question where images and styles come from in the first place and why we are reproducing them.

Maybe it is only in these Post-modern times that we can start to be objective about Modernity. In fine art, Modernity was not necessarily about white space. Painting, for instance, was most often about new subjects and ways of image making. On rare occasions, such as in the work of Malevich or Mondrian, simplicity of spatial arrangement was the major theme of their Modernist project; but mostly, the technical and expressive qualities of line and colour were at the centre of Modern creation. But this was not the case in any of the design related fields of expression. In graphic design, as in architecture, simplicity and less is more, governs the taste of the new age and you can only assume that this stylistic dictum derives from similar origins as, say, the Cubists with their drive to uncover the visual essence of structure and form. So I return to *starting from zero*[1] which lies at the base of Modern expression.

Part of the problem with Modernism is that it has become so value loaded. Modernism developed in controversy and opposition to Western bourgeois values. Its ability to shock and provoke was what made it avant-garde. At its best Modernism was always oppositional. Yet it is a frequently observed phenomena, that bourgeois shockabilty has been slowly modified by incorporation of once radical ideas, often gently introduced by the design arts, as desirable and constantly changing stylistic features. The factor which is so often overlooked in fine art analysis is economic. In any area of design analysis, to overlook the economic, should be impossible.

The battle Modern art fought with bourgeois complacency was simultaneous with the rise of consumer capitalism where every stylistic twitch was symbolic fodder for a new, different and often Modern codification of taste. Capitalism, of course, holds no special place for Modern values. Modern values simply serve to brand the image of one product or class of publication over the folksy or traditional image that another product might demand. Style is market driven. Style has no intrinsic worth apart from the image it ascribes to a product. So the white space presented in the abstract, asymmetrical qualities of a quality fashion layout is there simply to reinforce the market qualities of the fashion garment worn by the model who has also been chosen and photographed to amplify these same ends. In terms of graphic design, white space has been appropriated along with the Modern aesthetic, to represent the most expensive and desirable class of products being presented by modern consumerism.

TAKING ON THE MODERN AESTHETIC

The myth says that the Modern aesthetic is oppositional; that it challenges the complacent and mundane values of bourgeois hypocrisy. The history of the Modern movement in fine art is usually couched in these heroic terms. Design and architecture are couched in similar rhetoric, not helped by those manifesto-writing Futurists, Dadaists, and Bauhausists who describe the struggle to find the essence through function and truth to the material of construction, as the artists' greatest modern role.

This, at first, oppositional Modernist aesthetic came on top of an already developed bourgeois aesthetic—one that had itself developed in opposition to the aesthetic of ostentation and display left by the monarchies of the eighteenth century. So the bourgeois aesthetic sought to hide the presentation of wealth behind a diversion of interest into areas supposedly *outside* the economic and the necessary, and so elevated the arts and presentation of self through them, to become the principle cultural values. So the dominant bourgeois expression in material things is one of disinterest and detachment. Such an aesthetic focuses therefore more on the *form* of doing things rather than the material things themselves. So art and especially design related practices, were sitting ducks for incorporation into the bourgeois aesthetic. Add this to the consumerist economy of late capitalism and the expression of form in design becomes inextricably linked to the dominant bourgeois aesthetic. One expresses the other.

An aesthetic is an expression of value. Every time you symbolize something through aesthetic presentation, you are branding it with that value. If, for instance, white space is the ultimate value in graphic design as I claimed earlier, then to package perfume in a plain, glossy white box and to label it in the simplest, smallest black sans-serif lettering possible would be the most logical device to ascribe ultimate high class to that product. But to smother the box with flowers and add gold script is to use evocative elements but not to ascribe high class. So the use of one aesthetic is meaningful because its use evokes and correspondingly diminishes the value of the other aesthetic with which it can be compared. After all, aesthetics are not black and white. Aesthetics are general tendencies— more this than that—more simple white space than busy clutter—and necessarily comparative.

The strength of an aesthetic is not just demonstrated through its use, but also through its non-use. The aesthetic I use to praise the white perfume package is the same aesthetic I use to criticize the flowery packaging. We all incorporate an aesthetic into our system of taste and identify our own particular range of distinctions to represent us. This we show to the world in all that we own and all that we produce. What we produce as graphic designers, is all the more important because it is not only what *we* are; it is also perpetuating systems of taste which hold our readers/the public in their social position. By constantly producing and therefore reinforcing good taste design we are perpetuating the differentiation with bad taste. White space is our tool. White space is a tool expropriated from Modern design to create a sort of consensus of value—a sort of social engineering.

ON WHITE SPACE IN GRAPHIC DESIGN

White space is nothing. White space is the absence of content. White space does not hold content in the way that a photograph or text holds meaning and yet it gives meaning, through context, to both image and text. In fact, white space can make or break the effective transmission of image or text. This would be an effective experiment: find a simply presented fashion shot, preferably in black and white and compare its presentation: 1) as a full-page bleed; 2) with a white border; and 3) much smaller with asymmetric balance. The third wins every time. The former two fit within the code but the third uses the creative/unpredictable edge built into the code. The asymmetry symbolizes daring and innovation while still being safely within the Modern semiotic code.

In material terms, what is white space in graphic design? White space is extravagance. White space is the surface of the paper on which you are printing showing through and on which you are choosing NOT to print. If economy and conservation were your chief concern, then white space would be at a minimum; obviously you would use it all up. So white space is used for purely semiotic values; for values of presentation which transcend economic values by insisting that the image of what you present is more important than the paper you could be saving. It is likely that this aesthetic is more extravagant with paper than any other graphic design value—especially in Japan. Printing plates, separations, paper and four and more colour presses still have to be used and paid for with the inclusion of white space. White space is a negative cost right down the production line—except for giving style.

It is easy to name those sorts of publications where white space is not the first priority. In most paperback books for instance, where presentation of text in the most functional, economical, and readable way is the first priority, white space has minor importance. Historically newspapers have not been big on white space, although this is changing as newspapers are slowly shifting their function and provide colour and entertainment as well as hard core information. In these Post-modern times there has been an increasing competition for the eye in all media, so sales are promoted not through content, but through quick visual summaries made using the visual code in which white space plays a dominant part.

There is another important category of publication where white space is least dominant. This is the area of working class/mass market publications, where the main distinguishing variable is the category of class. This category of publications are common in most Western cultures. They share an international commercial aesthetic of clutter and busyness in every design element. Here we have a commercially motivated use of the polar opposite end of the quality/bourgeois aesthetic. Here is white space working as hard as ever to brand for class, but in this case it is working in the negative. Clutter has come to represent working class (just as white space identifies high class). Clutter clearly identifies a market in those who are immediately suspicious of white space and have no hesitation about what it means—that this publication is not for them/not of their class. So the quality aesthetic has been highjacked by bourgeois ideology, leaving the working class only trashy and *inferior* symbols to identify with. White space is the key *and* the tool.

Compare the mass market women's weekly magazines to *Vogue* (not to mention *Arena, Eye,* or *Emigre*). In the *quality* class of publication, white space is so dominant that even the advertising is simplified, highly visual, and heavily coded. Quality publications, in the 1990s, come as such heavily coded entities that no element can afford to be out of step. Compare these publications now to the relative anarchy of the early eighties and you can see that white space has once again gripped the design world in a new conformity.

THE HISTORY OF WHITE SPACE

White space has always been with graphic design. White space could simply be understood, in a *value free* sort of way, as negative space—that area not occupied by image, headline, and copy. The problem however, when assessing a void, is that a void so easily fills up with meaning.

Value, for instance, was represented by ornament up to and into the nineteenth century and so presented an aesthetic that was primarily historical, representing status by expressing a knowledge of past styling and reproducing it. This trend started in the Renaissance with the rediscovery of classicism and the recycling of classical motifs and literature. In graphic design, this period coincided with the invention of movable type, so historically inspired ornament has been a very important device to give value to design. When white space was used in Renaissance publications (and I am thinking here particularly of Aldus Manutius's *Hypnerotomachia Poliphili*) it was used not so much to give status through design, but out of that Renaissance sense of correct mathematical proportion so evident in Renaissance architecture. Hence the continuation of the medieval golden mean in book page design, which was only abandoned in the nineteenth century, when economy in publication became of greater importance than aesthetic tradition.

In the nineteenth century a new design aesthetic came about. This aesthetic grew out of the development of a mass media and of the newly competitive commerce of capitalism. The letterpress poster of the mid-nineteenth century, with its mad mixture of often highly decorative and newly designed faces, is often referred to as the crassest aesthetic to blot the supposedly constantly improving and modernizing world. The same was said of Victorian architecture.

William Morris in England led what became an international critique of nine-teenth-century design and industrial production and proposed a cleaner and leaner aesthetic for graphic design in the future. Though some of his frontispieces do not suggest it, most of Morris's work does give new values to white space and it is from this period that a new and generous aesthetic of white space grew for the twentieth century.

POST-MODERN WHITE SPACE

White space, is of course, always with us. The problem now is what we can make it mean. Can we rescue it from the class ridden value it has been overloaded with in *quality* design? Can white space be used in such a way that it is outside the bourgeois/Modern aesthetic?

The key is in understanding what white space signifies. If white space remains in the Modern code we are simply reproducing an appropriated formula; a code of acknowledged good taste. By reproducing the code we are working safely within the commercial system of design, despite its inbuilt change, modification, innovation, asymmetry, etc.

An interesting experiment is to change the colour of white space; first of all to make it black, but then to change it to primaries, to any PMS, finally to obliterate the white space with an image. All of these things have been appropriated by the code. Meanings do vary, but the code has been so extended and abused by repetition and commercial demand, that the graphic designer currently faces a dilemma of expression that allows little room for even the possibility of new form or signification.

Graphic design has become such a central part of our Post-modern visual language that it has developed into a carrier of meaning at least as significant as the words and images it is presenting. For this reason Post-modern white space becomes a very significant void.

In the late 1970s and eighties white space and its division came to be treated more irreverently. I am thinking of the mock commercial vulgarity of Jamie Ried and the anarchic grids and typography of *I.D.* et al. *Emigre* seems obsessed with the deconstruction of typography, a fine obsession in my view, but I am still not convinced that it is facing up to the fundamental question of white space. Until white space is liberated from the Modern code, it will continue to contain even the large-format deconstruction of *Emigre*. Until that time white space is captured by the extravagance of the Modernist avant-garde which can subsume format, colour, typography, scale—even to a minimum degree!

Originally published in Emigre *no. 26, 1993.*

Endnotes

1. See "Starting From Zero" by Keith Robertson in the next chapter.

KICKING UP A LITTLE DUST
by
Michael Dooley

Ding ding. *Ding* ding.

It *had* been a bright, quiet Sunday morning in October, but now the door's electric eye chimes are being triggered. Except no one is coming in. Rudy VanderLans looks out through the glass of the door to his studio, a stark white windowless bunker in a rapidly gentrifying industrial section of Berkeley, California, and sees scraps of paper debris tossing madly about by a big wind. "Strange weather," he distractedly comments.

He then gets back to the work at hand.

But every now and again, *ding* ding, *ding* ding.

At high noon, VanderLans goes outside to investigate. He stares at the sky, which has turned completely *black*, except for the sun, a blazing golden disk that cuts through the smoke. The scene resembles nothing so much as the die-cut cover of *Emigre* number eight, minus the logo.

He goes back into the studio, drags out the portable television and hooks it up. "There must be *something* on the TV." *Click, click, click.*

VanderLans finds a news report that a fire has broken out in the Oakland hills, and it's spreading. He calls his wife, type designer Zuzana Licko. Yes, she can see it from their home near UC Berkeley. No, they don't appear to be in serious danger at this point.

But VanderLans can't concentrate. The electricity is going crazy. *Ding* ding. The reports grow more ominous. The blaze will eventually claim several lives and hundreds of homes.

He drives home to Licko. They need to be prepared to start from scratch. They pack their valuables into the car. Clothes. Books. Passports.

Passports....

Back before the fire, before *Emigre* established itself as a highly influential and controversial showcase and forum for experimental design, back before some critics lauded it as innovative, inspirational, and embodying our cultural zeitgeist while others derided it as illegible, self-indulgent, and just plain *ugly*, way back in 1983 when VanderLans was assembling the first issue, he used his fingerprint, from his passport, as cover art. His resources were meager, so he would use what was on hand: photocopied resizings of typewriter type, clip art, torn paper, halftones shot by friends. He and the two other Dutch immigrants who founded the magazine had hardly any knowledge of publishing and distribution. They simply wanted to promote the artistic and literary projects that they and their acquaintances were producing.

Issue number one was subtitled "a magazine for exiles," a reference to the artist-as-outsider. After that, it was "the magazine that ignores boundaries." Fingerprints, and suitcases and airplanes and globes, were recurring motifs. Much of the subject matter dealt with traveling and being international citizens. There was a heavy emphasis on how exposure to various countries and different cultures generates inspiration.

The America VanderLans discovered when he arrived in 1981 inspired him to embark on his own personal journey of discovery, and *Emigre* was his vehicle. Its non-linear, free-floating hierarchy of visual and verbal information that sprawled and overlapped all over its poster-sized pages was a world beyond the rigid strictures of his Modernist design education. "I had been so brainwashed about designing according to a grid that I wanted to make *Emigre* look a lot more spontaneous. My only grid was going to be the four crop marks. And in California, anything goes. You could do whatever you wanted. People were always very encouraging. There was no finger-pointing, saying 'this was not the way it was supposed to be done.' That did not exist here. At least I didn't see it. And that might have to do with the ignorance of when you go to another country. You don't see many things. And that's sometimes in itself very liberating."

VanderLans first became aware of America's potential to help him venture beyond, in his words, "the dead end of Swiss Modernism" when he was still an aspiring illustrator at Holland's Royal Academy of Fine Art in the Hague and saw the work of a designer across the ocean. "Milton Glaser inspired me tremendously. It looked like he was a pure illustrator who taught himself how to be a graphic designer as well. I had been taught design functions around typography, whereas Milton Glaser's work was based around illustration. It was very expressive. And he could make that type of design function perfectly within society. People were excited about it and had fun with it and enjoyed it. And it was functioning at many levels. His posters were up in art museums. It was art, and it was also graphic design. And that touched something way deep inside me and I thought, *jeez,* if that is possible then a lot is possible."

Glaser's designs were the travel brochures that began to stir VanderLans's desire to explore new ground, and the ten issues of the eponymous magazine of Rotterdam design group *Hard Werken* were his maps. Published between 1979 and 1982, *Hard Werken* was a portfolio of their radical concepts doubling as an arts publication. They ran downbeat fiction, poetry, and articles about art, film, and underground music. They arranged idiosyncratic photos, illustrations, and typewriter text in anarchistic collages over a large page format. They painted directly onto the mechanical boards. They allowed for mystery and ambiguity in their designs. In short, they served as a guide for the early *Emigres.*

It was only after VanderLans came to the U.S. that he became involved with the work of his native countrymen. He remembers being attracted by their interdisciplinary talents. "These people were very much like Milton Glaser in the sense that they were not schooled as Modernist designers. Actually, most of them were fine artists. They had no knowledge of design. It was all self-taught. Their work was based on illustration and photography and their type was self-invented, and it was all just so incredibly vibrant, so uninhibited. They were designing magazines, they were designing book covers, they could do house styles and corporate identities in a very different way. But it worked. And people bought it."

But people weren't buying *Emigre.* Not for the first couple of years anyway. After a few issues, the other founders left for financially greener territories, and VanderLans became the sole publisher and editor as well as art director. With the second issue, Licko began contributing her fonts, whose architectural construction provided a rational counterpoint to VanderLans's grid-resistant layouts. Their bedroom piled up with undistributed copies. Yet they continued to pursue their labor of love at a time when other Bay Area designers were making their fortunes by providing the yuppie market with decorative designs in pretty pinks and beiges.

Their perseverance eventually paid off. With the worldwide distribution of the seventy-plus, and growing, number of fonts created by Licko and a handful of other designers, *Emigre* has become the mainstay of their business enterprise. Its print run has leveled off at 7000, up from the 500 of a decade ago. Its advertising is only for its own products. The fact that it makes a profit is attributable to VanderLans's continued belief in low-budget production values. "I am often disgusted with the waste that exists within graphic design. So much money is spent on the printing of materials the world can do so easily without." Despite the impression conveyed by feature articles about *Emigre* that tend to focus on select full-color examples, the typical issue strives to make the most of inexpensive monochromatic printing.

Economy, as well as inventiveness, is also the hallmark of *Emigre's* music label, which VanderLans recently created with company profits. He has released nine CDs so far, with categories ranging from hip-hop to industrial to folk pop to sixties West Coast music. As with the designers featured in *Emigre,* the only criterion for the selection of bands is the personal taste of Rudy VanderLans. So far, press reviews have been very favorable, and one band, Basehead, has already gone on to sign an eight-record deal with a larger label.

VanderLans figures his label needs more focus if it hopes to replicate the success of the magazine. *Emigre* became a viable commodity only after its contents became more clearly defined. This change began to take place around six years ago, when he found himself talking with friends about design topics and ideas not found in established publications. *"Print* was doing all their stories about Michael Vanderbyl and Eastern European design, which is all very valid and very good. There is no other magazine that does a better job. But I also felt there were other things going on in design and nobody was paying attention. Actually, if anyone paid attention to this work, it was to criticize it as bad or ugly or ungrounded or stupid or naive. But I thought it was just the most exciting thing happening.

"So I felt maybe there was a little bit of a niche there, to show the work of young graphic designers who had some radical ideas that the mainstream didn't exactly appreciate or understand or believe, people who were kicking up a little dust in the world of graphic design."

The dust-kickers included teachers and students from Cranbrook and CalArts who specialize in designing in ways that aren't supposed to work according to conventional standards. People like Ed Fella, whose vernacular style has earned him the reprobation of anti-designer. People like Jeffery Keedy, who, when asked by VanderLans why he doesn't design pretty typefaces, responded "well, it's been done, let's face it." *Emigre* has reprinted an essay by Dutch design dust-kicker Piet Schreuders in which he explains why "the profession of graphic design is criminal and really ought not to exist at all." It also has published an article by pixel-kicking computer design nerds Erik van Blokland and Just van Rossum in which they discuss the merits of creating a computer font virus that will "slowly transform Helvetica into something much more desirable."

Appropiately enough, *Emigre's* design is as extreme as its editorial stance. Although much is made of "the *Emigre* look," in truth, the format varies from issue to issue. It has ranged from an intricate weaving of text and graphics that challenges conventions of legibility to a stark simplicity, typical of recent issues. This is, again, in contrast to *Print,* which VanderLans considers poorly designed. He finds its covers to be nothing more than clever visual concepts and its department head designs to be much less than typographically elegant.

As fellow Bay Area designer Chuck Byrne points out, "*Print's* attitude is that the layout of the magazine should be neutral because it presents design. Rudy's attitude is exactly the opposite. Why does it have to look like the time before? The *subject matter* is different from the time before. The *people being covered* are different. To redesign the magazine every time would make the traditional editor or publisher hysterical. Well, Rudy just has this ongoing design problem that he goes about solving with each issue. Or he turns it over to someone else who is absolutely crazed."

Byrne discounts complaints that the layouts are often indecipherable. "Rudy doesn't design the way he does just to be radical. He has gotten extraordinarily good at making the type a sophisticated extension of the content of the story. Those pages are very well crafted. There is an organic relationship between the presentation of the word and its actual meaning. The only people who have tremendous problems reading *Emigre* are graphic designers, who have been trained to make type clear. The rest of the world doesn't live in that purist atmosphere. It doesn't know it's not supposed to read *Emigre.* Younger people look at it the same way they look at other magazines, because magazines are changing."

VanderLans simply stands by his philosophy that people read best what they read most. "If people read 'ugly' against-the-rules typography every day they will eventually get used to it and be able to read it without any problems. It's just a matter of giving it to them again and again and again."

Because he has taken such aggressive stances and published such inflammatory material, many consider Rudy VanderLans to be some kind of *punk.* So people expecting to meet the Sid Vicious of the design world are taken aback when they are first confronted by a charming, soft-spoken, wholesome-looking fellow with clear bright eyes and an easy smile.

VanderLans *is Emigre.* He may not agree with some ideas expressed in his magazine and, when he relinquishes editorial control to other designers, he may even consider some layouts hideous. Nevertheless, his fingerprints are deeply embedded in every issue. So much so that *Emigre* is often accused of being self-indulgent. Which he readily admits it is.

"*Emigre* is a *tremendously* self-indulgent magazine. It *should* be that. The one thing Zuzana and I have always done with all our work is to try to please ourselves, first and foremost. And then if people out there are also going to like it, that's just really great. But we have never believed in the idea of marketing, never believed in the idea that if we do *this* combined with *that,* then *those* people will like it. Marketing only looks into what people already like. Well, we *know* that. It's *boring.* We're interested in finding out what people *could* like in terms of what they haven't seen yet, or heard yet, which is a more difficult route to go but it's much more exciting for us."

As for the incendiary nature of the articles, "I know what we're doing is not always considered proper according to the mainstream. But it's not our intention to be provocative only. We really hope to contribute to how people look at graphic design. We are interested in people who have something very intelligent to say, who are very sincere, and who are really passionate about their work. And it just so happens oftentimes some consider what we publish to be provocative or obnoxious or vulgar or whatever. But that is not why we go to these people. That is not why we show their work.

"It's very easy to shock people. There's nothing to it, especially in America. We could just try to make nude photographs of every graphic designer we like and put them into center spreads."

April Greiman, whose computer-generated self-portrait for *Design Quarterly* showed her to be no stranger to full frontal nudity herself, has been a longtime fan, not only of *Emigre's* visuals, but of its adversarial stances. "Why *not* put out some startling articles saying 'let's create a virus to destroy Helvetica'? I heard Herb Lubalin say Helvetica was the most destructive face that was ever invented, it was just the total downfall of good typography. And that was twenty years ago. He said the biggest tragedy to typography is the invention of Helvetica because you can't make any mistakes. It just kind of numbs you out. It's so perfect, it's dead, stillborn. Personally, I think it would be great to put out a virus to put it to sleep."

Not surprisingly, *Emigre's* assaults on Modernism have incurred the wrath of several members of the established design community, who deride it as a visual abomination. Living legend Massimo Vignelli was particularly vituperative in a *Print* "Oppositions" debate (September/October 1991) in which he accused *Emigre* of being an irresponsible aberration of culture. When the debate was published, VanderLans was asked if he had spilled a cup of hot coffee in Vignelli's lap.

In fact, VanderLans has never met, or even talked with Vignelli. And although he is less than flattering about Vignelli's fashions, which he describes as resembling prison clothes, he has always admired his design work. "Massimo Vignelli is someone who was held up very high in art school in Holland. I remember so well when he came out with the New York City subway sign system. That was the big thing in the mid and late seventies in Holland, working on corporate identities and sign systems. And everybody looked at that as an example."

As for the criticism, "for all I care, Massimo Vignelli can *hate Emigre.* Esthetically. But then to go on and say it's bad for culture as a whole, that really hurts. Because how, then, do we go about making culture? By just copying Massimo Vignelli? Or is it maybe possible to create our own ways of expression?

"The problem I have is when people talk about our work as *wrong*, as if there was never any place for it anywhere. I believe *that* is wrong. I think for too long, Modernist designers have figured everything should be treated in this cold, rationalist way and that's *stupid*. It's naive, it's child-like.

"I know there are areas within design where there should not be any kind of mistake about legibility at all, like highway sign systems. Anything we've learned about legibility, we should apply there. People have a split-second to read a highway sign. You cannot put in any personality or anything like that. But there are so many projects in this world that could be done in very *irrational, illegible* ways, without any problem. There are punk magazines to be designed. Are you going to use Jan Tschichold's three rules of typography for that? That's silly! That doesn't make sense.

"To me it looks like the world of young designers, what they are thinking and what they are feeling, is passing Massimo Vignelli by. All I hope is when I'm his age, I'm not going to be that bitter and closed-minded."

Byrne detects a more personal agenda at work. "Part of the reason established designers don't like *Emigre* has to do with a turf imperative. Massimo believes Rudy is threatening his predominance in his field because of his following. Massimo and all those Modernists were revolutionary, but now when it comes time to change what they changed, they are proving to be the biggest fucking crybabies you've ever seen. They're just worse than the people they tried to change before."

Greiman, who views *Emigre* as part of technology's expansion of the paradigms of culture as well as the parameters of readability, perceives an even deeper issue. "The International Style was based on a simple set of values, and we're living in an age of enormous complexity. The tools that we have are much more complex and allow more levels of information. *Emigre* is one example, and a very good example, of a different kind of reading, a textural, emotional reading. And that's probably something that whole generation of Modernists just don't even begin to understand.

"I think the reason Vignelli would be outraged is that whole International Style represents a dinosaur that is definitely wagging its tail for the last time. Major capitalism and so-called democracy and all this corporate money that supported design so it had to have one look, one voice, one color, one typeface, all that neutral Swiss greedy stuff, that world is crumbling. We're in a different time. The power structures, the big-bucks people telling people at the bottom of the pyramid what kind of information they could have and when they can have it, is now being totally blown open by the information revolution and by being truly able to network. There can now be a participatory, interactive kind of information flow."

Besides having captured the spirit of an emerging technological democracy, VanderLans and Licko have also blazed a trail for others in the creation of their own fonts and designs. The computer provided the tool for designers to work with text in ways previously unimaginable, and *Emigre* provided the permission. As with punk music, the potential for freedom implicit within its pages has energized and empowered many others to take rule-defying risks. Byrne notes how "people saw an openness that had not been available before in Modernist design and they started to get really excited about it. Every issue seemed like a revolution. And that turning away from a strict discipline of the way things *should* be organized continues to have a dramatic impact on design."

VanderLans considers the abandoning of restraints and the receptivity to continual change as a fundamental distinction between his contemporaries and Vignelli's. "Back then, all those designers wrote books with guidelines on how design *has to be done*. None of the people in *Emigre* have this idea that rules should be laid down, particular rules like fifty-two characters on a line, twelve words in a line. I think those times are gone. We now see graphic designers much more as pluralists. And I think that's very healthy. That's true creativity, for them to work in many different ways according to the type of project given to them. And they will be very wild and incredibly brilliant."

Mark Treib, a designer-writer who was VanderLans's advisor at UC Berkeley's graduate program during the early 1980s, holds him in high esteem. "Rudy's work is pure research as in research-and-development, and it will be regarded in twenty years the same way we look at Constructivist photography." But Treib takes issue with some of VanderLans's emulators, those who confuse syntax with semantics at the expense of their clients. "I disagree with people who simply think if they make the design more complex it will have a more complex meaning. If they're designing writing on Baudrillard or Derrida or one of the fashionable people, they want something that represents deconstruction, but of course what they're doing is making it harder and harder to figure out what the hell's going on in the text, which is difficult enough. It's like getting a book that is already underlined, and if you have some idiot who is marking phrases that are unimportant in terms of your reading of the book, it's something you have to overcome to get back to the original message."

Still, there are several venues in which a spastic jumble of text, typography, and layout accommodates and appeals to the fits-and-starts reading habits of an audience plugged into the *click, click, click* of Macintosh computers and MTV. VanderLans admires the courage of mass-circulation youth-oriented magazines like *Beach Culture* that have incorporated structural as well as stylistic devices from *Emigre* into their editorial make-up. "You can't change magazine design by finding yet another way to use a pull quote or to insert a drop cap. You're going to change it by writing differently, by setting up the structure of your article entirely different." And, as if in an echo of the seminal punk rock band MC5's exhortation to "kick out the jams," VanderLans exclaims *"Throw out the headlines!"*

He regrets that *Beach Culture* was not a commercial success. "Eventually such magazines will make it, but there has to be people who continually work like that to have the mainstream accept it."

VanderLans has definitely established his place in mainstream culture. Styles that inflamed designers when they appeared in *Emigre* are now ubiquitous, having been disseminated and assimilated throughout the spectrum of print and electronic media. Licko's fonts, initially scorned and ridiculed as ugly, are now so established that other type foundries are knocking them off. Aspiring designers constantly show up with their portfolios, often without calling. *Ding* ding. *Ding* ding.

But their newfound status offers no protection from the brickbats of critics. Even as their work continues to be pilloried as deviant, it is now disdained for being too commonplace. Two designers, in separate articles from a recent issue of *Print,* stated they deliberately avoid using the fonts because of their identification with the magazine. Many others believe *Emigre* and its fonts have had their day in the sun and should move aside for the next hot new trend to set the design world aflame.

Byrne disagrees with this evaluation. "The best editorial concept I've seen in the last decade is the *Emigre* issue called 'Heritage.' It was absolutely fucking brilliant! There were these incredible interviews, the layouts were incredible, but there was also this great idea of 'let's go back to Switzerland twenty years later and take the pulse, the blood pressure, run a set of x-rays and see what's going on here.' And Rudy continues to come up with very sophisticated ideas, very advanced and perceptive themes for the magazine."

Greiman, who has been featured in *Emigre* herself, concurs. She believes it will continue to fill a void, at least in her own reading habits. "I just find people are stuck on style wars. That's why I don't read the middle America design mags. I think they're boring. *Print, CA, Graphis,* they're so superficial. It's just really slick printing and beautiful photos of well-printed items. And it's a waste of my time. It just puts me to sleep."[1]

Although *Emigre* is hardly in danger of becoming an oversize *Print,* VanderLans concedes the difficulty of continuing to travel along the cutting edge. Yet he maintains a steadfast optimism and determination to retain his resident alien status in the design world.

He even looks forward to new challenges to his turf. "I can still get excited over people who are doing things very different from how I do them, because I'm very interested in why they're doing it differently. And as long as I find those people for whom design is still this wide open area, I'll continue to publish."

British graphic designer Nick Bell easily qualifies as one of those people. A recent *Emigre* devoted to briefs Bell created as an instructor for the London College of Printing included an insert of random slashes on butcher paper. Accompanying text explains that this is an example of a typeface he created called Psycho. If Bell's gesture is not taken literally as yet another punk skewering of the carcasses of design establishment dinosaurs, it can be viewed as a jab at *Emigre* itself, taking its assaults on Helvetica and legibility to their absurdist conclusion.

VanderLans calmly explains that "there has never been a five year or ten year business plan for *Emigre*. I think I would stop publishing it when I myself get bored with it. But if I'm going to bore other people, then that's really too bad. The bottom line is if I can't make a living off it, then I'll stop doing it. Right now, Zuzana and I keep selling more magazines, we keep selling more typefaces, we continue to sell more records. So there must be people out there who enjoy what we're doing."

In fact, the operation has expanded to the point that it could no longer be contained within the bunker. This May, VanderLans and Licko emigrated to Sacramento. Their new office-warehouse has plenty of room for expansion. It also has a view through the windows of a tree-lined street in a peaceful, pleasant residential neighborhood just a short stroll from their new house.

VanderLans was contemplating such a move last October, as he stared at the sun asserting itself against the black, threatening sky. Since they make all their income through mail order, they could run the office from anywhere in the U.S. And so, the publisher of the magazine that ignores boundaries was "seriously thinking of moving up north, but still in California. California is too nice."

And anything goes.

Originally published in Print *magazine, September/October 1992.*

Endnotes

1. Greiman's comments did not go unchallenged. In *Eye* magazine (issue 8, 1993), Michael Bierut refuted her claims about the super-ficiality of design magazines, noting: "It's ironic that Greiman's scathing quote appeared (as part of an article on *Emigre* magazine) in a recent issue of *Print.*"

LANGUAGES
AND
DIALECTS

STARTING FROM ZERO
by
Keith Robertson

STARTING FROM ZERO. The will to eradicate the past with a new set of values and establish a new age is the Modernist mythology we inherit from the art books. These were political idealogues who rewrote history with a new brush. It was the Bauhaus groupies and Constructivists who designed a radical new workers' paradise and these movements helped create a new age; a future where the recycling of the past would be eradicated because the new theory exposed the past as corrupt and passe. Theory was above all a belief that justified action. Theory WAS ideology. Starting from zero was not the obsession of the Dada anarchist nor the naive optimism of the Futurists. "Starting from zero" was the catchphrase of one of the most influential, opinionated and ultimately conservative group of architects and designers who were ideologically working out theories of functionalism in design. Here was design governed by an idea.

Much of the nineteenth century was spent coming to terms with the machine age. The idea of being true to the materials of manufacture and of being utilitarian was the principal criticism of nineteenth-century British design and manufacture made by John Ruskin and William Morris whose ideas were later taken up by the Germans. Reeling after the death and destruction of the First World War, it is not surprising that the next generation should take a more hard line, apply the theory to their art, be supermen creating a bold new future. They, after all, created the new Modernism and called it the "International Style." It was international because it transcended the parochial national styles and traditions. It was the new art which expressed what was universal in the world—the new technology of mass production and standardization. In the past, it was claimed, the machine was used to express the foibles of fashion victims who chose historical motif for ornament. A truly utilitarian art, they argued, would be based on an accurate appraisal of mechanical production in order to develop the truest, purest mechanical aesthetic. Standardization and streamlining were the key to this approach.

TOWARDS A NEW ORDER

Walter Gropius is the best known idealogue of the International Style but he was only one of a phalanx of artists espousing the new art. He promoted a new unity where architecture became the center and the fine arts served the crafts which furnished the building with all its fittings and ornament. Theo van Doesburg was the principal theorist.

Neoplasticism was concerned with the hard-line geometric truth behind all human production—both artistic and industrial. El Lissitsky and Lázsló Moholy-Nagy were two of the principal practitioners of the new Neoplasticism or Constructivism. What they shared was the desire to transcend national styles by espousing what they had in common which was a response to a new technology through their art. Early in the Modern movement these artists were still developing what can be identitfied as parochial styles. But their theory was well ahead of their practice. They were working towards a new order even through the anarchy of Dada and the concrete poets.

In 1928, which was early in the development of Modernism, the first major manifesto on Modern design was published by Jan Tschichold called *Die Neue Typographie*. As with most radical movements, the most hard line ideas emerged first—only to be watered down in practice. In Tschichold's case, he was to become one of the finest classical designers who overturned nearly all of his early radical theories. His propaganda for the International Style however was to remain influential in Europe and even the USA long after the war.

Die Neue Typographie espouses a new approach to typographic design because Modern designers were working in a new modern age. Tschichold rejects the printed tradition from the position of style however, not of function, which is the flaw in his early argument which he was himself later to identify. So what was the new typography according to Tschichold? 1) It was essentially simple and pure design in harmony with the modern world; 2) asymmetry replaced symmetry because it was more functional reflecting the more complex rhythms of the modern age; 3) only sans serif type faces were efficient communicators of modern information—serifs were designated to the historicists' scrap heap; 4) where greater emphasis was to be brought, he insisted on using different weights of type (e.g. bold, italic, light) rather than different faces and even point size.

There was also emerging a new emphasis on "objective" and "scientific" approaches to the page grid—one planned less by tradition (the golden section) and more by mathematics. The mathematical grid can be most clearly identified in the early designs of Theo Balmer. The radical beginnings of the Modern movement started off with the mad fruit salads of point sizes and faces of Dada and the bold asymmetry of Tschichold, Bayer, and Moholy-Nagy, but slowly there was a formalization and ossification of the Modern movement culminating in Switzerland after the war.

HELVETICA HELVETICA

Post-war Swiss design developed a new classicism, a new conservative benchmark to which most later designers seem to retreat at times of crisis. Swiss movement artists based their designs on the Constructivist traditions of prewar Europe but they strove to perfect the theoretical position espoused by Tschichold and others in their practice, emphasizing the bland, depersonalized, mechanical and objective principals of design which were close to being theoretically correct. It is interesting that the most successful examples of International Style design were in the area of poster designs for various cultural events— art exhibitions, film festivals, industrial exhibitions and the like. It is rare for these recessive, stylized designs to be sufficiently engaging to serve a more commercial function.

Theo Balmer was the first great International Stylist. In 1928 when using strictly mathematical grids he created posters with a hard-line purity not bettered stylistically till the fifties. He is distinguishable from his Constructivist contemporaries by his insistence on square grids and relatively small, single point sized sans-serif asymmetrical type. Such discipline deserves a place in the pantheon.

Max Bill was student at the Bauhaus in 1928 but he had to wait till the war was over to sufficiently reduce his style to the barest of elements. He used strict mathematical proportions, asymmetry, and generally small sizes of sans-serif type but always with a superb sense of balance between black and white space.

Armin Hoffmann was the classic fifties designer who mastered the combination of disciplined asymmetric typography and often striking details from photographic sources. This element of his work was, however, eclipsed by the leading International Stylist Josef Muller-Brockmann who established himself as their leading writer and propaganist.

It was Muller-Brockmann who spread the word that International Style was about to adopt the mannerisms of machine art where pure spacial harmony would reign, governed by mathematical logic and a few self-imposed restrictions designed to down-play individual talent and create an objective and reproducible style. In 1960 he produced his black, white, grey and red "der film" poster; surely the masterpiece of the fifties (for that is the decade to which it stylistically belongs). Designed with mathematical logic and using typographical elements alone to create a low key but impressive poster, Muller-Brockmann sought to strip his work of all but the essential meanings. "Der film" was surely close to zero.

POOR ZERO

Since the fifties, zero seems to have slipped as a role model. Far from announcing the end of graphic design, because the machine age had at last found its true expression, International Style has simply become one of a number of what are now recognized as being design options. Each decade since the fifties seems to have spawned a range of graphic styles but only aspects of psychedelic and Post-modern design can be described as being primarily historicist in orientation. Pop, Punk, and New Wave (or Post-Punk) do at least relate to their contemporary industrial cultures just as legitimately as International Style did to the consolidation of the corporate giants after the war.

There have, however, been some interesting reverberations of International Style through most of this period. More often than not, it performs the role of the safe haven to which many top designers can retreat especially after their innovation has been ripped off by the style vultures who make up the rest of the industry.

Milton Glaser, for instance, must rank as perhaps the greatest graphic innovator of the sixties. Glaser is best known for his eclectic themes, flat color and outlined illustration style; but each one of his designs is based on what is essentially a mathematical grid. Typographically, Glaser would either use austerely small and simple Helvetica or he would invent some of the most vulgar decorative faces that even the drug-obsessed sixties couldn't manage. Who could explain the lapse? Nevertheless, Glaser was a major inheritor of the International tradition.

Instead of reaching back into history, Pop simply reaches across to its contemporary commercial culture for inspiration and symbology. This approach to design is less critical, in terms of being less insistent on an aesthetic that comes from outside the symbols being represented. It is more imitative/appreciative simply of what exists—a value-free acceptance of the status quo whether that status quo be commercial, capitalist, or popular.

To understand Post-modern sensibilities in design is to bring to contemporary design both the critical and uncritical aesthetics. Part of the appeal of Post-punk design is the juxtaposition of the refined and the vulgar, the classic and the gaudy, the kitsch and the technocratic.

Of the British Post-punk designers only Jamie Reid presents himself as the consistent anarchist. Jamie Reid's designs are mostly concerned with making usually critical/outrageous sociopolitical statements which purposely reject the Modern design aesthetic. Reid's aesthetic has more to do with graffiti and the randomness of found objects—the same anti-aesthetic used in the hand made Punk fanzines.

Starting with Barney Bubbles, there was an insistence on marrying Modern-movement good taste with pop-culture products, whether they be for mass production or the entertainment industry. Most interesting from this point of view is the design work of Malcolm Garret, Peter Seville, and Neville Brody.

From the Modern movement has come the reawakening of the potential of typography as the primary communicator in design. Typography is the hook on which Post-modern design hangs. At first this "new" typography followed the same progression as the Modern movement had taken itself—first the anarchist Dada fruit salads of ransom-note type to classic, controlled, centered and seriffed elegance.

Along with a new type consciousness there is also a new grid awareness which tends to wear its design process on its sleeve. The process of design, of preparing finished artwork, of being printed in four-color printing process, of being laid out using mathematical precision and geometry is something that is often being exposed through the artwork. Post-punk design, when it is plundering the rules of the Modern movement for ideas, tends to use Modernism simply as the formal layer of their artwork. Most likely, the contemporary layer, be it an illustration, a photograph or even a digitally distorted device will be there by nature of its juxtaposition and incongruity.

Poor Neville Brody! What a dilemma to be the world's most ripped-off designer. Brody was not exceptional in the British context, but out of context (which is a position he was projected into with the international distribution of *The Face* magazine and *The Graphic Language of Neville Brody*) he is seen as a lone innovator. He is fast becoming yet another of those art geniuses Thames and Hudson are so keen to generate. For most of his time at *The Face* Brody was reworking Modern movement design history. His most original contribution however (and he claims only to have resorted to this out of sheer ripped-off desperation) was to design his own type faces which give an element of Post-modernity to an otherwise shared art-school awareness of recent design history. It seems that the role of taste trendsetter is one that *The Face* seeks for itself, but it is not apparently the role Brody wishes to contribute to. So where do you go to as a Post-modern designer when you are ripped off by the system? Where else but the safe refuge of International Style. At least the bland and mechanical is a safe harbour where the logic of construction belongs to history rather than a new boy genius.

Originally published in Stuffing/Art, Graphics Stuff Publications, Australia 1990. *Also published in* Emigre, *no. 19, 1991.*

PICTURES, PHONEMES,
AND TYPOGRAPHY
by
Marc Treib

Visual languages convey both sound and meaning, although whether they address one or both, alone or in balanced measure, will vary with the graphic form used. If the picture bears sufficient resemblance to its referent, and the code being used is obvious,[1] there should be little trouble in linking the idea with the representation. But as we develop graphic systems which represent aural rather than pictorial ideas, the communication vehicle inherently becomes more abstract and the gap between the concept and its graphic form increases. To bridge this gap, vernacular sign-makers and designers create hybrid forms we might term *"eye-konic;"* letter forms enriched with pictorial content.

To trace a single idea/sound pattern through the range of its possible representations, we can use the sausage in American argot called the *"hot dog,"*[2] and trace it through the various non-verbal (perhaps non-oral is a better term) notation systems. We can witness the exchange of phonetic expediency for meaning, and the changes in signification dependent on context and familiarity within the cultural context of which the concept, hot dog, is a part.

If we begin with the Chinese character, or in this particular case, the Japanese version of the Chinese character, we immediately discover complications. A native speaker explains: "The art of *kanji* (characters) is very complicated. *atsui* (hot) can be written in two alternate ways."[3] The first has the connotation of hot for humans, because the temperature is hot or the weather is hot. So one wears a *yukata* and fans oneself because it is *atsui*. But the alternate character signifies heat, hot, calorific heat. In the case of our dog, he's not howling and complaining because of the heat; so it might be more appropriate to use this character still meaning, in English, "heat" and thus "hot dog."[4] Neither of these characters is historically derived from a picture, since the concept of heat would be difficult to abstract or stylize; although the second is derived in part from an abstraction of fire, while the first includes the radical for sun. Of course neither of these concepts, even with the character for "dog," conveys the idea of sausage, since the *dog* portion of the example, even in English, is totally metaphorical. And the pronunciation, *atsui inu*, in addition, has nothing to do with the English pronunciation, although the meaning of some sort of dog (but not a sausage) which is hot in some way is understood.

Using the phonetic writing systems creates different problems. Even in Japanese, a rough approximation of the English hot dog could be written with the *katakana* syllabary (or even in the *hiragana* syllabary). Although the pronunciation of the *katakana "hotto doggu"* smacks of a Japanese accent (precisely for this reason, the utilization of a syllabary devised for Japanese rather than an alphabet adopted for English), the Japanese would be unfamiliar with the sausage unless grounded in American culture, or at least the more noted of America's eating habits.

The learned sounds of the alphabet recreate the sounds *"hot dog,"* but do so only at the expense of meaning. To an American, hot dog is a relatively easy concept to comprehend, its meaning probably acquired at an early age and its written form only a little later. He or she might also be familiar with alternative terms such as wienies, red hots, wieners, franks, frankfurters, and even Coney Islands, although this is really beyond the realm of the current discussion. But in context the American would also be able to recognize great distortions in pronunciations in the word hot dog, and in this sense one really doesn't read the word as the combination of the letters *d* and *o* and *g*, but together as *dog.* Thus the written form of the word dog in itself becomes a sort of pictorial symbol, like the Chinese characters for the concept, denotive or metaphorical, dog. We can even recognize eccentricities in spelling, for example *hot dawg,* as representing speech used in the South, hinting that we can read letter by letter when the word or spelling is unfamiliar. As John Downing points out, we really don't usually use the alphabet as a system of single letters, but following Whorf's notions of words, "sentences not words are the essence of speech, just as equations and functions, not bare numbers, are the real meat of mathematics."[5] Letters exist not in isolation representing single sounds or phonemes, but only in combination asserts Downing: "An alphabetic writing system's units are not merely the individual characters. The alphabetic system is primarily a code for phonemes. English has approximately forty phonemic units (varying with dialect), which are supposed to be signaled by the graphemic units of the writing system. Obviously, twenty-six individual letters cannot be enough for forty phonemes. Ellis (1845) a nineteenth-century linguist, analyzed all the alternative ways of printing and writing the forty or so phonemes of English and found more than 2,000 alternative graphemes."[6]

Downing adds that the redundancy in certain sounds and the complications of utilizing upper and lower case letter forms, in serif, sans-serif, cursive, and the various other alphabet variations, we can see that reading even in a supposed phonetic system is a complicated matter indeed.

We must also notice that increased difficulty in comprehension accompanied the move from a pictographic to a more abstract system of notation like a syllabary or an alphabet: one must physiologically convert the visual sensations through a complex cognition process until the idea is finally registered in the brain. Thus from the more emotional, immediate, and visceral reaction, one shifts to the complex and intellectual. Increased time in perception and mental registry is necessary as a result.

If in place of any abstract writing form we substitute a pictographic image of the hot dog, we might be able to increase the rate of processing. We still must assume that viewer knows that a sausage is to eat; though it is no longer necessary to know what is called. When words are included, usually highly evocative adjectives added to the picture which represents the noun, meaning becomes enhanced. The expansion of size may increase some aspects of comprehension. A building with a sign saying or depicting a hot dog *might* be read as a hot dog stand, but a building in the *form* of a hot dog will be understood with some degree of certainty, unless by some chance it happened to be used metaphorically.

The above discussion examines the range of devices used in the visual languages of various cultures to communicate a single message. It becomes apparent that the production and interpretation of meaning is a very complicated process which has no single and universally applicable solution.

Originally published in the AIGA Journal of Graphic Design, *vol. 7, no. 3, 1989.*

Endnotes

1. The presence and effect of the graphic code should not be underestimated. We do not see the world in black and white, nor as flat forms represented by thin black lines, following the "rules" of linear perspective, for example. We learn to see *within* these codes and to see images that follow the codes as representations of our reality. See E.H. Gombrich, *Art and Illusion: A Study in the Psychology of Pictorial Representation,* Princeton: Princeton University Press, (1960), 1972.
2. I am aware of the problems caused by choosing a slang and metaphorical term such as hot dog. It was chosen because it shows just how complex metaphorical ideas are and how difficult they are to communicate, although the idea has been treated in a multitude of graphic ways.
3. In Chinese the two meanings of *hot* are expressed by two words and hence two characters. In Japanese, the one word, *atsui,* expresses both concepts. *Atsui,* however, can be written as two different characters borrowed from Chinese. Thus, greater and more subtle distinction is found in writing than in speech.
4. Yuko Honjo, Note to the author, March 1974.
5. Benjamin Lee Whorf, "Language, Mind and Reality," *Language, Thought and Reality,* p. 259 (Cambridge: MIT Press, 1973).
6. John Downing, "Is Literacy Acquisition Easier in some Languages than in Others?", *Visible Language,* VII: 2 (Spring, 1973), p. 150.

TYPE AND DECONSTRUCTION
IN THE DIGITAL ERA
by
Rick Poynor

Type is going to be as abstract as sand on a beach.
In that sense type doesn't exist anymore.
—Max Kisman

In the age of the desktop computer, font design software and page make-up pro grams, type has acquired a fluidity of physical outline, an ease of manipulation and, potentially, a lack of conceptual boundaries unimaginable only a few years ago. Everyone agrees that the new digital tools remove typography from the exclusive domain of the specialist—whether type designer, typefoundry or typesetting company—and place it (not always firmly) in the hands of the ordinary graphic designer. The results of this freedom, however, are the subject of intense and continuing debate. Traditionalists argue that the accessibility of the technology will accelerate the decline in typographic standards that started when the first clumsy photocomposition systems began to replace lead type. Evangelists enthuse about a soon to be realized digital paradise in which everyone will compose letters in personally configured typefaces as idiosyncratic as their own handwriting.

This essay is an interim report on these changes, filed while they are still under way. It addresses new work—from America, Britain, Germany, France, and The Netherlands—which is redefining our approach to typography. Some of these designs are entirely dependent on the new technology—in production terms it would be simply too time-consuming, costly, or awkward to generate them in any other way. Some of them anticipate the aesthetic concerns of the new digital typography, or reflect the freedoms that typography makes possible, while still being produced at the drawing board, or by letterpress. Some will stand the test of time; others will prove to have been representative of their period, but of no greater significance. All of them demonstrate their designers' reluctance to accept that the conventions of typography are inscribed inviolably on tablets of stone.

Among these articles of faith, legibility is perhaps the first and most emotive. If there is one characteristic that links the many visual strategies of the new typographers, it is their combined assault on this most sacred of cows. Swiss Style Modernism composed orderly, linear, well-tempered messages using supposedly objective, and certainly inexpressive, sans-serif letterforms. The new typographers, reacting against this bloodless neutrality, justify their experiments by arguing that no typeface is inherently illegible; rather, in the words of type designer Zuzana Licko of Emigre Graphics, "it is the reader's familiarity with faces that accounts for their legibility."[1] We might find it impossible to read black letter with ease today, but in prewar Germany it was the dominant letterform. Baskerville, rejected in 1757 as ugly and unreadable, is now regarded as one of the most serviceable typefaces for long text setting.

Type design in the digital era is quirky, personal and unreservedly subjective. The authoritarian voices of Modernist typography, which seem to permit only a single authorized reading, are rejected as too corporate, inflexible and limiting, as though—it may be a forlorn hope—typographic diversity itself might somehow re-enfranchise its readers. "I think there are a lot of voices that have not been heard typographically," says type designer Jeffery Keedy, head of graphics at CalArts. "Whenever I start a new job and try to pick a typeface, none of the typefaces give me the voice that I need. They just don't relate to my experiences in my life. They're about somebody else's experiences, which don't belong to me."[2]

Another American type designer, CalArts graduate Barry Deck, speaks of trading in the "myth of the transparency of typographical form for a more realistic attitude toward form, acknowledging that form carries meaning."[3] The aim is to promote multiple rather than fixed readings, to provoke the reader into becoming an active participant in the construction of the message. Later Modernist typography sought to reduce complexity and to clarify content, but the new typographers relish ambiguity, preferring the provisional utterance, alternative take, and delayed punchline to the finely honed phrase. "If someone interprets my work in a way that is totally new to me, I say fine," says Keedy. "That way your work has a life of its own. You create a situation for people to do with it what they will, and you don't create an enclosed or encapsulated moment."[4]

For Keedy, Deck, Emigre Graphics, and colleagues such as Neville Brody and Jonathan Barnbrook in Britain, and Max Kisman in The Netherlands, designing typefaces for personal use is a way of ensuring that graphic design projects carry their own specific identity and tone of voice. The pre-digital typefaces that Brody drew for *The Face* emphasized the new perspectives on contemporary culture embodied in the magazine's editorial content. They also functioned as a medium through which Brody could develop a socio-cultural commentary of his own. Typeface Two, designed in 1984, was deliberately authoritarian in mood, in order, Brody said, to draw a parallel between the social climate of the 1930s and 1980s. The typeface's geometric rigidity was persistently undermined by the light-hearted manner in which it was applied. Other designers take an even more idiosyncratic approach. For Barry Deck, the starting point for a type design is not traditional notions of legibility or elegance, but a highly subjective and seemingly arbitrary narrative founded on what he perceives as the correlation between sexuality and letterforms. "With this in mind, I began imposing narratives of angst, deviation and perversion on the design of my type. Because the *F* is a particularly important letter in the language of sexuality, it came to be a major point of activation in all of the alphabets."[5]

In this polymorphous digital realm, typefaces can cross-fertilize each other or merge to form strange new hybrids. Kisman's Fudoni Bold Remix conjoins Futura and Bodoni; Barnbrook's Prototype is collaged from the bodysnatched parts of ten other typefaces, among them Bembo, Perpetua, and Gill; and Deck's Canicopulus Script is Gill Sans Serif with the satirical addition of puppy-dog tails. Other typefaces are more polemical than practical in their acknowledgement of the contingency, impermanence, and potential for chaos which is a basic condition of the digital medium. Erik van Blokland and Just van Rossum's Beowolf is a family of unpredictable random fonts programmed for three levels of randomness, whose broken, antique outlines shift and reform every time a letter is produced so that no character is ever the same twice. Van Blokland and van Rossum, mavericks with a semi-serious message about the shortcomings of computerized perfection, speculate on the possibility of developing fonts that will cause characters to drop out at random, or to print upside down, and typefaces that will slowly decay until they eventually become illegible in a digital parody of hot-metal type. Jonathan Barnbrook goes a step further by extending this randomizing principle to the text itself. As if to imply an extreme suspicion of content, his typeface Burroughs (named after the novelist with a penchant for textual "cut-ups") replaces whatever is typeset with a stream of gibberish generated at random by the software.

Hand-in-hand with this investigation of the new aesthetic possibilities of the computer comes a revaluation of the artless and the ugly, the hand-made and the ready-made. For designers who are dissatisfied with the glib solutions and formulaic perfection of professional graphics, naive vernacular approaches to type (and imagery) appear to offer a rich seam of authenticity, allusion, expression, and meaning. *Hard Werken,* The Thunder Jockeys, John Weber and Barry Deck value letterforms—hand-drawn and mechanical—for their impurities and flaws. "I am really interested in type that isn't perfect," says Deck. "Type that reflects more truly the imperfect language of an imperfect world inhabited by imperfect beings."[6] Deck's typeface Template Gothic, based on an old sign he found in a laundromat, is an attempt to capture the spirit of crude lettering templates by using truncated serifs, erratic tapered letterforms, and letters that look like they are the degraded product of photomechanical reproduction. Edward Fella, a former commercial artist, creates poster/flyers that break every known rule of typographic decorum and designer good taste. In Fella's agitated hands, type is spun, tilted, stretched, sliced, fractured, drawn as if with a broken nib, and set loose among fields of ink-blotter doodles and deranged networks of rules. He is perhaps the most extreme example of the typographer as artist, an innovator who assumes and achieves the same level of creative freedom as the painters and sculptors whose exhibitions he promotes in catalogues and posters.

Fella, significantly, is a graduate of the Cranbrook Academy of Art, the source of many of the most interesting developments in new typography. Few Cranbrook exercises, however, are entirely typographic; the most typical concentrate on the relationship of image and text. Cranbrook has been at the forefront in exploring the dense, complex layering of elements that is one of the most salient (and frequently criticized) characteristics of the new typographic design. Unlike the earlier work of the New Wave designers, this is not simply a formal exercise in collage-making; the method arises directly from an engagement with content. The Cranbrook theorists' aim, derived from French philosophy and literary theory, is to deconstruct, or break apart and expose, the manipulative visual language and different levels of meaning embodied in design in the same way that a literary critic might deconstruct and decode the verbal language of a novel. "When the deconstructionist approach is applied to design," write American critics Chuck Byrne and Martha Witte, "each layer, through the use of language and image, is an intentional performer in a deliberately playful game wherein the viewer can discover and experience the hidden complexities of language."[7] Work by Cranbrook co-chair Katherine McCoy and academy graduates Allen Hori and P. Scott Makela is a direct challenge to its audience, which must learn to "read" these allusive, open-ended image/type constructions with the same close attention that it would bring to a demanding piece of text.

Although the idea of deconstruction is gaining ground among designers in the U.S., and enjoys some currency in Europe where it originated, few typographers at this point would feel sufficiently confident of the theoretical basis of the term to describe themselves as deconstructionists. Yet the visual strategies of deconstruction, driven by the layering capabilities of the computer, are already widely dispersed. The Californian surfing magazine *Beach Culture* rapidly became both *cause célèbre* and designers' *bête noire* for the deconstructive frenzy with which its art director, David Carson, dismantled the typography of contents pages, headlines, and text. In London, Why Not Associates bring similar typographic abandon to their catalogue dividers and covers for the clothing company Next. In each case the visual delirium is formally stunning, but its relevance to the content is not always clear. Both in their different ways are examples of what Andy Altmann of Why Not Associates calls "type as entertainment." The designs function decoratively as a means of engaging, amusing, persuading and no doubt sometimes infuriating the reader, rather than as vehicles for extending meaning or exploring the text.[8]

Such issues are unavoidable when it comes to the design of long pieces of prose. The questions of legibility and personal expression that preoccupy the new typographers become far more acute when the aim is to hold the reader's attention over the course of many pages. Are the new fonts suitable for any purpose other than exotic display? Or is it time, perhaps, to re-examine the rigidly drawn distinction between typefaces for text and titling? Emigre Graphics, which is able to road-test its typefaces in its own magazine, *Emigre*, has demonstrated the surprising readability of even the most bizarre and apparently unpromising fonts, given a little familiarity with their quirks. *Emigre*'s designer, Rudy VanderLans, mixes seemingly incompatible faces, varies point size and line depth, centers text over extra-wide measures, changes column width within articles, and runs two or more text-strands in parallel—most of the time without undue loss of legibility.

But *Emigre* remains the exception. Most designers experimenting with radical approaches to page structure and typographic hierarchy work with a far more restricted and conventional selection of typefaces. The British typographer and letterpress exponent Phil Baines has turned to medieval manuscripts, media theorist Marshall McLuhan's *The Gutenberg Galaxy,* concrete poetry, and artists' books for alternative models of textual organization. Baines' autobiographical postcards and his highly accomplished undergraduate thesis "The Bauhaus Mistook Legibility for Communication" combine editorial rigor and sensitivity to language with a playful sense of typographic possibility. "Legibility presents information as facts rather than as experience,"[9] says Baines. There is nothing wrong with logic and linearity, he argues, but these qualities satisfy only the rational side of the brain. For Baines and his colleagues, it is equally important that typography should address our capacity for intuitive insight and simultaneous perception, and stimulate our senses as well as engaging our intellect.

Baines' most experimental work is still to be found in his personal projects, but in the last two years there have been a number of striking attempts to deconstruct and redefine the syntax of the conventional book. Tibor Kalman and Marlene McCarty's catalogue for *Strange Attractors: Signs of Chaos* (1989), an exhibition about chaos theory and the arts, subjects the essays to extremes of typographic distortion in an attempt to embody the exhibition's theme. In one essay, the word-spacing increases progressively until the text disintegrates into particles; in another, bold and under-sized characters are sprinkled randomly throughout the text. Avital Ronell's *The Telephone Book* (1989), a discourse on the history, philosophy and Psychoanalytical implications of the telephone, subverts the traditional elegance of a university press publication by assembling a directory of typographic mishaps and metaphorical wrong numbers. Lines of type ripple with size changes, sections of text are crossed out or tilted at angles, whole pages are obscured by over-setting or photographic erosion, fragments of setting float free of the grid, and arguments break off like a bad connection and are never resumed. It is as though the entire book—a collaboration between "switchboard operator" Ronell, designer Richard Eckersley, and compositor Michael Jensen—is in the grip of some fiendish message-scrambling gremlin playing havoc with the telephone system.

Ambitious publishing projects such as *Emigre* and *The Telephone Book* suggest that the tradition of experimental typography initiated by Futurism, Dada and the Bauhaus, and sustained by the work of Robert Massin, Wolfgang Weingart, Warren Lehrer and others, is being refreshed. None of these projects is part of the typographic mainstream, or reaches a particularly wide readership, yet they are exerting an influence well beyond their milieu. Textual designs such as these make large demands on their readers, but they make equally large demands on their designers. If this kind of typography is not to become simply an exercise in style, or fashionable deconstruction, then designers must be able to function as visual editors who can bring acute perception to their readings of the text. In some cases (*Emigre* and *Octavo* magazine, published by London design group 8vo, are examples) the designer might combine the role of editor and typographer. If this is not possible, then author and typographer must work together much more closely than is usually the case to establish and amplify textual meaning. Only then will there be a satisfying relationship between typographic expression and text.[10]

This is a revised version of an essay originally published in Typography Now: The Next Wave, *edited by Rick Poynor and Edward Booth-Clibborn, London: Booth-Clibborn Editions, 1991.*

Endnotes
1. "Do you read me?", *Emigre*. no. 15, 1990, p. 12.
2. *Emigre*. no. 15, pp.16–17.
3. Designer's statement, August 1991.
4. *Emigre*. no. 15, p. 17.
5. Designer's statement, undated.

6. *Emigre*. no. 15, p. 21.

7. "A Brave New World: Understanding Deconstruction", *Print*, XLIV:VI, November/December 1990, p. 83. See also Katherine McCoy and David Frej, "Typography as Discourse", *I.D.*, vol. 35 no. 2, 1988, pp.34–37.

8. In fairness, it should be noted that David Carson has challenged this reading of his designs—"The work is very much concept-driven. Without question, it is attempting to extend meaning, and certainly tries to explore the text" (*Emigre* no. 27, 1993, p. 17). Readers will have to make up their own minds about whether or not he achieves this aim. I would argue that the "meaning" of *Beach Culture*, and more recently Carson's work on *Ray Gun* magazine, lies less in the detailed design decisions of individual spreads than in the super-heated environment they combine to create. Here, the medium really is the message, and the message—like the subject matter, be it surfing or grunge—is a highly specialized form of subcultural entertainment. It embodies an attitude and, for many readers, a way of life.

9. "The first consideration of typography is to be clearly read", public debate, Chartered Society of Designers, London, 11 March 1991.

10. On this last point, it should be borne in mind that the original printing of this article tried to achieve just that—a satisfying relationship of typographic expression and text. Its design, by Why Not Associates, was an attempt to apply some of the main ideas in the essay. For a detailed discussion of this strategy, see my letter in *Emigre*, no. 28, 1993.

LOGOS, FLAGS, AND ESCUTCHEONS
by
Paul Rand

"It reminds me of the Georgia chain gang," quipped the IBM executive, when he first eyed the striped logo. When the Westinghouse insignia (1960) was first seen, it was greeted similarly with such gibes as "this looks like a pawnbroker's sign." How many exemplary works have gone down the drain, because of such pedestrian fault-finding? Bad design is frequently the consequence of mindless dabbling, and the difficulty is not confined merely to the design of logos. This lack of understanding pervades all visual design.

There is no accounting for people's perceptions. Some see a logo, or anything else that's seeable, the way they see a Rorschach inkblot. Others look without seeing either the meaning or even the function of a logo. It is perhaps, this sort of problem that prompted ABC TV to toy with the idea of "updating" their logo (1962). They realized the folly only after a market survey revealed high audience recognition. This is to say nothing of the intrinsic value of a well-established symbol. *When* a logo is designed is irrelevant; *quality*, not *vintage* nor *vanity*, is the determining factor.

There are as many reasons for designing a new logo, or updating an old one, as there are opinions. The belief that a new or updated design will be some kind charm that will magically transform any business, is not uncommon. A redesigned logo may have the advantage of implying something new, something improved—but this is short-lived if a company doesn't live up to its claims. Sometimes a logo is redesigned because it really needs redesigning—because it's ugly, old fashioned, or inappropriate. But many times, it is merely to feed someone's ego, to satisfy a CEO who doesn't wish to be linked with the past, or often because it's the thing to do.

Opposed to the idea of arbitrarily changing a logo, there's the "let's leave it alone" school—sometimes wise, more often superstitious, occasionally nostalgic or, at times, even trepidatious. Not long ago, I offered to make some minor adjustments to the UPS (1961) logo. This offer was unceremoniously turned down, even though compensation played no role. If a design can be refined, without disturbing its image, it seems reasonable to do so. A logo, after all, is an instrument of pride and should be shown at its best.

If, in the business of communications, "image is king," the essence of this image, the logo, is a jewel in its crown.

Here's what a logo is and does:

A logo is a flag, a signature, an escutcheon.

A logo doesn't sell (directly), it *identifies*.

A logo is rarely a description of a business.

A logo derives its *meaning* from the quality of the thing it symbolizes, not the other way around.

A logo is *less* important than the product it signifies; what it means is more important than what it looks like.

A logo appears in many guises: a signature is a kind of logo, so is a flag. The French flag, for example, or the flag of Saudi Arabia, are aesthetically pleasing symbols. One happens to be pure geometry, the other a combination of Arabic script, together with an elegant saber—two diametrically opposed visual concepts; yet both function effectively. Their appeal, however, is more than a matter of aesthetics. In battle, a flag can be a friend or foe. The ugliest flag is beautiful if it happens to be on your side. "Beauty," they say, "is in the eye of the beholder," in peace or in war, in flags or in logos. We all believe *our* flag the most beautiful; this tells us something about logos.

Should a logo be self-explanatory? It is only by association with a product, a service, a business, or a corporation that a logo takes on any real meaning. It derives its meaning and usefulness from the quality of that which it symbolizes. If a company is second rate, the logo will eventually be perceived as second rate. It is foolhardy to believe that a logo will do its job right off, before an audience has been properly conditioned. Only after it becomes familiar does a logo function as intended; and only when the product or service has been judged effective or ineffective, suitable or unsuitable, does it become truly representative.

Logos may also be designed to deceive; and deception assumes many forms, from imitating some peculiarity to outright copying. Design is a two-faced monster. One of the most benign symbols, the swastika, lost its place in the pantheon of the civilized when it was linked to evil, but its intrinsic quality remains indisputable. This explains the tenacity of good design.

The role of the logo is to point, to designate—in as simple a manner as possible. A design that is complex, like a fussy illustration or an arcane abstraction, harbors a self-destruct mechanism. Simple ideas, as well as simple designs are, ironically, the products of circuitous mental purposes. Simplicity is difficult to achieve, yet worth the effort.

The effectiveness of a logo depends on:

a. distinctiveness
b. visibility
c. useability
d. memorability
e. universality
f. durability
g. timelessness

Most of us believe that the subject matter of a logo depends on the kind of business or service involved. Who is the audience? How is it marketed? What is the media? These are some of the considerations. An animal might suit one category, at the same time that it would be anathema in another. Numerals are possible candidates: 747, 7-Up, 7-11, and so are letters, which are not only possible but most common. However, the subject matter of a logo is of relatively little importance; nor, it seems, does appropriateness always play a significant role. This does not imply that appropriateness is undesirable. It merely indicates that a one-to-one relationship, between a symbol and what is symbolized, is very often impossible to achieve and, under certain conditions, may even be objectionable. Ultimately, the only thing mandatory, it seems, is that a logo be attractive, reproducible in one color, and in exceedingly small sizes.

The Mercedes symbol, for example, has nothing to do with automobiles; yet it is a great symbol, not because its design is great, but because it stands for a great product. The same can be said about apples and computers. Few people realize that a *bat* is the symbol of authenticity for Bacardi Rum; yet Barcardi is still being imbibed. Lacoste sportswear, for example, has nothing to do with alligators (or crocodiles), and yet the little green reptile is a memorable and profitable symbol. What makes the Rolls Royce emblem so distinguished is *not* its design (which is commonplace), but the *quality* of the automobile for which it stands. Similarly, the signature of George Washington is distinguished not only for its calligraphy, but because Washington was Washington. Who cares how badly the signature is scribbled on a check, if the check doesn't bounce? Likes or dislikes should play no part in the problem of identification; nor should they have anything to do with approval or disapproval. Utopia!

All this seems to imply that good design is superfluous. Design, good or bad, is a vehicle of memory. Good design adds value of some kind and, incidentally, could be sheer pleasure; it respects the viewer—his sensibilities—and rewards the entrepreneur. It is easier to remember a well designed image than one that is muddled. A well designed logo, in the end, is a reflection of the business it symbolizes. It connotes a thoughtful and purposeful enterprise, and mirrors the *quality* of its products and services. It is good public relations— a harbinger of good will.

It says "We care."

Originally published in the AIGA Journal of Graphic Design, *vol. 9, no. 3, 1991.*

READING OUTSIDE THE GRID: DESIGNERS AND SOCIETY

by

Frances Butler

Perfection of means and confusion of goals seem—
in my opinion—to characterize our age.
—Albert Einstein

Modern kitchen—where the pot calls the kettle chartreuse.
—Anonymous

We're now living 200 years per annum. When you're moving at
that clip there's no place to stand. Its like putting a Model T
on the highway at 100 miles per hour. It breaks down.
—Marshall McLuhan

All that is not eternal is eternally out of date.
—C. S. Lewis

Willi Kunz began questioning the operation of the grid system of page layout through typographic experiments in the early 1970s. (The grid, as we all know, but no one else does, provides columns with margins between them in both directions; it provides for multiple but similar starting points on a page.) Kunz pushed especially on the conflict, or at least difference, between text placement or punctuation, which implies stasis around points, and word sequence, which implies both physical and mental movement from word to word. Somewhat later Wolfgang Weingart also began to dismantle the Swiss grid system, using it as a three dimensional support for illusions of planar overlay generated by differences in grey value. Instead of horizontal linearity, his text layout involved depth perception, certainly a new direction for the ordering of thinking or reading. But, following the same procedure followed by architects who, in pursuit of a style of spatial articulation called Modernism, had turned from ornamenting construction to constructing geometric ornament, these early graphic experiments were soon replaced by stylists using the dismantled grid as an ornamental motif. Now dismantled Swiss layout is a fad in the United States, usually featuring the full range of Univers or Helvetica type strewn over the pages of avant-garde tabloids and school posters. Different designer intentions support this style of text layout, ranging from historicism—reopening the Futurist's experiments with *Parole in Liberta*—to generating a new style of physical manipulation and visual acrobatics that could be called "sporty reading," or at least opening up possibilities for more reader control of narrative syntax.

But now that this mode of free writing, and/or freed reading, has been institutionalized (i.e., taught in design schools), it is time to ask whether these announced intentions coincide with their actual social operation, and if they do, how and why they work. We must understand what this evolving layout tactic means in order to know if, once more, graphic designers are making up a style that is interesting to them alone, or if this new layout system reflects changes in the nature of institutional thought. For in late twentieth-century democratic culture, institutions and their founding assumptions control all of our big decisions. We are a culture of committees, in business, government, and education, and although we make personal decisions, these are either marginal or irrelevant to the main operations of power. There is nothing more important to institutional culture than its organizational systems, big or small. And the systems we use to organize either thinking or living, be they modular sizes for the manufacture of building materials or the models governing text layout, are all based on the assumption that placement *is* information.

Beginning the questioning process about place on the page, we need to question the grid with more speculation about its origins. So far the origins given have been symptoms of its existence, not causes for its generation. For, as in the development of most new underlying social assumptions, or founding epistemologies as the anthropologists call them, practices precede theory. The origins of the grid structure do not lie in academic or aesthetic teaching or theorizing. Alan Hurlbut contends that the early twentieth-century books of Jay Hambidge were a contributing influence on the grid. Now it is true that Jay Hambidge, Claude Fayette Bragdon, Mathilde Ghyka, Darcy Wentworth Thompson, and others around the turn of the century discovered, or demanded, an underlying geometry in the world, finding the golden mean and the Fibonacci series to determine everything from the arrangement of plants to countless systems for generating ornament, ranging from that of Islam to that of dynamic symmetry. Lydia Dalrymple Henderson has gathered the writings of these neo-Platonist enthusiasts into two main groups; those that gave time, the "fourth dimension," a physical, geometric form, and those, who like the Theosophists, connected physical geometry to the service of a religious spiritualism. But the grid as a page organizing system predates these geometricizing spiritualists by about a century. It originated in the need for more precise indexing systems to make, market, account for, and transport the products of the Industrial Revolution. Newspapers, catalogs and railway schedules all provided the multiple vertical column. Order forms, bills of lading, sales receipts, and account books provided multiple horizontal locations.

The Swiss grid simply divided the page, or the double spread, into more possible points of significant separation. It was a logical conclusion in a culture that had been developing a profound conviction that place was an active component of abstract thought ever since the place system in counting and calculation was learned from the Arabs in or about the twelfth century. The two dimensional grid was very slowly assimilated into the accounting practices of the Italian and German bankers and merchants, but by the sixteenth century was in wide use. It was then supplemented by a three-dimensional version when Descartes proposed the grid as a locating system for the properties of the physical universe. The Cartesian grid was considered so useful, or so glamorous, that Thomas

Jefferson used it to structure the Land Ordinance of 1786 and determine the property boundaries of all new lands subsequently acquired and sold by the United States. And at the end of the eighteenth century J. H. Lambert (1728-1777) and William Playfair (1759-1853), began to develop time-based graphic charts based on a grid of two intersecting horizontal and vertical variables.

In this atmosphere of significance designated by place, the development of a grid layout system, doing for text what the multiple entry system had long done for numbers, cannot be explained by the existence of any one group of geometricizing enthusiasts at the turn of the century. And furthermore, the grid system of page layout simply expanded on the basic tactic for information access already used in the classic page layout of the codex. Guides to the information on a traditional page were usually found on the top and on the left margin of a page. At the top of the manuscript page the Diminuendo gave entry into the text. In printed texts the running head gave a continual summary of the contents of the chapter or that page. On the left margin indentations or marks announced changes of subject. Sometimes the folio numbers were on the top or side of the page, and extra material (elaborations, definitions, concordances) was printed in smaller type in the outside or central margins. But like the other elements of the traditional codex layout, these emendations sought to make the center of the text block more accessible through marks on its edges. The grid system dissolved that block, moving the top down, and the left margin over progressively so that the entire page was open to the devices of traditional indexing.

By the mid-nineteenth century, the multiple column format was used for the structure of some books, especially almanacs that had to incorporate many different kinds of information. By 1931 layout guides like Andrew Tuer's *Mise en page* were advocating a rudimentary grid of vertical and horizontal page divisions to accommodate different kinds of text and pictures. And in the 1950s, the grid was given final form in the work of Swiss designers like Max Bill, Armin Hoffmann, or Emil Ruder.

The next question that needs to be raised about the grid system relates to how texts presented in grid formats are read. The grid system not only organized textual material, it affected reading by changing the kind of language that was used within its confines. A grid system can exist with only two columns of text or images per page, but more typically it has three or more vertical columns, and three or more horizontal divisions. As the number of columns goes up, their line length goes down, and many newspaper columns are not more than 12 or 15 picas wide. The argument used to justify short line length ties together the small forward eye movements used to read, the saccadic movements, with reading by contending that the sentence length which most nearly corresponds to the amount of text seen at one time is most easily read and comprehended. Now this may be true, but it is also true that the kind of idea best presented in a short sentence is short, or uncomplicated; one without ambiguities or qualification. (Remember, the columnar grid originated in numbers, or in the one or two word categories found in accounts, graphs, train schedules, and catalogs.) Such short entries, and short thoughts, work like codes which are deciphered by reference to information given outside the sentence, outside the text, in general culture. This kind of idea can be called conventional wisdom, common sense, the cliché, or implicit knowledge; but whatever the name it is never a *new* idea. Ideas which are not "common sense" frequently need explicit development in longer sentences for anyone to comprehend them. First Ludwig Wittgenstein and then Marshall McLuhan, both of whom presented not new ideas, but new arrangements of old ideas, found to their dismay that if an idea is not already so well known as to be implicit in the culture, there could be no substitution for precise language, carefully deployed around the dimensions of the idea. Both tried to present their ideas in aphoristic language, in the short sentence; and McLuhan, at least, finally reaped nothing but resentment and scorn. Now, a generation after his death, his ideas have been quietly assimilated and many academic writers have found his writings useful in thinking and are writing entire books to fill in the gaps left in his abbreviated dicta.

McLuhan's fate highlights the fact that other ideas, many of which are still useful for thinking, have fallen out of general circulation because we can no longer read their sentences. Many earlier English writers, and contemporary writers in other languages like Italian, use long sentences. It is not appropriate to put either Henry James or Italo Calvino into a 12 pica line. It is difficult to sustain reading of their long sentences when these are forced into narrow lines, and therefore extend half-way down the page. The combination of saccadic eye movement and frequent line returns sets up excess noise that interferes with the smooth remembrance needed to keep the multiple subtended clauses of such sentences in order.

But for the common-sense idea, the assumptions that implicitly govern culture, the grid system and the short, encoded sentences that the grid supports, provide a simple reading system that is open to every level of reader. The wide range of type weights and set widths in the sans-serif type families typical of the Swiss style grid layout, and the generous white spaces, help frame the information and make it memorable much as the shape of a chart serves as a mnemonic for its data. Ease in reading the grid layout supports equal access to information, which equals democratic opportunity for employment and economic survival. And democratic access to information is critical to our corporate business and bureaucratic structure, for, to flourish corporations require a large pool of potential employees characterized by intellectual skills like literacy, conceptual inventiveness, and organizational talent. Such skills do not necessarily occur in sufficient numbers in the privileged populations created by blood-based dynasties or caste hierarchies.

It cannot be said that our corporate culture does not support some blood-based social exclusion from information and social opportunity: we seem to be deeply and irremediably racist. But in so far as our institutional bureaucracies do need literate clerks, the grid system supports literacy. The dismantled grid does not. Reading the dismantled grid is only open to very determined and very sophisticated readers. The unskilled reader simply cannot regenerate enough text from the reader-syntaxed stew to find the implicit assumptions of institutional culture needed for their sustenance or interest. The style of the presentation, *dismemberment*, becomes the subject of the presentation.

It is possible to say that graphic designers are simply acting out the behavior of late practitioners of any art style outlined by historians of cultural shift like Henri Focillon, George Kubler, or Thomas Kuhn. These writers on the history and uses of style would perhaps have said that graphic designers long for variety and novelty but, not yet being able to generate a new style, exaggerate and ornament the old one. Or it might be possible to project from the writings of a number of late-nineteenth century art historians, the most important of whom was Alois Riegl, that this late style of fragmentary sentences, requiring active reader participation for the reconstruction of sentence sense, reflects a new preference in comprehension habits. Riegl wrote about late Roman sculpture, once considered unskilled, degenerate, by art historians because instead of the skilled transitions from one plane to another differences were crudely drilled in; roughly defined. Riegl contended that although skill may have declined, viewing preferences had also changed. He felt that these sculptures demonstrated a change in responsibility for making the complete image from the sculptor to the viewer, who, with the activity of their own eye and mind made from the light and shadow generated by the rough surface of the sculpture a complete, and dramatic surface more interesting than the smooth one provided entirely by the sculptor.

Applying Riegl's idea that a change in style reflects a change in the habits of cognitive practice in the groups that use that style, it is perhaps possible that the designers using the dismantled grid may reflect profound cultural changes; changes in organizational preferences, that is to say, changes in the very mode of comprehending information.

Joshua Meyerowitz, one of the many writers mining the seams first opened by Marshall McLuhan, has written a book, *No Sense of Place*, about his finding that the place system of authority which has sustained our culture for such a long time is collapsing. He notes that television, which sells the illusion of capturing the live moment with such close-up realism that it shows the red blood vessels in the skin of a politician's nose, has so effectively demystified public figures that it is no longer possible for them to gain authority simply by speaking from a position or place of power; a place like a church pulpit, a political seat, or an academic lectern. He found that even in popular culture, no one cares about contemporary "stars" the way they did about Gary Cooper or Elvis Presley, because their lives are no longer separate or mysterious enough from the rest of us. And he cites the newspaper editorials which made it clear that a president, who was televised tripping on his untied shoelace, could not regain the charisma that traditionally supported his authority simply by sitting behind the desk in the oval office.

There is evidence that belief in the fixed place as a condition of authority, truth, and power is slipping away at other scales of human activity. Einstein and his theory of the relativity of physical phenomenon has been jokingly accepted in popular culture for two or three generations, and popularizing books like *Chaos Theory* and television science programs continue to develop the theme of the fluidity of physical reactions. Now, the scale of the points or *places* described by fractal geometry mathematics has become so fine, so miniaturized, that it is too fine for visible distinctions of direction at all.

At the literary level, deconstruction of the process of assigning qualities to something by naming it, begun in the late nineteenth century by Ludwig Wittgenstein, has by now reached the level of popular culture. Deconstruction of the connection between naming and belief in the reality of the named qualities is now central to popular entertainment; the slow trajectory from Laurence Sterne to Samuel Beckett, who merely broke down literary conventions by making them the subject of their stories, accelerated off the charts as David Bowie and Boy George dismantled gender by making it their subject. In short, it may be that the incomplete story, the particle, the fragment, is now the preferred unit of information for our culture, and lack of place is more useful for presenting these fragments than to fix them into sentences or grids.

Fashions are a mode of asking questions and an experimental range of answers. "Running it up the flagpole" may provide answers that last fifty years, or may provide answers that last for centuries. In the thirteenth century the zero and the place system used in counting and mathematic calculations was a fashion. It proved to be such a useful adjunct to the development of accounting that accompanied mercantilism that it has lasted for centuries. The place system is but one example of our cultural reliance on grid systems for organization, evidence that the grid has been a fruitful tool for thinking. Now it may be that the fashion among graphic designers for the deconstruction of the grid, and of some kinds of traditional punctuation like the continuous sentence may auger a new kind of idea for thinking, a new textual organization system, of floating fragments, combined by the readers the way Riegl contended fourth century Romans combined vision of light and shadow to make up the images of their sculpted gods and generals. Perhaps this new spatial system will produce texts in which the connection of word to word will be, as it is in Japanese, very much more flexible. In Japanese the reader runs any two contiguous words through a wide and open range of connections at every stage in the deciphering of a sentence. In effect, reading Japanese, or reading the post-Swiss or fragmented sentence expands the possible connections beyond the scale of the grid that has served us so far, into a new grid, with so many connections that the intersections are no longer visible. We are now, with computers, truly gathering and using information on a new scale, through a grid that is sub-miniaturized.

Change of scale is not a simple additive or subtractive process; change of scale is absolute, with consequences which cannot be comprehended by projection from previous experience with the earlier scale of organization. For example, the change of scale of our business and governmental institutions into ever larger bureaucracies required the development of simple communication matrices, language and work practices, which could be understood by a large and varied work force. But this change of scale has unexpected consequences: these engrossed bureaucracies could not even deal with many of the very social problems they were established to handle, because society is not one large body but many individuals, with many specific, personal, idiosyncratic needs.

Scale change is absolute change. Converting the visible grid that we have known into a sub-miniature grid is a change of scale that has produced not additive but absolute changes. The sub-miniaturized grid is too small to be visible and punctuation can no longer be seen to fit into it. A new punctuation system may be devised by the same kind of experimental repetition that generated the earlier grid over time, but as yet the new grid is only a fashion, a question. As yet the fashion for the floating sentence is too abbreviated for many to make use of it. It is not unlike the aphorisms of Wittgenstein or McLuhan, without the necessary bulk of different interpretations and experiences swathed around their skeletons to make them comprehensible to the out-size groups which support the scale of our social institutions. Designers may provide enough variations on the freed sentence, inserting it into many different kinds of reading products, and ultimately make it familiar to different populations so that they can either use it or reject it. Academics will then analyze the ways in which the freed sentence works, write theories about it, and produce teaching texts to support it. If the freed sentence is to be a major reading and thinking tool, the time it takes to establish it is one of those unknowns that results when organizational scale is changed. A few years or a few hundred years from now the freed sentence may provide our major reading, and thinking, tool.

Originally published in ADC Statements *(American Center for Design), vol. 4, no. 3, Spring 1989.*

THE WRITTEN WORD:
THE DESIGNER AS EXECUTOR,
AGENT AND PROVOCATEUR

by
William Drenttel

L ate last year, America elected a reader as President. Bill Clinton read through– throughout the campaign to ease stress and to save his voice (ironically taking in words to keep himself from uttering words). A chief campaign spokeswoman then caused a stir by noting that his favorite book was the *Meditations* of Marcus Aurelius. Clinton usually reads a couple of books simultaneously: a work on contemporary politics or economics and a spy novel. As of this writing, he is reading Martin Cruz Smith's *Red Square*, a novel of black market intrigue in contemporary Moscow. He is also reported to have asked the CIA to turn over its vast collection of spy novels—on which the Agency has undoubtedly spent millions trying to decode—to the White House for his private library. Some reporters have remarked that they felt better knowing that the President was readying himself for the challenges that lay ahead.

Compared to his predecessor, President Clinton is a bookworm. William Honan of the *New York Times* reported that in 1984 George Bush was innocently asked to name a book he had recently read. He stumbled, eventually naming the twenty-two-year-old best seller, *The Guns of August*, by Barbara Tuchman. During the 1992 campaign, the same question was asked, and President Bush floundered again, not remembering a title. While hardly illiterate, President Bush just was not a reader. And after the infamous *potatoe* incident, it was clearly established that his running mate just was not a speller!

I feel more comfortable knowing that the President is a reader, that he is both capable of reading policy reports and reading for its sheer pleasure. With all the discussion about literacy in America, the truth seems to be that much of our country is losing its taste, perhaps even its appetite, for the written word. The issue is not what you read so much as whether you read—and if the illiterate can't read, the literate increasingly don't read. If the illiterate don't know where Burma is, the literate probably don't know that Burma is now named Myanmar. In either case, the new atlases read like Greek to many of us— who, after all, can remember the eleven new countries that comprise the Commonwealth of Independent States (the former USSR, without Georgia and the Baltics) much less the emerging cacophony that makes up the rest of the former Ottoman Empire? In this context, it is no surprise that few understand the historical complexity of the crisis in Bosnia or that public discourse on the economy is at best shallow. Our reliance on the written word seems to be at an all-time low, and with dramatic effect on general knowledge and communication.

For this state of affairs, we hear many explanations: the influence of television, in general; the rise of MTV; the rise of the sound byte and the corresponding decline of television news; the expansion and complexity of new forms of media; the popularity of Nintendo; the decline in educational quality; the proliferation of languages in a multicultural society; and the propensity to engage in other forms of leisure activity. Among my contemporaries, I most often hear that reading and having children just don't mix. The explanations are many; more concerning is the facile way in which they are invoked to explain away the issue. The very acceptance of these rationales has become self-fulfilling, the prophecy of a dead end.

This evolution of the role of the written word is having a profound affect on graphic designers. The fodder of graphic design is, after all, words and pictures. Yet how many times have you heard, "Well, people just don't read anymore" offered as a rationale for de-emphasizing the role or amount of writing (copy, text, language, whatever it's called) in a design project? Some designers seem to acquiesce to the logic of this statement. Other designers seem more cynical, taking this situation as license to render words fundamentally illegible, engaging in dense shenanigans under the guise of avant-garde typography. Still others view this as one of the challenges of being a designer today.

Of course, it is true that reading seems more and more a luxury given the frantic complexity of modern life. In a commercial sense, these changes are equally extreme, affecting the nature and form of business communication. How do designers produce brochures or promotional literature for their clients, yet trash most of what they themselves receive? (The answer that "my" work is different doesn't, of course, get the profession very far.) When was the last time you saw someone actually read CD liner notes or an employee handbook? When a magazine editor or publisher says they want their magazine to be easier to read, more scannable, they should be taken literally—they are praying that readers actually do scan it. If you are a graphic designer producing such brochures, leaflets, magazines, or direct mail, wouldn't you rather just go home for the day? Doesn't this feel like a professional dead end? Alex Isley, the principal of Alexander Isley Design in New York City, succinctly noted, "I just have to believe that people still read."

Many people, of course, still do read, especially the staples of books, magazines, and newspapers. I believe the reason is simple, and that hidden within this reason is a way for graphic designers to approach this issue. These books (or magazines, whatever) were meant to be read. They were written to be published, sold, taken home, and read. Generally, the better they're written, the more they're read. (If some of them become decoration on the coffee table, that's okay too. Books have a way of taking on a life of their own: someone else picks it up off the coffee table, and a new reader is found. It is this glow of an afterlife that makes a good bookstore interesting and a large urban magazine shop exciting.) There is the assumption that these objects of commerce are for you—that you might be interested, that they're worth your time, and they might educate, entertain, or just relax you.

The crux of this equation is their good intent—that they were meant to be read. Roland Barthes, the French critic, has written of the implicit contract between the writer and reader—that despite the image of the solitary artist, there is always a reader in the mind of the writer. Designers seem to have the image of a "viewer" in mind, even as they produce printed materials. The catch is that the "viewer" is a generic category, a composite consumer of imagery. The same can be said of "audience" and "public," perhaps even of "readers." As the novelist Paul Auster recently observed, "I don't think of 'the public.' 'The public' doesn't exist, because books are not a communal experience. They're a private experience. Every book is read by one person. No matter how many people read it totally, it's always one person reading the book. So I don't think of the physical mass of the reading public." Designers, too, can imagine a single reader and then set out to create work that is intended to be read. It is here that something like a contract can occur.

Instead, the intent of graphic design is usually posited as having something to do with "communication," another term more generic than specific. As the editor of this column, DK Holland, has written, "The graphic designer is a key player in the development of *intelligent communication* tools ..." If one designs something and never really expects it to be read, then what kind of communication is being created? Why does so much award-winning design include language that was never meant to be read, or does any text longer than a byline, caption, or design credit seem too long? "Well, people just don't read anymore."

These are traps for contemporary graphic design. The use of the word "communication" often sounds hollow, a camouflage for delivering sales points without an idea on the page. Look through a design annual and try to read the words—most of the time it's just a surface, a façade. This is what wins awards, and it's this level that other designers then try to emulate. Design firm self-promotions suffer from the same affliction—one is seldom supposed to look further, or to actually read anything shown. Recently, I was pleasantly surprised by a self-promotional book by MetaDesign of Berlin—one caption said to simply read the work pictured, which *could* be read and which explained itself.

It is as if some designers have grown fearful of language, and are, like some audiences, only capable of thinking in visual terms. As one designer told me: "We may argue endlessly over the copy, but when it's done the comment is always just that it 'looks good.'" If editors sometimes play the role of the visually illiterate, then there is something out there like the "dumb designer" syndrome, the desire to hide behind the right side of the brain. This, in some cases, flows directly from the historically inferior position designers hold in many worlds. Magazine art directors seldom have the power of editors; advertising art directors are often not equal to their copywriting counterparts, who create the slogans of the industry; and corporate art directors are usually in staff positions without line responsibility.

Nonetheless, many of the best graphic designers working today are or have been editorial designers. Learning from books is obviously the longest tradition in design history. In magazines, the structural link between editorial and art departments rewards talented designers who are comfortable with the written word. Also, the editorial process, even at its worst, still seems to focus on the reader as reader.

In corporate communications, other tendencies are apt to predominate. Paper companies are a case in point. Designers aspire to have the freedom and printing budgets of paper promotions, and then often produce homages to collections of dusty objects or meaningless explorations on vapid themes. They are meant to be printed, but seldom meant to be read. Recent environmental concerns have resulted, at least to some extent, in a sensitivity about how much paper and ink is used to produce such fluff. A few companies are grappling with these issues by encouraging promotional efforts that have enough content to be worth printing, with some recent promotions placing greater reliance on quality writing.

In the business world, writing incorporated by designers in corporate communications projects is seldom well written, much less communicative. The usual recipes include idyllic fluff (flowery metaphors that say nothing), the hyper-clarity of bullet points (well thought out snippets of services, features, capabilities that numb any reader), or strategic hard sell (barely re-wording client strategies and pretending this is the way people speak).

Yet, designers frequently control the editorial content of such projects. They are given a business need, an audience, a budget, and then the creative juices are supposed to flow. They become, in effect, the editor, determining the "story," hiring the writer, assigning the artwork. It is sometimes instructive to define a project in these terms, to think of the strategy as requiring a story. For a good editor, telling the story is the key thing, and writing and visualization are both important. Designers often put photographers and illustrators on a higher plane, with the writer considered just another freelance function. When designers describe their favorite writers, the compliment used most often is "professional"; i.e., the manuscript is delivered on time, ideally on a disk, with a flexible attitude about changes necessary to fit into the design. This is writing on demand, filler that fits. Used in this way, writers have as much importance as mechanical paste-up. One way to raise the importance of writing in an everyday office environment is to change the vocabulary. Referring to "writing" or "text," as opposed to "copywriting," is a way of signaling that the writing you use in your work must be real writing. (One step further is to hire real writers as opposed to copywriters, but here the argument becomes unintentionally inflammatory.)

For most of us, there is much to learn from the editorial world. Respect for editors leads to an understanding of what is a good story, what is a tightly written argument, and the power of a concise headline. Just as designers need a good brief and then a lot of freedom, so, too, with writers. Designers who work with writers a lot are also more comfortable with longer texts and more complicated, in-depth arguments. Some designers find that occasionally trying their own hand at writing is a way to get close to the words; it also helps to integrate writing and design. These and other efforts can be made by designers to elevate the role of writing in design projects, and to grow more comfortable working with writing and writers.

In the end, though, writing that gets read must be intended to be read. Using the written word does not solve illiteracy, but it at least speaks to the literate as if they were living and breathing—rather than assuming they are brain dead. If Roland Barthes was right about the contract between writer and reader, then perhaps there is also an implicit contract between client and audience, with the designer as executor, agent, and provocateur? This is perhaps where one can speak of responsibility, of the need to take seriously the written words that are used in graphic design. It is here that communication starts to happen, when a reader knows that you mean it.

Originally published in Communication Arts *magazine, vol. 35, no. 1, March/April 1993.*

I LIKE THE VERNACULAR...NOT
by
Jeffery Keedy

The most familiar "use" of vernacular is to produce nostalgia. The problem with the nostalgic vernacular is that it steals steals from the past to deny the future. The past is robbed of its authenticity and historical context (or specificity) to be rewritten as if it were an episode of *Happy Days* or a Norman Rockwell painting. Absence makes the heart grow fonder, and there's no fiction like "the good old days." This kind of nostalgic reverie is an escape from the anxiety of an uncertain future; it's not so much historical quotation as it is nostalgic sound bite. Authenticity is not a high priority for graphic designers because its usually the feeling we're after, NOT the fact. This allows us to play fast and loose with history to construct feelings, like that of the art deco thirties or the fifties, that never really correspond to any specific time, place, or people. It's not the past, it's better than the past—and the present and the future. Retreating into nostalgia is turning your back on the present and running in fear of the future. If graphic designers are busy daydreaming about the good old days, then who is going to show us what the future looks like? Who's in charge of inventing tomorrow? Are we all so embarrassed that the Modernist visions of Herbert Bayer, Raymond Lowey, and Bucky Fuller didn't exactly come true that we must retreat to some imaginary past life that didn't really exist, either?

The commercial artist was transformed into the graphic designer with the help and encouragement of Modernism. Graphic design's identity is so co-dependent on Modernism that one does not dare contemplate design outside of the Modernist paradigm. Now, in an era of Post-modern plurality and technological change, the good old days of the easy and unchallenged answers of Modernism are gone for good. That's why graphic design is suffering from an identity crisis. When you are having trouble defining something it is often easier to define what it is NOT, and the vernacular is what we (professional graphic designers) are NOT.

I think much of the current interest in vernacular is a symptom of the lack of direction and a groping for self-definition of the design profession. So many times I hear designers waxing poetically about some lovely little match book cover, menu design, or hand-lettered sign and how terrific it is—what graphic designer doesn't have a stash of such found goodies to "borrow" from? And there's nothing wrong with that; after all, the capacity to appreciate something will e x p a n d your understanding, NOT define it.

Appropriation of the "other" (to use the current art world vernacular) means taking something from a culture "other" than your own. You can appropriate something without reference to its original context (pastiche), or in a way that calls attention to its original context (parody/irony). Other cultures are not just literally other national cultures but can be high, low, pop, and sub-cultures. When one culture borrows from another there are often problems that arise due to issues of dominance and equality. For example, when the high-culture graphic designer (trained in a design school) borrows clip art illustrations or crude lettering from the low-culture hack (trained in the school of hard knocks) it can be a condescending act of elitism that deliberately draws attention to the difference in status between them as if to say, "Hey look at what this so-called illustrator did ... isn't it corny? I could never do anything that silly, I'm too sophisticated, I really wish I could but I'm just too clever to do anything like that. In fact, I'm too clever to do anything at all, that's why I have to use stuff from these poor hacks." This appropriation/nostalgia thing has not only become a bit tiresome lately, but is increasingly mean spirited as well; and only in the most covert fashion because the plunderers are always the first to proclaim how much they love the one they are plundering. The idea of "borrowing" in graphic design is so pervasive that it's often done unconsciously. What is needed is an awareness of what crossing cultural/historical barriers actually means, as well as an understanding of the importance of context.

The culture that is perceived to be the high or dominant is not the only one to be empowered. In this negotiation of status, the plundered underdog is given the unassailable status of the authentic, capable of true, natural, or honest expression. The so designated dominant culture, on the other hand, is a vacuous imitator/manipulator plundering the TRUTH from the real "other" culture. Thus, the price of dominance in the culture war is authenticity. "They" used to be great, but now that they're mainstream/commercial they're just crap! In this exchange of tit-for-tat, the high and low cultures are leveled out into one pop culture. Is it the graphic designers task to please everyone in this pan-pop culture? Or to affirm their client's status as the high, and the audience/consumer's status as the low?

You can't please some of the people some of the time, but you can please all of the people all the time!

Today, cutting-edge vernacular users are the designers creating rave graphics. (For those of you who live in a cave, a rave is an illegal underground party of a thousand kids on ecstasy [DRUG], dancing in puddles of their own sweat to techno-house music until the cows come home, or the cops drop in [FUN]!) The old and low cultures that rave designers borrow from is primarily American corporate and package design of the seventies and eighties (now there're some hacks)! Rave designers love logos, lots of color and outlined type, and hey, who doesn't? The fact that the "professional designer's" work is now being reworked like any other bit of ephemera might be some kind of poetic justice, but it fails to be a very interesting design strategy. That's because their work (like their predecessors) is essentially a one-liner that has little resonance beyond the "shock of the old." What little invention there is in rave graphics is provided mostly by the computer.

I remember the late eighties ... now those were the good old days!

At this point it would seem the vernacular idea in graphic design has pretty much played itself out. The only thing the cutting-edge appropriator can do is continuously reuse what they just did last year. This strategy couldn't really be called vernacular design, after all there are already a lot of designers who do this and call it "timeless design." Have you ever seen a dog chasing his own tail? Now that's timeless.

The past used to be considered a classic example or ideal for the present. In the postindustrial, Post-modern world the past is just another place to go shopping, except most of the past has been bought up, just leaving yesterday's news. Retro-fitting a popular old song is the easiest way to get a hit. It is a very different thing to recycle the past for the purposes of "instant gratification" than to reinvent the past as an ideal for the present. Reinventing the past is a lot of hard work (scholarship), and who wants to wait for the future (it may never come). When the general cultural mood is here-today-gone-tomorrow, all history is reduced to one undifferentiated vernacular (no linear hierarchies, please).

Is there a "correct" way to use the idea of vernacular in graphic design, or is the whole idea of the vernacular overly simplistic and not very useful?

Isn't getting "inspiration" from your *Print, How, I.D.,* and *Emigre* magazines using the vernacular?

Why is it that graphic design history includes cave painting, cuneiform alphabets, and woodblock engravings but doesn't include sign painting or clip art?

When is the vernacular just history?

What is the point of asking all these questions if you aren't going to answer them?

Currently, graphic design practice and history is neither specific nor general in its scope; rather, it is elusively constructed out of fickle self-interest and unchallenged ego. Unchallenged, because for the most part the rest of the world doesn't give a shit about graphic design anyway.

Maybe we should either expand our notion of what constitutes graphic design or become even more specific and rigorous in our self-definition of graphic design practice. Maybe graphic designers should go back to the old business of inventing the future instead of regurgitating a past that's been digested so many times that it has no taste (not to mention style).[1]

Deep down inside I think most designers suspect that "using vernacular" is a chicken shit's easy way out. It's a retreat from style, or at least from expressing one's own style forged from your own experience and time. Graphic designers should be responsive to and responsible for the development of their own style. Instead of just "using" the vernacular we are creating it, and it tells us not only who we were and are, but who we hope to be.

Originally published in Lift and Separate, *Cooper Union, 1993.*

Endnotes
1. I realize most graphic designers today find these two words (taste and style) problematic, since we allegedly are problem-solvers instead of tastemakers and trendsetters; anyone with half a brain can see what the larger culture values most in graphic design.

LOW AND HIGH:
DESIGN IN EVERYDAY LIFE
by
Ellen Lupton

In 1990 the Museum of Modern Art held the exhibition *High and Low: Modern Art and Popular Culture,* which showed how Modernist artists have incorporated elements of low culture into their work: the curators presented newspapers, advertising, comic books, and graffiti as raw material for the hermetic experiments of the avant-garde. In each instance, the "low" was transformed into a higher form, its crude energy cultivated into a new aesthetic value.

Graphic designers have engaged in their own transformations of low into high with their recent fascination with the so-called "vernacular." Echoing the pattern set forth in the MoMA exhibition, many appropriations of ordinary commercial artifacts have worked from the top down, viewing the "vernacular" as an external artifact to be studied and adapted with detachment. Yet the question of high and low can also be viewed from the bottom up—from the worm's eye view of everyday life rather than the bird's eye view of the distanced critic. While the bird looks *down* at the world from the *outside,* the worm looks *up* at the world from the *inside.* In this essay, I argue that in order to take a renewed critical view of contemporary life, designers must find a place to speak from *within* culture, and not position themselves above it.

The opposition between low and high *culture* parallels oppositions found in *language,* where the words "low" and "high" refer first to a simple spatial relation—as do under/over, down/up, fall/rise, bottom/top, etc. These relative spatial conditions are matched by value judgments loaded with cultural connotations: lower class/upper class, lower species/higher species, downstairs/upstairs, and hell/heaven to name just a few. Again and again, the English language classifies features of social and spiritual life as a proximity to the earth.

The conflict between high and low is not a question of *content* but of *structure.* High and low is a pattern, a conceptual shell, whose specific referent shifts from situation to situation. What is high in one setting is low in another: in the space of a decade, a style can cycle from current chic to dated convention to camp nostalgia to neo-conservative revival. The term "vernacular," like the high/low pair, is also relative: it positions a standard language against a lesser dialect, a dominant culture against a secondary subculture. The vernacular is the *other,* and every discourse has its other.

The current attraction to vernacular styles is fueled by a search for spontaneous, unpretentious voices belonging to the idealized aura of a romanticized past (the roaring twenties, the flamboyant fifties) or to the noble savagery of a visual underclass (hand-made signage, ethnic food packaging). Nostalgia, a key ingredient in raising the market value of a vernacular style, is not a *return* to history but a falsification of history; it treats the past not as the roots of the present, but as a distanced other. Appropriations of contemporary vernaculars often project a barrier between a sophisticated "us" and a naive, spontaneous "them"—the ordinary commercial artifact is an innocent object that fails to comprehend its own genius. As in nostalgia, such borrowings relegate the vernacular to a space safely removed from the aesthetic world of the designer.

The belief in a distance between design and everyday life was one of the founding principles of Modernism, which posed a divide between the consumer culture and a critical avant-garde. Thus William Morris designed objects which stood against the machine ethic of the day: he opposed naturalism with abstraction, artifice with honesty, and the illusion of depth with the affirmation of surface. Morris created a *conscience* for design, and also a *consciousness*—a sense of distance between a philosophical *minority* and a commercial *majority* governed by the appetites of the marketplace.

Morris initiated the Modernist ideal of the designer as critic, a figure who stands aside from the mainstream and presents alternative visions. The designer-as-critic is not simply an obedient extension of marketing, but aspires to go *beyond* what people already want, and *teach* them to want something better. The lofty mission of the designer/critic carries with it, however, an elitist attitude towards the public. The designer is a cultural expert occupying a view from above. Hovering beyond the teaming crowds, the designer hands down master plans for reform.

As Modernism became an academic creed in the 1950s and sixties, museums and universities became critics of the junk products and street graphics of everyday consumer culture. This paternalistic view was attacked by the Pop movements of London, New York, and Milan; for American designers, the Post-modern rebellion was canonized in *Learning from Las Vegas* in 1972, which rejected highminded reformism in favor of embracing the existing landscape of capital.

Yet the distanced stance of the critic returns in the voice of Venturi, Scott Brown, and Izenour, whose claim to "learn from Las Vegas" positions their book as a lesson directed *at* Modernists, *not* at the creators of ordinary commercial art—their target audience was an academic elite, the late inheritors of Modernism. *Learning from Las Vegas* views its subject like an ethnographic specimen: an innocent sample of popular life to be studied by the knowing specialists of high culture.

Parallel to the Pop urbanism of Venturi and Scott Brown was the eclectic style of the Push Pin Studio, which recombined elements of avant-garde art, historic ornament, and popular media. The Push Pin artists chose America's permissive marketing ethos over the normative theories of European Modernism—they treated Modernism itself as a kind of vernacular, one dialect among many rather than a standard grammar. For example, Milton Glaser transforms his sources—from comic books to Constructivism—into his own signature style, sifting his borrowed material through the filter of a personal "touch." Reflecting the logic of "learning" from Las Vegas, Glaser turns low forms into something higher, refashioning them into his distinctive artistic style.

A similar alchemy of the ordinary appears in the post-Push Pin eclecticism of Charles Anderson, who has tapped the vernacular—along with other graphic languages— as a source of familiar codes, ready to be updated into old-yet-new styles. Anderson's appropriation of "naive" commercial art from the 1940s and fifties capitalizes on the nostalgia epidemic which gripped middle-class America in the 1980s and has yet to loosen its hold. Anderson describes the commercial art of thirty years ago with phrases like "naive, simple, in your face, not intellectual, not slick, bone-head." Beneath his admiration, however, is a sense of condescending distance from the culture he quotes. Anderson's nostalgia projects a distance between "us" in the knowing present and "them" in the bone-head past.

M&Co championed the vernacular in the 1980s as a source of clean, honest inspiration; a cold, invigorating shower to cleanse the conscience of style-happy and client-rich designers. Alexander Isley, Marlene McCarty, Emily Oberman and other designers employed at M&Co in the 1980s converted the everyday lingo of quick-print wedding typography, felt-board lobby signage, and phone-book iconography into a new urban chic. M&Co's ironic use of over-the-counter graphics suggests a self-effacing modesty—the absence of art, the erasure of ego, the disappearance of the designer. Yet while creative director Tibor Kalman publicly promotes non-design as an instrument of salvation from the moral sins of our profession, he has built his career on the mystique of the designer-as-witch-doctor, the impresario of taste capable of turning lead into gold, and low into high.

Working out of the same New York milieu, Stephen Doyle of Drenttel Doyle Partners also claims mundane commercial sources for his signature style of mixed fonts, graduated type sizes, and literary interventions. In many of Doyle's appropriations, however, the low source is transformed beyond recognition, providing a hidden energy for the chaotic classicism of his final pages. As Doyle explains, he has adopted tabloid typography for "civilized use"—he is interested in the *ideas,* not the look, of such crude artifacts as the *World Weekly News.*

The commercial vernacular became part of a distinctly Modernist experiment at Cranbrook beginning in the mid-seventies. Students were asked to submit an ordinary typographic object—such as a Yellow Pages ad or a ketchup label—to a series of formal operations, from rational grid studies to free-form compositions. The exercise is an object lesson in discovering the distance between "us" and "them," between the esoteric laboratory experiments of graduate students and the specimens they skillfully dissect. What these studies *overlook* is the fact that the apparently naive "commercial vernacular" often belongs to a sophisticated marketing strategy. The Heinz company, for example, helped invent corporate identity in the late nineteenth century, by pioneering modern packaging, advertising, and image management.

An act of transformation is performed by each of these quotations of the everyday. From the Pop make-overs of Milton Glaser, to the sweetened-up nostalgia of Charles Anderson, to the class-conscious incorporations of Drenttel Doyle Partners, the low *redeems itself* by turning into something better, by offering a source of energy to the higher life form which feeds up on it. A comparable transformation was the subject of MoMA's *High and Low* exhibition, in which commercial art was presented as a body of *source material,* a fertile mass of potential nourishment ready to be turned into the hermetic visions of Modern artists. Hence curators Kirk Varnedoe and Adam Gopnik reiterated the transformation from the public to the private, the external culture to the internal artifact, the low to the high. The MoMA exhibition treated newspapers, packaging, advertising, and comic books as modern-day equivalents to the landscapes, bowls of fruit, and naked ladies which have traditionally offered subject matter to secular artists.

Many critics of modern culture have argued that mass media and mass production altered the entire conduct of both public *and* private life, and thus they cannot be treated merely as an innocent source of subject matter, imagery, or style. The modern museum has itself become a form of mass entertainment and a vehicle for corporate promotion—the *High and Low* exhibition was, among other things, an ad for AT&T, the project's sponsor. From Walter Benjamin in the 1930s to writers from the new field of "cultural studies," critics have asserted that mass culture has changed the very *structure* of art, both high *and* low. We cannot simply draw a line *between* the inside and the outside of culture, or *between* public and private experiences of mass media, or *between* low and high forms of expression. The line must also be drawn across them, through them: *linking* the two sides of the divide as well as separating them, *canceling* the opposition as well as defining it. [See Meaghan Morris, "Banality in Cultural Studies," *Discourse,* Vol. X, No. 2 (Spring/Summer 1988): 3-28; and Stuart Hall, "Notes on Deconstructing the 'Popular'," in Raphael Samuel, ed., *People's History and Socialist Theory* (London: Routledge and Kegan Paul, 1981) 227-239.]

It is, in fact, this contradictory break between the low and the high—at once there and not there, dividing and connecting—on which Modernism was founded. The vanguard opposition to middleclass society, the search for a place above and beyond the mainstream, the need to magically transform the ordinary into something new: these are features of the Modernist vision. The desire to find a space *outside* of culture was inspired by the very omnipresence of products and media, a socializing force from which no-one is exempt.

Many contemporary uses of so-called "vernacular" styles assume a distance between the civilized designer and the raw material to be transformed, while other work acknowledges the position of the designer as someone who is *both* inside and outside of culture: the designer is a spectator of his or her *own* world, rather than a connoisseur of a nostalgic past, an exotic other, or a visual underclass.

For example, a common strategy among urban subcultures is to remake national trademarks into emblems for alternative ideas. Appropriations like these are made not from *above* mass culture but from *within* it: a view from the street rather than the laboratory. Such designs represent vernacular images not as examples of a naive and innocent dialect, but as the visible traces of corporate power. By taking back and rewriting the hieroglyphic speech of everyday products, these subcultural groups are making a new language of the ordinary that borrows time from the dominant corporate monologue.

A critical refashioning of a vernacular language is the information graphics of *Spy* magazine, initiated by Drenttel Doyle Partners in 1986 and crafted by Alexander Isley into a ruthlessly funny yet rigorously archival typographic language. The vernacular model for the charts, maps, and diagrams of *Spy* is the authoritative lingo of newspapers and science textbooks. *Spy's* info-graphics—which are now widely imitated across the American magazine industry—parody the typographic style of Objectivity, Facts, and Information. They appropriate a vernacular belonging not to a visual underclass but to the vocabulary of "knowledge" itself.

Jeff Keedy's typeface Manuscript offers an alternative to the nostalgic use of history. Based on the geometry of grade-school handwriting, Keedy's font refers not to a quaint, romanticized past but to the tedious disciplines of childhood. It refers not to a "lower" class of typographic expression, but to the standardized vocabulary of literacy in general—the ability to read and write is a minimum requirement for membership in American society.

Because designers are taught to focus on visual *style* over social *function,* we often overlook the relation of design to institutions of power. The tendency to see styles as working in a free space encourages a romantic view of the "commercial vernacular" as an innocent other rather than as a major player in the politics of everyday life. The heroic aspect of the avant-garde lay in its vision of design as a liberating social force. The *crisis* of Modernism lies in the contradictory desire to occupy a place outside of society while at the same time transforming it; its critical stance must now be relocated as an analysis from *within* culture, rather than a critique from *above.*

Originally published in Eye *magazine, no. 7, vol. 2, July 1992.*

LEGIBLE?
by
Gerard Unger
translated from Dutch into English
by Rudy VanderLans

S uddenly legibility is under siege. While printed text, just like God, has been declared dead a few times, legibility, until recently, was still considered sacred. However, during the past few years, many doubts have surfaced. In trade magazines, panel discussions and in the hallowed halls of graphic design, new interpretations of legibility are being considered. Wim Crouwel (graphic designer and director of the Museum Boymans-van Beuningen) was recently quoted as saying that everything we knew about legibility twenty years ago is now invalid because the notion of legibility has been stretched so much since that time. We are inundated with so many different texts in such varied manifestations that we have become used to everything and can read anything without difficulty.

In *Eye* no. 3 (May 1991), Michele-Anne Dauppe suggests that legibility relied on set rules and could be measured against absolute standards that were obtained through optical research. Those rules no longer apply, she believes. The standards are shifting and legibility is pushed to extremes. Two issues of *Emigre* magazine (No. 15, 1991 and No. 18, 1991) contribute to this discussion. In issue number fifteen, Jeffery Keedy states that too many people strive to omit ambiguity (which is exactly what good, legible typography aims at). Keedy believes that life is full of ambiguity, which is what makes it interesting. His typefaces emphasize this belief.

In that same issue Zuzana Licko proclaims "You read best what you read most." She hopes that her typefaces will eventually be as legible and easy to read as Times New Roman is today. She also states that letters are not inherently legible but become more legible through repeated usage, and that "legibility is a dynamic process." In issue number eighteen, Phil Baines fully agrees with these statements and goes one step further when he adds that "the Bauhaus mistook legibility for communication." There seems to be a general consensus that the ultimate legible typography is extremely dull. It overshoots the mark because no one feels invited to read it.

Printed text is far from being dead. On the contrary, every day more and more text is being produced on paper. But don't we have to be concerned with its legibility anymore? It is possible that the existing rules are too strict. How about those rules that Michele-Anne Dauppe believes were established through research? Who performed these tests and where can we find the results?

In the book *The Visible Word*, published in 1968, Herbert Spencer presents a summary of over a hundred years' worth of investigations of legibility. The conclusions in this book are very general, such as: "Words typeset in upper case are considerably less legible than words set in lower case. Italics are also less legible and bold type can work, provided the inner spaces of the letters are clearly visible. Medium bold is very legible. Many readers prefer a text set in medium bold." The last chapter of this book shows attempts at creating completely new letter shapes.

Since 1968 several additional investigations have been performed, but the results have added little to what Spencer had already scraped together. They offer no shocking conclusions that would lead designers to permanently renounce certain typefaces or to accept one particular typographic arrangement as the only correct one. The rules that Michele-Anne Dauppe refers to, in fact, do not exist.

Yet rules for legibility continue to proliferate. For instance, efforts have been made to establish sans-serifs as the only truly legible letters, or, simultaneously, to declare them entirely illegible. Spencer describes how scientists have researched this problem and have come to the conclusion that sans-serifs, under certain circumstances, are less legible than letters with serifs (Burt, 1959). Yet a few years later, some other scientists conclude that there is no significant difference between reading sans-serifs or serifs (Tinker, 1963 and Cheetham and Grimbly, 1964).

Where can we find those fierce opponents of serifs and sans-serifs? Here we have some clear statements: "Of all available typefaces, the so called 'Grotesque' […] is the only one that spiritually fits our time." And: "The best experience I have had was with the so-called 'Normal Akzidenzgrotesk,' which generates a quiet and easily legible image." They are by Jan Tschichold from *Die Neue Typographie* published in 1928. In this beautiful book, he shows how developments in typography are connected with those in the arts, such as Suprematism, Neoplasticism, and Dada. Tschichold was searching for a typeface for the modern age and sans-serifs fit the bill. And just as many other graphic designers, whose ideas he represented and developed, he made a case to set text in lower case only. In 1929 he designed a typeface with mixed upper and lowercase letters.

As early as 1925, Tschichold had written down some ideas about new typography in an essay titled "Elementary Typography." Here he suggested using a sans-serif as a matching elementary typeface. But he was still qualifying his viewpoint by stating that typefaces with serifs were better for use in longer texts. It was also his opinion that as long as there were no good sans-serifs available, it was better to use a neutral font with serifs, which is what he did for this 1925 text. Three years later, those ambiguous statements had disappeared. The ideal sans-serif was not there yet, but Paul Renner's Futura was a step in the right direction and no mention of serifs was heard again.

During those three years, between 1925 and 1928, Tschichold had not performed any scientific research that forced him to adjust his opinion of 1925. His preference for sans-serifs, and his opinion that they were quite legible and more legible than typefaces with serifs, were based upon emotional considerations. They were based on the desire to be modern and in 1928 Tschichold must have felt more modern and more certain of his opinions than in 1925.

In that respect, nothing has changed. The recent pronouncements about legibility are still primarily based upon emotion and are prompted by the need for change.

Why quote Tschichold so extensively? More quotes will follow, not only by Tschichold but also by Stanley Morison. I do this because the texts of Tschichold and Morison come closest to a serious theory about our profession. There are other authors who have published theories on typography, but those by Tschichold and Morison have had the most visible influence on our profession.

Books on graphic design are often filled with practical knowledge acquired through hundreds of years of experience, with rules developed through intense observation and a deliberate use of typographic means. There are rules for preferable line length, letter size and line spacing, for the arrangement of the page, the use of initial caps, footnotes, etc. Yet a deeper, underlying theory supporting these customs hardly exists. The best these theories can offer is that clarity and readability are the highest goals, which means that the typographer should remain invisible. It is curious that both the supporters and opponents of traditional typography held on to these basic goals. Tschichold mentions "Klarheit" (clarity) as the highest goal in 1928 and Morison wishes for "consummate reticence" in 1930. Publishers, typographers, printers and users have, since the days of Gutenberg, agreed within reasonable limits on what is considered legible. Anybody who consults a historical collection of books will quickly realize that those limits allow the designer quite some room—much variation can be detected.

Due to rapid and drastic changes that took place during the beginning of this century (and not just in the fine and applied arts), traditionalists and innovators alike dug themselves in and the previous voluntary agreements were replaced by strict rules, dogmas, and slogans. Against what or whom do those who demand change today direct themselves? The only thing that seems necessary is to use those agreements again in a reasonable and relaxed manner. In numerous typographic works, the concern with legibility is taken with a grain of salt. There seems to be more freedom than in the seventeenth, eighteenth, or nineteenth century.

In 1948, the same Jan Tschichold who was quoted before, wrote in an essay titled *Tön in des Topfers Hand* (Clay in the potter's hand); "Personal typography is faulty typography. Only beginners and fools will pursue it. [...] As typography addresses everyone, it leaves no room for revolutionary change. We cannot even fundamentally change one single letter form without destroying the typeset representation of our language and render it useless. Comfortable legibility is the supreme canon of all typography." With that, he radically denies his previous point of view. Tschichold was not the same typographer anymore. After a rough encounter in 1933 in Munich with the emergence of Nazism, he escaped to Switzerland and also moved away from his ideas published in *Die Neue Typographie*. Those ideas suddenly appeared too dictatorial and too closely resembled Nazi ideals, he thought. It is not without significance that he wrote the 1948 essay in London, because some of the ideas closely resemble Stanley Morison's, whose text *First Principles of Typography* had appeared in 1930. This publication quickly became very influential, particularly among book designers. "Typography is the efficient means to an essentially utilitarian and only accidentally aesthetic end, for enjoyment of patterns is rarely the reader's chief aim. Therefore, any disposition of printing material which, whatever the intention, has the effect of coming between author and reader is wrong. It follows that in the printing of books meant to be read there is little room for 'bright' typography. Even dullness and monotony in the typesetting are far less vicious to a reader than typographical eccentricity or pleasantry." Another lengthy quote from Morison: "It is no longer possible, as it was in the infancy of the craft, to persuade society into the acceptance of strongly marked and highly individualistic types—because literate society is so much greater in mass and correspondingly slower in movement. The good type designer knows that, for a new font to be successful, it has to be so good that only few recognize its novelty. If readers do not notice the consummate reticence and rare discipline of a new type, it is probably a good letter." Here convention is required to go down on its knees. If these rules had been applied, then the profession would not have changed its appearance since 1930. However, the path didn't run this narrow.

In *Typ G,* published in June 1991, Max Kisman writes: "The institution of the letter will be abolished. The power will be defeated. Since their digital manifestation, letters have been outlawed. The prevailing conceptions have lost their value. Graphic design is a fake and aesthetic-based page filler. Graphic design and typography will be banned." He adds: "The printed message is old-fashioned and of the past." We will forgive him this latter nonsense. However, I do agree with Kisman that there is frequent evidence of superficiality and that much design only draws attention to the work of the designer—narcissistic design without respect for either the authors or readers. Are those striking new typefaces produced to offer the readers more pleasure or to impress fellow graphic designers?

Kisman suggests, as a last convulsion of graphic design, "… to mix all design styles during a wild party in order to lay to rest the profession. So that with the resulting hangover, we can position ourselves to start the restoration."

Before the party begins, I want to know where the restoration is going to come from. How do we find out what legibility really is? To break with the past does not solve anything. It isn't possible; this is what even the most powerful revolution has taught us. By gratuitously repeating historical standpoints, the discussion is not served well, either. To live for the here-and-now and fun of it all, without concern for serious depth, as *Typ G* suggests, is oppressively restrictive.

I chose to once again carefully reexamine what reading essentially is. The following observation is not complete by a long shot, but is my starting point for a broad and detailed reflection of legibility.

DISAPPEARING LETTERS

A man is reading in a bar in Madrid. We have just entered after looking around to find a nice place to eat. From the loudspeakers come shrill singing and the sound of trumpets. We don't feel like leaving and searching for another place. The restaurant is well occupied and at the table next to us there is loud debating with wild gestures. Strong scents come from the kitchen. All the senses are activated.

The man sits reading at the bar while absentmindedly cracking nuts. He has a short beard, sits on the stool with one foot positioned on the floor. He is reading a book. I order a drink at the bar and try, inconspicuously, to find out what he is reading. It is a translation of Hemingway. Next to him glasses are being washed and filled. He quickly looks around from across his reading glasses and then reads on.

The culture philosopher George Steiner presented a lecture in early 1990 about the future of reading. He limited himself to books and classical literature in particular. Silence, he believes, is one of the most important conditions for careful reading. And silence is a disappearing cultural commodity. There is even a growing need for noise out of fear of loneliness, according to Steiner.

He is not the only person subscribing to such a pessimistic view. For many, the declining sales of books implies that it is not going well with reading. At high schools, the interest in literature is dwindling and more and more we hear about increasing illiteracy. Commercial television makes it even worse and there are many more influences that could turn reading into a threatened human activity. In all truthfulness, we know very little about reading, which is why unfounded opinions can easily catch on. It is important to know how reading functions because it is still the way to acquire knowledge and printed text is still the most used medium for the storage and transfer of ideas.

Take silence. It is true that there are quite a few activities in which noise disturbs concentration and limits people in their pursuits. However, reading is not one of them— certainly not to the degree that Steiner fears. Whenever a reader gets absorbed in the reading matter, the surroundings will quickly become less noticeable than the magazine, book, newspaper, or computer screen. The text becomes the world. The surroundings dissolve and with them will most outside signals. It becomes quiet around the reader.

Reading creates its own silence. I have often observed how, even in the midst of noise, someone who is reading and is spoken to does not reply until after repeated appeals. Fascinating writing pulls the reader in; the man in Madrid was a good example.

Reading has been extensively researched. Eye movement, and the number of characters that can be taken in per movement, has been studied just as reading speed in relation to the amount of surveyed and remembered information. The influences of paper color and lighting have been measured, as is the time that someone can remain fully attentive while reading, and much more. The results of this type of research are interesting but offer a one-sided notion of what reading is; they give the impression that people read like machines, that you can turn on and off at will, and that reading is all about gathering dry information. Such research tells you little about the need to read and the pleasures and intimacy of reading. Also not touched upon is reading as a way to escape reality and to engulf yourself in other people's realities.

There are many different ways of reading, tied to rather varied reading objects. You can read to research, read to study, read to be informed, or read to relax. Sometimes you look more than you read, sometimes you read just a bit, or with interruptions, and then you read for a while again. Telephone directories and dictionaries you obviously read differently than the newspaper, and a novel, too, demands to be read in its own particular way. With every form of reading, this silence arises. Most people don't realize this. And that's exactly it. That silence arises out of the concentration through which your consciousness is narrowed. You turn inward and surrender to reading. It is a semi-conscious or even subconscious action.

Simultaneously, with the silence that causes one to read, something else quite wonderful happens. Not only do the surroundings dissolve but also the object on which your attention is focussed. The black, printed letters dissolve in your mind like an effervescent pill in a glass of water. For a short moment, all those black signs disappear off the stage, change their outfits and return as ideas, as representations, and sometimes even as real images. It doesn't matter whether the reading matter concerns news, literature, relaxation, or science. First your environment dissolves and next the reading object disappears; or at least, both are placed at a subconscious level. When this type of artistry succeeds, the contents of the text flow directly into the mind of the reader.

Although typographers would like to pride themselves on the logic and precision of their profession, it is in fact not so clear-cut. Typography seems exact because much of it has been done in the same way for so long. There are really only a few fundamentals that are set: we read from left to right and from top to bottom. Letter shapes and letter sizes are reasonably limited. But beyond that we rely primarily on emotion. Common sense, experience, and practical limitations are what have regulated typography. The profession is founded on empiricism but leaves much room for interpretation. We don't have to keep up this façade of exactness. Typography and typefaces fare well by the acknowledgement that emotion plays an important role because it allows texts to be designed with more passion.

Wait a minute! This introduces a contradiction. I just explained that reading is a fantastic disappearing act, a double one at that, and now I start talking about designing with passion. Doesn't that imply that designers want to be noticed and that they produce striking or even flirtatious products? Together with this disappearing act, don't we need the often praised invisible typography? This is a noble principle, derived from book typography, which preaches respect for both author and reader. Book typographers fulfill a subservient task that restrains them from manifesting themselves and positioning themselves between author and reader. Craftsmanship yes, artistry, no.

According to Morison's *First Principles of Typography,* this is the way to do it. Actually, the notion of invisible typography is best verbalized by Morison's friend Beatrice Warde, one of the few women who has written about typography, in an essay titled *The Crystal Goblet, or Printing Should be Invisible,* (1932). Both texts offer crystal clear starting points guiding author, typographer and reader back to the few essentials of reading. According to this principle, beautiful "naked" books have been produced, without decoration, that are a pleasure to read. In the hands of a master typographer, with an excellent eye for proportion, this ascetic typography can render monumentally plain books—pure typography, pure text, realized with plenty of devotion and the finest materials. They are also very expensive books.

With the average, mass-produced book, typographic simplicity is usually the result of forced restrictions instead of self-imposed restraint. That's why many of these books are typographically quite "undressed."

Typography becomes a balance sheet. Typeface, type size, proportions, and other elements are defined by the demand to fit the text on a limited number of pages of restricted size. The text is not allowed the space it ideally deserves. That's also why many of these books, particularly on the inside, have been designed decently at best, but usually look indifferent and cold. The covers are often designed conversely. As signposts for books, covers have become louder and more colorful. To the readers it must be a strange experience, after some nicely spiced hot sauce, to bite into sodden, cold rice.

It is particularly these typographic products that can use a little bit of warmth on their pages. Besides this I have little to complain about. Newspapers, magazines, and other printed matter are usually designed with sufficient emotion, and more than sufficient on occasion. Restraint and invisibility are as good as absent. Yet here too, the double disappearing act succeeds. Loud newspaper and magazine page designs create their own silence and dissolve. Visible typography is read also. This leads one to believe that Morison's principles sound good but don't connect with reality. To find out if this conclusion is correct can be seen upon closer inspection of the most important typographic ingredient: the letter.

Invisible typefaces do not exist. Nobody will choose a typeface that doesn't look like anything. Everybody I know who regularly uses typefaces does this with conviction and dedication, even with passion. Advocates of invisible typography, too, will get emotional when discussing their favorite typeface. The basic forms of typefaces remain uncomplicated. Not much can be changed. It is very simple: when we deviate from the basic shapes, reading becomes less easy. This is no problem for short texts or headlines, but in long texts its effect is unfavorable.

Let's stick with text faces because headline faces are there to be both seen and read. But for real reading, you need experienced text faces with conventional basic shapes. Not conventional typefaces, that's something entirely different! Only the basic shapes need to comply with what we are used to. To this conventional frame, the type designer applies the features that supply typefaces with their characteristics. Every designer has particular habits that ooze through in the typeface designs: typical curves and corners, idiosyncratic transitions from thick to thin, a personal approach to endings, a peculiar movement throughout all letters and elements. The ideas of the type designer are dipped in the styles of the times, which help define the characteristics of the letters.

Furthermore, there are influences of technology, such as the rough paper and thin ink of newspapers, and the fast turning printing presses that newspapers are printed on. Such technological influences make demands on typefaces that lead to pronounced characteristics—in this case, an entire category of typefaces better known as "news faces." Typefaces for use in books are generally a bit more refined due to less severe production circumstances.

Typefaces endow printed matter with a character. They turn newspapers into newspapers and books into books. Together with page layout, paper style, binding method, and format, they turn a text into an individual product. As soon as the product is picked up and the reading starts, the attractiveness of the typeface will help the readers on their way. Briefly they show themselves and then they retreat.

For the designer of new typefaces, it is a challenge to create an exciting combination of familiar and unfamiliar elements. How far can the type designer go when the basic shapes are dressed up with little-known, or even unseen, elements? Are the basic shapes perhaps open to some alterations? This is how two converse qualities are united within letter shapes: common sense and attractiveness. This latter characteristic does not function when invisible. One of the reasons why there is a constant demand for new typefaces is the fact that we get used to the peculiarities of older typefaces. What you see too often doesn't work anymore. This is how typefaces play their double role until we're fed up with them.

Originally published in Emigre no. 23, 1992.

A BRAVE NEW WORLD:
UNDERSTANDING DECONSTRUCTION
by
Chuck Byrne and Martha Witte[1]

When it comes to aesthetic theory, designers today perceive themselves as originators, not followers, and most are loath to admit that they are influenced by much of anything other than their own inner creative resources.

To suggest that there is a link between new directions in design and ideas or developments taking place in contemporary society ought not to give offense to this ideal of creative individualism. Believing it does is a relatively new phenomenon and one that many respected figures in the history of graphic design would probably find puzzling. For the seeds of many a historic movement in graphic design are found in contemporaneous literature, painting, philosophy, politics, and technology.

In a January/February 1960 *Print* article, "The Bauhaus and Modern Typography: The 'Masters' Liberate the Typographic Image," Sibyl Moholy-Nagy discusses the relationship of the designer to culture and technology. She points out that one of the most significant reasons for the success of the Bauhaus was its artists' abilities to make creative use of the inventions of the time. Under the aegis of a fundamental group philosophy, Bauhaus designers were able to capitalize on new, and seemingly alien, construction procedures and materials, exploiting them for their production and esthetic advantages. They did not resist change, but embraced it and engaged in meaningful discourse about it.

Today, the technological changes taking place in typography have been brought about by the personal computer. Relatively inexpensive and easy-to-use desktop publishing equipment and software have given those designers choosing to take advantage of them direct control over typographic arrangements which were previously dependent upon expensive typesetting techniques or laborious handwork.

The ability of the computer to allow variations at low cost gives the designer the freedom to experiment until the page seems "right," whereas previously, tried-and-true formulas were necessary in order to predict the outcome more certainly, and avoid undue expense at the typesetter. Today's seemingly boundless freedom precludes the need for many typographic conventions and even brings into question the need for that most sacrosanct of mid-twentieth-century graphic design devices—the grid.

Grids are but one means of organizing visual material—a means to an end, not an end in themselves. Ostensibly, the best grids are based on a general evaluation of content and reflect the particular character and presentational requirements of that content. Besides being useful to designers from the Middle Ages to the present as visual organizers, they are useful to those designers who, because of the expense involved, are unable to visualize or mock-up accurately more than a small amount of the total material that will be controlled by the grid. Based on this sampling, the designer using the subsequent grid, with its inherent regimentation, can predict the visual outcome of the entire body of the material. At the same time, however, general assumptions about all or portions of that material are made that may not be specifically responsive to the content, nor in its best interpretive interests.

The computer permits the designer to view all the material that needs to be organized at one time. It does this by allowing the designer to place into the machine, and then maneuver and accurately view, the actual copy and images before even the most rudimentary of design decisions are made. This versatility includes the particulars of the page itself, the style, size, character, and position of type; as well as the size, shape, position, and other features of all kinds of imagery. Just as important, the designer is able to experiment freely with the relationship of these elements one to another—left to right, top to bottom, and even front to back. These capabilities allow the designer to organize empirically, that is, from within the actual environment of the material thus permitting the development of a more responsive grid, or the exploration of other means of visually organizing materials, or quite possibly eliminating the need for any kind of restrictive structure. The grid may be dead, and if so, the computer will have been the culprit.

But while the computer provides the technical ability to accomplish a seemingly new look in typographic design, it is certainly not the only inducement to aesthetic innovation.

The evolutionary temperament of general culture is capable of producing an atmosphere that stimulates a variety of creative disciplines to respond simultaneously, sometimes similarly, sometimes dissimilarly. And designers often find concepts and images generated by disciplines remote from design seductive and worthy of appropriation.

Sibyl Moholy-Nagy writes that two of the most dynamic revolutions in twentieth-century typography, Futurism and the Bauhaus, were fueled by the excitement of ideas generated by such seemingly unrelated developments as the automobile, Einstein's theory of Relativity, and Freud's theories of the self. According to Moholy-Nagy, the inventive quality in all of these ideas had to do with motion, and so typography, "in it's age old function of filtering the great artistic movements down to a residue of simple communication, then took upon itself this restlessly evolutionary trend…."

Within the last few years, typography and design in general have been influenced, either directly or indirectly, knowingly or unknowingly, by the concept of "deconstruction."

Most designers moving in deconstructionist directions vehemently deny any knowledge of deconstruction, much less admit to being influenced by this encroaching concept from critical thought and philosophy. But design does fall under its influence, if for no other reason than because designers live in the culture that gave birth to deconstruction. We live in a deconstructed world, a world agitated by more and more complexity, where the attention span diminishes hourly (turning us into a society of information grazers), and values appear to change weekly. It is inevitable that heretofore clear and supposedly resolved notions about what design does and the way it does it will begin to blur and ultimately reshape themselves.

Deconstruction, which began as an avenue of literary criticism, involves the examination of texts in terms of the language and ideas of which they are composed. Evolutionarily, deconstruction (also referred to as post-structuralism) grew out of but later disputed—an earlier movement called structuralism, which, led by the linguist Ferdinand de Saussure, sought to establish language study as a science in and of itself. Deconstructionist ideas were first introduced in the U.S. by the French philosopher and critic Jacques Derrida, who, in 1966, was invited to speak at Johns Hopkins University. Beginning in the late sixties, Derrida's writings, including *Of Grammatology, Writing and Difference,* and *Dissemination,* became available in English and are now widely read, albeit with some difficulty.

As the word itself suggests, "deconstruction" refers to the breaking down of something (an idea, a precept, a word, a value) in order to "decode" its parts in such a way that these act as "informers" on the thing, or on any assumptions or convictions we have regarding it. Its intention, revolutionary insofar as critical thinking is concerned, is to activate the discussion of ideas by demonstrating how their interpretation is influenced less by their actual meaning than by the amount of play in the fabric that holds them together.

For example, think about deconstructing the word "whole." We think of a whole as one complete thing, but in actuality we never understand any one thing except in terms of its parts, and at the same time our understanding of the details is conditional, or informed by an idea of how they are a part of and make up a totality. In concept therefore, "wholeness" is inherently incomplete. Its meaning depends on the multileveled, mental play of the parts that hold it together. This kind of deconstructive thinking has moved philosophy away from meaning-centered discourse and into a sort of flirtatious game-playing *around meaning,* or with multi-meaning.

One deconstructs something for a variety of reasons, which may be political, artistic, philosophical, or otherwise expressive. Political/cultural positions such as feminism and Marxism work deconstructively when they uncover aspects of our society which, while appearing to be universally humanistic, actually suppress the needs of one social group while serving those of another.

While several branches of art and design, most notably the practice of architecture, have been heavily influenced by deconstructionist ideas, typographic design is probably the most logical *visual* extension of deconstruction because of its basis in words and text. Deconstructionist writings are linked with the visual world, in that their authors often utilize graphic nuances in order to illustrate difficult concepts or subtle contradictions in meanings. Derrida, in the essay "Différance," demonstrates *in print* the concept of something being present and absent at the same time, by cleverly inserting a "rogue" vowel to replace one of the correct characters in the French word *différence.* The new word reads *différance,* in which the "a" is a misspelling—in French, this change is visible (present) but inaudible (absent). Thus the distance between two seemingly contradictory concepts, presence and absence, is remarkably abbreviated, collapsed into one typographic solution.

Similarly, deconstructionist Jacques Lacan, a French psychoanalyst and structuralist, uses an illustration of two side-by-side, identical lavatory doors, over one of which is the sign "ladies" and over the other, the sign "gentlemen." With this simple picture, he attempts to show the impossibility of there being only one point of reference or "meaning" for any one word or concept. The difference again is graphic: The lavatory doors look the same, but the designation over them—and each viewer's reference point to either sign—is different.

   The deconstructionist view asks that a reader comprehend and account for complex differences in signification, at one level meaning one thing and at another level meaning its possible opposite—to point out that "meaning" is an elusive business. For designers, using different layers to create a sort of comparative visual vocabulary in order to present the evolution of a particular idea has become a fairly common, and sometimes arbitrary, practice. But when the deconstructionist approach is applied to design, each layer, *through the use of language and image,* is an intentional performer in a deliberately playful game wherein the viewer can discover and experience the hidden complexities of language. While this approach is effective when the purpose of the game is to extend or enhance the message being conveyed, it can be a communications paradox when merely used for stylistic purposes.

   The intricacy of this kind of work virtually requires the designer to participate in the writing process, if not actually be the writer, something more and more designers seem willing, able, even anxious to do.

   Some graphic designers may be inclined to think of a process like deconstruction that is so deeply involved in theory as absurd and remote. But the very essence of contemporary typography-driven design lies in the process of determining the characteristics and arrangement of type relative to the interpretation or presentation of the text or words in order to enhance communication or expression. With this in mind, it is easy to realize the susceptibility of typographic design to this kind of deconstructionist visual discourse. The Modernist movement advocated simplicity, and so it is understandable that many of today's designers view the visual complexity found in much de-constructionist design as extraneous and alien. Far from being the mere application of style, however, deconstructionist design potentially clarifies or extends certain aspects of communication that the uniform treatment of elements inherent in Modernism has a tendency to obscure. Some signposts of deconstructionist design are: empirical page design and juxtaposition of elements based on context rather than traditional presuppositions (for example, the entire character of a particular page being determined by the subject of that page alone); typographic coding and modulation arising from content and language rather than convention (for example, articulating the content/context of significant words in the text by visual or literary punning); and/or meaningful layering and contrast to create discourse rather than adornment (for example, superimposing selected portions of text directly over the appropriate area of a related photograph, in order to comment on or emphasize aspects of their association).

   Throughout the history of graphic design, there have been reinterpretations of the contextual assumptions concerning the typographic page, and it is possible to find isolated examples of fascinating deviations from the norm that rival in typographic intricacy anything being done today. But for the most part, until the revolutionary explosions of the early twentieth century, and much later the work of Wolfgang Weingart in the late sixties and the seventies, changes have been evolutionary rather than revolutionary.

   The way was prepared for the introduction of deconstruction to graphic design by the reissuing in 1982 of *Pioneers of Modern Typography,* first published in 1969, and the publication of *The Liberated Page* in 1987, both by Herbert Spencer. These books made it possible for designers to see a substantial collection of the work of those twentieth-century innovators, the Dadaists, Futurists, De Stijl artists, and Constructivists through examples by designers such as Filippo Marinetti, El Lissitzky, Piet Zwart (who often wrote his own copy), Kurt Schwitters, Herbert Bayer, László Moholy-Nagy, Jan Tschichold, and Theo van Doesburg.

Spencer points out that the visual interpretation of the meaning of words to provide emphasis, and even the portrayal of the sounds of words, was of interest to both Dadaist and Futurist typographers. The Futurist Marinetti proposed a revolution against formulaic design, and began by refuting the uniform integrity of the text block: "My revolution is aimed at the so-called typographical harmony of the page, which is contrary to the flux and reflux, the leaps and bursts of style that run through the page. On the same page, therefore, we will use three or four colors of ink, or even twenty different typefaces if necessary."

Regardless of whether Marinetti might reconsider the idea of using twenty different faces on a page upon seeing the progeny of the average "desktop publisher," his work and ideas as well as those of his contemporaries have had a direct impact on work from the studios of Rick Valicenti, Neville Brody, Ross Carron, Katherine McCoy, Nancy Skolos, Gordon Salchow, Rudy VanderLans, Tom Bonauro, Stephen Doyle, Lucille Tenazas, Tibor Kalman, and others. Some of these designers also reflect the influence of the turn-of-the-century French poet Guillaume Apollinaire and the American concrete poets of the sixties, writers who understood the importance of the visual presentation of words and chose to make typography an extension of poetry by taking direct personal control of it. The work and ideas of these designers is in strong contrast to the aloof minimalist typography generally seen in the fifties, sixties, and seventies.

Deconstructionist design continues to collapse traditional typographical harmony even further than Marinetti's claim. The visual coding accomplished by style, size, weight, and position of each typographic element on a page, from initial caps, text, and headlines to captions, has begun to disintegrate. Evidence of this can be seen in the new work of Joel Katz, Michael Mabry, David Carson and Joe Miller, where what are still obviously initial caps are distorted or appear in unexpected places, or the contrast, in weight, of a portion of the text causes the eye to begin reading in a non-traditional location.

In graphic design as a whole, formulaic structures seem to be blurring in favor of a kind of empirical context for the page that serves to create a new relationship between form and content specific to an individual piece of work. Although pages from different issues of *Emigre* bear a family resemblance to one another, for example, the resemblance does not spring from traditional graphic structure. John Weber's work exploits these methods not only in traditional print graphics, but also in type animations that take place on a computer screen, or in video, where the relationships between typographic elements constantly change.

At the MIT Visible Language Workshop, designers are experimenting with the very nature of the perception of typographic information. Their work goes so far as to tamper with presumptions about the eye moving from the top to the bottom of a body of information. Here, powerful computers allow the viewer to control interactively the sequence or movement *through information,* rather than over it. Moving a pressure-sensitive pen up or down, left or right, and in or out, causes text and images on the screen to be moved or selected, indicating to the computer the interests of the viewer. The computer reacts with the new information in the form of new type and visuals on the screen.

Deconstruction brings into question and reshapes the entire typographic vocabulary, the orientation of the page, whether there should be a page, and whether type itself should do more than perform its basic historical function of being readable.

Discussing legibility, both Rudy VanderLans, designer and publisher of *Emigre,* and Tibor Kalman of M&Co are quick to point out that there are many ways to approach reading and that type and text can have a purpose other than to be read.

While saying so might seem heretical to some, type can have purposes which are illustrative, atmospheric, interruptive, and expressive in addition to, or beyond, mere legibility—what Sibyl Moholy-Nagy refers to as "the non-communicative function of type." Designer Paula Scher, who occasionally uses typography executed by hand, maintains, "The legibility of type is dependent upon the goal: If it's supposed to be legible, it should be. If it's not supposed to be, it shouldn't be." With this observation, she clearly points to the need for the designer to understand the reason for a particular approach rather than merely engaging in meaningless stylistic mimicry.

If the computer has been an important influence on typographic design, it promises to challenge equally the traditional use of photography in design. With the new-found ability to capture images, manipulate, crop, and mask them on a screen, designers are beginning to rediscover the power of the photographic image. Photography is being used less and less to isolate rectangles of "reality," and is instead becoming more fully integrated in the "reality" of the entire page—a circumstance that quite naturally serves deconstructionist ideas about the discourse and play between language and image achieved through positioning and layering. The visual expression of these ideas can be seen in the work of April Greiman, Lorraine Wild, Chuck Byrne, Katherine McCoy, Rudy VanderLans, Ross Carron, Lucille Tenazas, Edward Fella and Jeffery Keedy.

Sibyl Moholy-Nagy states that her husband's special contribution to his era was the integration of photography with typography. He would surely have recognized and appreciated the significance of the introduction of the computer into the two, and the potential for that relationship to be more synergistic. Doubtless, László Moholy-Nagy and his contemporaries would have embraced the computer with a passion.

The most extreme deconstructionist reassessments of design precepts tend to distinguish themselves clearly from other forms of reinterpretation, such as those of the early twentieth century. A recent issue of *Emigre,* titled "Heritage," is devoted to the state of Swiss design today. In it, Richard Feurer, a founder of the studio Eclat, states the goals of his work in a discussion with other young designers. "To me, it's neither a question of bringing across a significant message, nor of being 'understood.' I don't expect to be understood in the way that I myself understand my visual message.... My task is to generate an effect. You can't define what exactly, or how, the viewer will take in your visual message. There are an endless number of possible ways of looking at it. The only thing I can do as designer is to animate the person through my message. He himself should act, should analyze, and reproduce the visual message for himself."

These designers, as do most, grouse at the suggestion that what they are doing involves deconstruction. But the new thinking behind their work stands in strong contrast to Modernist concepts of visual clarity and reduction of complexity and reflects the introduction of deconstructive ideas, directly or indirectly, into graphic design.

While some critics feel that these ideas are a moral transgression of the designer's commitment to clear visual communication, it can't be denied that reading and the perception of visual information is a learned skill the practice of which can be altered. Interestingly, many designers who find great fault with the legibility of this kind of typography tend to forget the hue-and-cry that was raised concerning readability when the use of small-size, unjustified, sans-serif type was introduced in the early 1960s—the model held up today as the ideal of readability! The pages of *Emigre,* and many of its mainstream visual imitators, are not only widely admired, they are even read—suggesting that human perception, or at least young human perception, is more flexible than it seems.

Some designers are more closely tuned than others to the world of ideas outside design, and the educators and writers among them are beginning to disseminate these ideas in the classrooms and various design publications. But these designers, too, respond cautiously when it is suggested that deconstructionist characteristics originating in fields such as literary theory, semiotics, linguistics, and philosophy are apparent in their work.

Hans Allemann, an instructor at University of the Arts in Philadelphia, finds that training in semiotics is a useful "tool" for graphic designers, but warns against the complexity of "signs" brought from the vernacular environment distorting communications on the printed page. Allemann argues that, for the most part, it is still a designer's responsibility to communicate clearly, regardless of his or her facility with complex language. In discussing the influence of literary theory and criticism on graphic design, Katherine McCoy at Cranbrook is similarly cautious. "Some of these ideas," she says, "fit the role of art better than design, since designers have an implicit agreement to accept the client's message as their primary content."

The ultimate effect on graphic design of deconstruction and computers can't be known. What is apparent is that even though they tend to isolate themselves from its philosophical origins, many designers today are engaged in deconstructive design. That they should wish to isolate themselves from the origins of a philosophy so intertwined with the visual is unfortunate, as it seems to be the source for a significant change in graphic design. They should instead follow the example of the early pioneers of twentieth-century design: seek to understand these sources and engage them.

Originally published in Print *magazine, November/December 1990.*

Endnotes

1. Many of the ideas and much of the thinking contained in this article were suggested by the poet and scholar David Orr, who died during the summer of 1989 while preparing research for a book to be titled *The Ecology of Information.*

TYPEFACES ARE RICH WITH THE GESTURE AND SPIRIT OF THEIR OWN ERA

by

Michael Rock

We were sitting around the other night (a group of survivors from the seventies), marveling that bell-bottoms were actually looking good again. I swore it could never happen to me, but somehow the retro clock is working its way around and there's Deee-Lite or Jody Whatley or Vanessa Williams on MTV looking like the past twenty years had just disappeared. The mechanism of retro-izing is mysterious. It seems styles have to be reviled before rising from the ashes of old fashion magazines to fill the pages of new fashion magazines. The retro-glorified moment is brief; notice how the fifties craze—first revived in the late seventies' "New Wave"—has vanished, left to die out in the malls, suburban bop bars, singles parties, and *Happy Days* reruns.

DESIGNING TYPE TO EVOKE AN ERA

This is getting around to the idea that letter-forms, like fashion silhouettes, are one of the overt indices of style; as type designer Herman Zapf put it, "they are one of the most visual expressions of an age." Flipping through a type manual's back pages is like perusing old high school yearbooks and ogling at the haircuts. "How could we have thought… how could anyone in their right minds…." But scattered amongst the painful reminders of the near past—the Smokes, the Baby Teeth, the Rhapsodies—there are bound to be a few gems. It may be a face that just last year seemed as awkward and dated as the rest but there you are, shaking your head, thinking that maybe, just maybe Optima (my personal least-favorite, the bellbottom typeface) doesn't look so bad after all.

Letterforms intended to be contemporary or futuristic—like the future shock projections in *Popular Science* magazine—are the most susceptible to premature aging. The 1970s' 2001-look or the OCR "computation" style suggest that today's futurism is sure to be tomorrow 's anachronism. But there is a constant demand for newness and today, thanks to an unprecedented array of innovative technologies for designing typefaces, there are new font designs flooding the market to satisfy that hunger.

Type design used to be one of the most obscure of professions. W. A. Dwiggins wrote that to most people, letters are as transparently connected to ideas as the ticking of a clock is to telling time, but "… however unconscious of type the reader may be, there is something communicated to him by the aesthetic quality of the page he peruses—a vague something." Letterforms frame the message; they place the content in historical and cultural context. While the canons of readability and legibility are usually stressed (perhaps because they are more easily defended), fonts are rich with the gesture and spirit of their own era—even Helvetica and Univers can seem downright evocative.

In fact, the sensibility that gave rise to the consistency and unity of Univers (designed by Adrian Frutiger in 1957) says as much about the late fifties mindset as Beowolf (by Just van Rossum and Erik van Blokland in 1989)—a face that uses random computer generation to produce a font in which no two letters are ever exactly alike—says about the culture of the late eighties.

Contemporary letter design is influenced by two somewhat antithetical forces: the need to be recognizable within the accepted conventions of the alphabet, on the one hand, versus the varied goals of expressiveness, semantic value, reference and distinction. By distinction, I am referring to a marketable difference—it's a simple economic reality that a new font must be different in some way from an old one, or else no one will buy it.

Part of the impetus behind a project like Beowolf comes from the desire to challenge current technology, to capitalize on the digital production process and rethink the invisible conventions imposed on type design by the metal-casting process. But a reaction to the mid-century penchant for sanitized design is also evident in many new fonts. These faces are unabashedly irregular, idiosyncratic, and personal. Beowolf takes that idea about as far as it can go, disregarding one of the most basic aspects of moveable type, namely, the consistency of letters.

INTERPRETATION VERSUS EXPERIMENTATION

Notable twentieth century designers like Eric Gill, Paul Renner, Jan Tschichold, and Rudolf Koch produced fonts that now seem suffused with historical and nostalgic evocation. Renner was particularly adamant that designers continue to create experimental type forms and not endlessly duplicate the perfected forms of the past: he wanted to invent alternate writing systems based on aesthetic and formal requirements. In contrast, Zapf sees the contemporary type designer as working within history, drawing on the work of Gill, Rogers, and Dwiggins for "inspiration, recognizing that our cultural and commercial conditions are different from theirs." In other words, designers should be updating conventional structures to more contemporary forms. Today both trends—historical interpretation and formal experimentation—are evident and sometimes overlapping. Early avant-garde experimentation is now firmly part of our design history, and so revivals of these alphabets have aspects of both the interpretive and experimental impulses.

There are a lot of reasons to design a new font but, according to Matthew Carter—a type designer who has worked in metal, photocomposition, and digital technologies and is one of the founders of the computer typehouse, Bitstream: "Far and away the great majority of type designs come about for the purest reasons, just because someone wants to do them … it is related to the instincts that people may have in the fine arts, a kind of self-expression." Since fonts are usually created on speculation, rather than at the request of a paying client, their design is one of the specialties most open to personal initiative. Many of the new commercially available alphabets represent first attempts by designers or, like Barry Deck's Template Gothic or Tobias Frere-Jones' Dolores, are the creation of designers who are either still undergraduates or recently graduated.

Carter argues that this trend results from the technological developments that are transforming the industry. "Now it's perfectly possible for someone to set up a Mac using Fontographer [a font development software program] and get into the font-making business on a shoestring budget. In the early days of photocomposition, let alone in hot metal days, you sort of took a deep breath before you developed a new type series. It was a project of absolutely architectural scale."

AN INCREASE IN MEDIOCRITY

The labor and capital-intensive aspects of designing type disappeared with the refinement of desktop publishing systems and the release of powerful new software programs. The entire process of creating a fully functional font has been democratized, demystified. And as with any democratization there is a parallel increase in competition and mediocrity. We may have to suffer through a lot of useless junk designs or second-rate knockoffs in the near future. But the advantages of having increased flexibility outweigh the drawbacks. Ultimately it will give designers more control over the production of their fonts and—if the laws of capitalism function as promoted—greater competition should spur an increase in quality and choice.

Many type designers are now approaching the problem of font design with new expectations. Readability, legibility, proportion, or balance may no longer be their primary concerns. For example, Zuzana Licko, designer of many of the innovative Emigre faces, sees her designs as informed by several factors: the technology by which they are designed, the output devices for which they are intended, and her own personal experimentation within the structured forms of the alphabet. "One of my aims," she says, "when designing typefaces is to see how much the basic letter shapes can be changed and still be functional."

As Licko suggests, embracing the new technology and the forms that it gives rise to can lead to a reexamination of conventional letterforms. Carter believes that this reexamination may call the whole process of typography into question. "People are experimenting with the relationship between the writer, the reader, and the typographer," he says. "I don't have any problem with that at all. These designers are saying there is more to the experience of assimilating information from a document than just transparent reading, a transparent transmission of information." As Modernist critic Marshall Lee predicted forty years ago, "The evocation of mood becomes a primary concern of the designer. It is not enough for the designer to be 'unobtrusive.'"

THE RISE OF TRIBAL TYPOS

New digital technology has not only made "personal fonts" economically feasible but has allowed designers to create or customize fonts for specific purposes. Jeff Keedy has created several limited-use postscript fonts. His recent face Skelter was designed specifically for the "Helter Skelter" exhibition catalogue for the Museum of Contemporary Art in Los Angeles. In this case, the line between type design and graphic design is practically indistinguishable, a condition impossible—for both economic and technological reasons— before the advent of desktop publishing. Keedy says, "To make new typography, you must have new typefaces. The old typefaces are exhausted of meaning: the new ones will revive meaning."

While one of his fonts, Keedy Sans, is commercially available, most of his faces are created with specific purposes in mind. Occasionally, if a font seems to be especially interesting, Keedy circulates it amongst his friends and colleagues. Carter sees in this one of the most far-reaching implications of the industry as it is now developing. "We're actually a long way along the path to what I have heard referred to as tribal types," he says. "These are typefaces that don't have to deal with the huge problems of legibility and universal acceptance in the Latin reading world … they can be project-specific."

Already many of these new faces are making their way into mainstream usage. Letterforms created by—or knocked off from—Zuzana Licko or British designer Neville Brody turn up in "Saturday Night Live" and the *New York Times*. "Traditionalists" who grumble that type died with the passing of hot metal miss the point that these new faces suggest. Innovative designs don't threaten the integrity of typography. On the contrary, they document and codify the "current," generating the artifacts that will serve to frame our own generation. As Carter says, "You never know when something is going to be assimilated. There are historical faces that people now take completely for granted that caused a terrible uproar when they first appeared. In the early days of Futura, for example, people threw their hands up and said, 'God forbid we should ever have to use anything as mechanical and cold as this!'" In my old typography textbook from art school, *Typography; A Manual of Design*—about as close to a canonical text as you are going to find in design— author Emil Ruder wrote, "The fact that the typographer has no contribution of his own to make to the form of the typeface but takes these ready-made is of the essence of typography … The typographer must be able to take the impersonal view; willful individuality and emotion have little place in his work." As students, we took this Modernist argument seriously. Ironically, it is now the very notion of universality that seems so peculiar to Ruder's generation. That attitude of timelessness appears particularly temporal. Doubtless, the idiosyncrasies of the present (or, to use Keedy's phrase, its "willful ambiguity and rigorous inconsistency") will be considered equally remarkable to the next generation.

NOVELTY IMPACTS ON THEORY

Which brings us back to the recycling that is one of the inevitable by-products of the style industry. Sideburns or no? Medallions, platform shoes, leisure suits, all are sure to be high fashion again in time. Is a "bad" typeface really any worse than a shag haircut? Looking new is often simply a function of looking different or referencing the correct historical moment. But novelty impacts on theory as well as on visual artifacts: every stylistic movement comes with a supporting ideology, or perhaps with a ready-made alibi.

I suppose each generation imagines itself at the peak of some great historical refinement; the idea of progress is central to the mentality of newness. I mistakenly believed that everyone would see 1976 as the nadir of our visual culture. The idea that anyone might want to revisit it will always be astonishing.

Originally published in I.D. *magazine, May/June 1992.*

TYPEFACE DESIGNS AND TEXT
by
Jonathan Barnbrook

I used to be a Modernist. Although I still agree fundamentally with the socialist ends of Modernism, I feel that its visual language is quite redundant. Its ends were to the good of society, but it has, like all ideologies which attempt to affect the status quo, been appropriated and corrupted for the systems of authority to carry on. Its application has been misunderstood in the most barbaric of ways. There has been a complete misunderstanding of what "function" is. Not the most cost effective way of producing an object; instead something which helps the individual to create some theatre in their life or resonates to reflect human experience.

Modernism seems very anti-English, whatever that means. Although I am not patriotic, I am interested in producing work that is true to my own culture. Culture is the only worthy thing about political borders. I dislike the way America exports its low culture, it affects everything—a kind of political subversion far more effective than military power. Marketing policies are increasingly becoming tied up with political ideologies. Most of the conflicts between America and the Middle East have been due to the arrogance of American culture.

"Modern" roots come from a signifier of new political ideologies. Britain is the only major European country not to have undergone any extreme upheaval in the past few hundred years, which means that the visual vocabulary of Modernism is not necessarily appropriate to England. "Post-modernism," though, is no antidote for England—in with the property developers, visual meaning as fashion—no thank you.

When I was younger London seemed a very romantic place. It is something that I find difficult to put into words. This quality manifests itself in many things—the lettering on an old post box which says "LONDON, COUNTRY, ABROAD" or the old usage of Johnston typeface on the London Underground. In general, my work has more to do with the layout of a 1940s tube station rather than any contemporary graphic design. I would like to make it clear, though, that I am not into "heritage" or "nostalgia." It is only worth using these influences if you can change their context and make a comment about today with it. "Pastiche" is something I hate.

I am not certain why I started drawing type. My initial attraction was to the absolute beauty of the serif letterform. When I saw the lettering on the Trajan Column and in churches, it seemed that their beauty had an effect on me much more than any of the sculptures they were on. The lettering also seemed to give a more direct clue to the people who drew and carved them. It reaffirmed that typography was both a lasting and an ephemeral product: lasting in beauty this long but being designed absolutely in the spirit of the age.

I never really understood the idea of serif type until I experienced drawing it with a brush. There are various theories as to how serifs came about. One attributes them to the pull of the brush, another to the ending of a letter when using a chisel. I tried both methods as it was useful to understand the fundamental structures of letters. Working with the brush was useful for seeing exactly how the quirks of a typeface come about. Designers who say they would rather use a pencil as they find it more "true" than a computer for drawing type, should in fact use a brush and cut out the technical qualities that a pencil gives to type design.

Another reason for wanting to draw type, is that I am interested in the sort of authority you can give with a letterform. I think this may be a result of being quite insecure all throughout my childhood. During my adolescence I started to believe that if I produced work that looked as though it had authority, then people would believe I was a "legitimate" person. Most typographers are males and this is no coincidence. It has to do with the male ego and how it needs to be affirmed as right, to have authority; it has to do with the appropriation of power. The only power I wanted though, was a visual one—complete control even down to the typeface in a design. I was getting tired of using letterforms which carried the idiosyncracies of the type designer. Often this is what makes a typeface so interesting. But it is also something which means that you don't have a say in all the visual aspects of your work.

The first typeface I drew, called "Mulatto," was designed before the Macintosh came out. I was nineteen. The idea was to produce a typeface with serif and sans-serif features in each character (it seemed a reasonably original idea then). The roughs, which were drawn in pencil, lay in the bottom of my drawer for two years until I started using the Macintosh at the Royal College of Art, London. Mulatto soon developed into "Prototype," which was partly inspired by the idea of "sampling" which was just starting to be used in contemporary pop music—the idea of taking digital bits, using them in a new context, but realising their source. I tried to take existing parts of upper and lower case characters from existing typefaces and graft them into a universal form. This had been attempted before, most notably by Bradbury Thompson. Since I am primarily interested in the visual quality of the letterforms, I tried to "trick" people into recognizing that the characters had all aspects of the shapes that go to make up the identity of what a letterform is. After I completed the sampling process, I decided to redraw them to make them a workable typeface as the weight was critical to emphasis on serif and sans-serif. After this, the project was extended to come up with new punctuation marks for processes such as simultaneous or ambivalent thought. The marks were to work as nodes between sentences, rather like a molecular diagram. It is an extra part of the project and is not strictly typeface design, but is involved more with the expression of thought in a pictogram form.

When at the RCA, I also designed "Bastard." This came from a need for a black letter font, but having no money to buy one. Instead I tried to draw it myself. After a few attempts at trying to mimic a broad nibbed pen, I realised this sort of thing was completely inappropriate for a font drawn on a computer. Instead I drew a rigid grid for the construction of the font, and then used a few simple parts and replicated them to use in all the letters. I hope it acknowledges the heritage and the technology.

I'd like to stop here for a moment to talk about the names that I give my typefaces. They are very important. The names are unusual, often understood only by other graphic designers. Since you are working to an informed audience, you can communicate in a more complex way. It is a chance to do many things: make people laugh, or link the poetry of language to the poetry of typography. One of my most recent typefaces is called "Exocet." This was designed for a book (*Illustration Now*) which showed the best of European illustration. I made the theme of the design about how Europe markets itself. The Exocet missile seemed to be one of Europe's most successful exports, since every conflict that Europe or the U.S.A. were involved in seemed to involve the use of these missiles by the other side. The contrast of this use of technology, the summation of thousands of years of knowledge with the primitive act of killing, seemed in a strange way quite "poetic." The phonetic sound of the word is precise, engineered, beautiful (I would rather be killed by an Exocet than a Scud). I hope people see it as an ironic name—that you could look into yourself and question what beauty and cruelty are. "Manson" was named after the mass-murderer Charles Manson. I am not interested in serial killers. The cult where they obtain celebrity status is quite sickening and could only happen in the good old U.S. of A. This was a different way of looking at naming. Here I tried to create a double-take—whilst reading the word "Manson" other associations come up which have to do with the look of the typeface, such as "mason" or "mansion." The surname, in addition, sounds quite sophisticated, but then (hopefully) you realize that it is in fact the murderer and you look again at the context the typeface was drawn in, i.e. not in a monastery 500 years ago but in contemporary society. The font itself is taken from drawings I have made in my notebook. Manson is an ongoing project that will probably never be finished.

"Nylon" is based on characters from pre-eighteenth century paintings (only slightly more expressionistic). I arrived at the name because the word "nylon" is made up of N(ew) Y(ork) Lon(don), which was an attempt to override the cold, scientific image of man-made products and to give "glamour" to the product. I find glamour nauseating, it is a soft word for the creation of envy through image. "Nylon" now means cheap motels rather than anything glamorous.

You may have noticed that my typefaces are nearly all uppercase. I try never to use lowercase as I find the shapes boring on the page. If I have to use them I will use an italic. Lowercase letters are far less iconographic, less "believable" and just less beautiful. As a graphic designer there is no way I look at typography the same way as other human beings—which I think is true for most graphic designers (you're kidding yourself if you think it is not). This is one of the reasons I hate it when people rant on about legibility. They usually base it on some scientific, or other principle which doesn't acknowledge the multitude of complex messages given out by different bits of design and their context.

Personally I have found it difficult to use my own typefaces as I am so close to them. I start to see them as individual elements rather than part of a larger discourse.

This is a revised version of an article originally published in Emigre *no. 23, 1993.*

THE (LAYERED) VISION THING
by
Mike Mills

Like acid-washed jeans and theories about oat bran, the word Post-modernism now elicits an embarrassed—aren't we over that?—reaction. There is a general suspicion that Post-modernism is a conspiracy set loose by pretentious academics and ambitious designers inclined to overestimate the meaning of their work.

But simply to go along with such an anti-intellectual standpoint is too easy. Out of respect for Post-modern thinking and its rich potential for design practice, we need to understand how certain visual concepts have come to represent the ideas of Post-modern writers in design terms. From coffee cups to rock magazines, from April Greiman to the Cranbrook Academy of Art (see *Eye,* vol. 1, no. 3), we see a range of more-than-Modernist visual techniques that are vaguely associated with "Post-modernism." How have the layering of type and imagery of Allen Hori's *Too Lips* poster (1989), or the use of diagrammatic charts as in Katherine McCoy's Cranbrook design poster (1989), or even the lacerated, stretched, butting columns of type of David Carson's *Ray Gun* magazine come to stand, for Post-modernism? Are these "deconstructed" graphics, as McCoy has stated, "a visual analogue" for Post-modern theories? Would anyone who hasn't been exposed to the language of a graduate school design program see this work as a "provocation" to "construct meaning" and "reconsider preconceptions"?

Post-modern theory, or more accurately the ideas embodied in post-structuralist writings, has caused a radical questioning of conventional attitudes towards the creation of art and design and the way we interpret the meaning of the objects created. While structuralism attempted to demystify the humanist, Romantic understanding of art and literature as the mystical creation of heroes and geniuses by turning interpretation into a critical, rational science, post-structuralism tends to emphasize the instability of meaning, the limitations of objective analysis and the importance of the social and historical contexts in which the object is interpreted. Post-structuralist critics have shifted our attention away from the intentions of the designer and have critiqued the idea that a cultural product (whether a novel, a car, or a typeface) has an "essential" and "transhistorical" meaning. Instead, they treat books, cars, and typefaces as "texts" which are continually filled with new meanings by the different cultures and changing historical contexts in which they exist.

For instance, a Post-modern analysis of Helvetica would not center on the "inherent" qualities of the letterforms or the goals of its designer. Rather, it would analyse how those letterforms were encoded as "functional" when used in the context of Armin Hofmann's studies in Basel in the 1950s, or as "classy" when used by Massimo Vignelli for the Knoll logo in the 1970s, or as "trendy" when used by Neville Brody in the 1980s. By focusing on the cultural and historical frameworks of different viewers, we can see that universal or even national legibility is unattainable. As McCoy rightly states in her introduction to the catalogue *Cranbrook Design: The New Discourse,* after Post-modern theory, design is "no longer one-way statements from the designer to the receiver."

But there is a troubling contradiction in the way Cranbrook interprets Post-modern theory. A post-structuralist critique has shown that Modernism endowed visual forms with too much power—it assumed that if a typeface were made geometric, for example, it would be interpreted universally as rational, enlightening, and neutral of style. Yet while Cranbrook employs Post-modern theory to reveal the hollowness of such a claim, McCoy nonetheless describes certain of its own favorite visual strategies (such as decentering, manipulating type, and layering) as if they will automatically be interpreted as critically "self-referential" and "subversive" of our culture's conventions. Similarly, while post-structuralist theory decentralizes the agency of individuals, Cranbrook's catalogue primarily discusses the designers' intentions. "Personal content" and "hidden stories" are encouraged as a rebuttal to Modernism's demand for objectivity. Even when they reject "personally generated original 'design' forms" by appropriating "vernacular" icons such as the Heinz logo, this is synthesized and personalized through the visual techniques of collage and layering to become the "high" design of an individual.

We must remember that the majority of people who sat in a Breuer chair, looked at Paul Rand's IBM logo, or read Vignelli's New York subway signage interpreted that work in terms other than Modernist design theory. Is it likely, therefore, that viewers uninitiated in Cranbrook's thinking could interpret its designers' "layers of meaning" as just one visually challenging but unmeaningful layer? While the "receiver" is often discussed as an integral part of a Post-modern approach, that person, their social environment and their interaction with Post-modern design is rarely enlarged on.

The pioneering work of McCoy and Cranbrook has greatly broadened the design community's acceptance of theory. I would even argue that it has changed the perception of the work of designers not involved in theory—for example, Rick Valicenti's design has probably been both derided and given more conceptual weight due to a tendency within the design community to read diagrammatic, typographically experimental and irreverent work as the product of Post-modern thinking. Yet much of the design which has loosely been called Post-modern—the work of April Greiman, Dan Friedman, Robert Nakata, Allen Hori—still works largely within the confines of Modernist thinking. It concentrates on visual techniques and individual solutions rather than on cultural contexts. Much of this "Post-modern" design uses a visual vocabulary pioneered by the 1920s avant-garde, yet without the critique of cultural institutions that informed the found-object collages of Kurt Schwitters, the typographic havoc of the Futurists, or the socially engaged design of the Constructivists. Our attempts to go beyond Modernism are often realized by referring to visual techniques that we have been taught represent radicality: avant-garde design of the 1910s and 1920s.

The influence of post-structuralist theory could radically alter not only the appearance, but the organization, study, and historicizing of design. Much of the work we call Post-modern lacks an analysis that goes beyond the aesthetic into the institutions that give us the tools to conceive, evaluate, and produce design. Such an approach would look beyond the crop marks to analyse how schools, clients, award contests, history books, and magazine articles create a value system and language which enable us to read graphic design. Such an approach would look at typefaces and visual techniques like layering not as the sole source of a design's meaning, but within the larger support system (an article such as this, a design conference, a cocktail party) which enables us to interpret a dotted line with an arrow pointing to some scattered type over an image as "Post-modern."

Originally published in Eye *magazine, no. 8, vol. 2, 1992.*

SURFACE
AND
STYLE

NEOMANIA: FEEDING
THE MONSTER

by
Anne Burdick

Style is something to be used up. Part of its significance
is that it will lose its significance.
—Stuart Ewen, All Consuming Images, 1987

A fifteen-year-old girl has filed a $50,000 claim against the Burbank school district for suspending her because the sweat shirt she fashioned to mourn a slain classmate was imprinted with Old English style letters that school officials regard as gang symbols," the *Los Angeles Times* recently reported. The cover of the Constitution is printed in the same lettering, the student's ACLU lawyer observed. "'We thought that was the nicest looking writing. Even Disneyland uses it on some of its signs,' the girl's mother, Ruth Cisneros said … 'How can they object to a typeface and not the message?'"[1]

From the Halls of Justice to Sleeping Beauty's castle, forms gain their meaning through cultural agreement, rather than through an intrinsic nature of their own. Within each new context, the style of Old English lettering acts as a signifier, encoded through its use. "Gang style" or "Authoritarian style" or "Storybook style" are descendant mutations of *texture,* a calligraphic writing style prevalent throughout much of medieval Europe. In the Gothic era it served a functional purpose: its compact design helped conserve the expensive parchment of the educational and liturgical books that were produced in monastic scriptoria.

Historic forms are up for grabs. As the pace of our culture accelerates, surfaces are stripped away, their skins lifted, reapplied and reassigned meanings with increasing frequency. In this cultural condition, graphic design is both participant and product. In practice, the design profession embraces stylistic fashion and fleeting design stars. Yet at the same time, the rapid turnover dizzies the Rational Functionalist in each of us; the apparent reign of surface style leaves us on unsure footing.

SURFACE VALUES

Style is viewed by many as a shallow obsession with disembodied surfaces. However, our activities as designers are based on style's function as a cultural communicator. A recent *Domus* article entitled "Applied Style *vs.* Intrinsic Style" makes the distinction between style as a "natural" outgrowth of internal parameters (a legitimate or appropriate style) and style as an empty skin merely applied.[2] Style that develops from within is considered pure, while style applied from without is presumed to corrupt the marriage of content and form. Such value distinctions overshadow the issue of how style moves within the culture and the profession.

In a more neutral realm, style refers to the way in which form is handled. A vocabulary or set of formal characteristics constitutes a particular style, recognized most frequently in retrospect. Style itself is the visual language of a culture: in fashion, in consumer goods, in art, in literature, in all varieties of media. Style is ephemeral: it is timely. To be "in style" is to embody the influences and values of your time.

The presumed legitimacy of so-called intrinsic style has been absorbed into the prevailing value system as an outcropping of "objective client problem-solving." While at the same time the cult of individual style is fostered in publications and annuals: (admittedly! enthusiastically!) no two designers would "solve" a design "problem" the same way. This contradiction is symptomatic of a profession that has adopted a public self-definition in answer to commercial concerns, while obscuring (or hiding?) the more personal motives behind much of the actual work. Graphic design, in its adolescent phase, is still loosely defined: its membership ranges from store front sign painters to Madison Avenue art directors, to designers with graduate degrees, to desktop publishers—a competitive environment that perpetuates the need for a quasi-professional value structure to elevate status and salaries for those on the "high" end. Formulated within a culture dominated by industry, this structure has transformed over time to suit the needs of industry. Commercial relevance has caged our self-definition. To openly embrace our very own sumptuous surfaces solely for their formal qualities dilutes the authority we have contrived through the mandates of Rational Functionalism. This does not keep us from making decisions based on aesthetics or personal interests alone, it just means we keep quiet about it.

However good looks are not enough. A value system can sustain (and confine) the internal dialogue of our profession; it can construct a framework for our decision-making, a structure we can work for or against. For the most part, the predominant ideology relies on an oversimplified variation of Modernism: rational, functional, and socially responsible. While these values have their merits, they can at times limit the discussion. In the *AIGA Journal* on Modernism,[3] Kathy McCoy, Dan Friedman, and Massimo Vignelli, in spite of their differing viewpoints, all make note of the disparity between the complexity and richness of the original Modernist ideologies and what has become merely an applied Modernist style. Yet the real contradiction lies between stripped-down Modernist precepts *in theory* and that which the profession values *in practice,* where formal novelty is most frequently rewarded, and each new fashion is consumed and spent overnight. As our ideals wither in the face of this dilemma, style itself becomes the scapegoat and the discussion grinds to a halt.

FORM FOLLOWS FASHION

The History of Modern design is very much about
a history of style developing independently of ideology.
—Dan Friedman, Modernism: Style vs. Ideology, 1991

Wolfgang Weingart participated in the revolt against the strict minimalist approach of his Swiss predecessors. While his work is considered within the Modernist idiom, his experimentation with form and structure rejected the "neutral envelope" approach of ostensibly objective form-making in favor of intuitive choice and personal expression.[4] When visiting CalArts in 1991, Weingart commented with disdain that he was no longer in fashion, as though the design-of-the day that served as his replacement was merely a trend somehow not as worthy as the trend his work once embodied. Which aspect of his work was no longer considered relevant? Had the visual expression of his ideas lost its power to communicate as time had altered its context? Or were the ideas themselves no longer popular? Or was it just that designers had seen the style of his work for too long (never mind the concepts) and now looked to something new, out of boredom alone? I asked Weingart, given the breadth of his experience, if he could elaborate on what appears to be a preoccupation with formal fashion (style) within the graphic design profession. What is this affliction that makes graphic designers crave perpetual stylistic (r)evolution? Weingart evaded the question, inhibiting inquiry into a realm that makes most designers uneasy, for it calls into question an aspect of our work we like to overlook or deny: the trend.

Weingart's reaction is not uncommon. In the world of so-called legitimate style, "trendy" is a death sentence. When stylistic change in graphic design is tied to the rapid turnover and imitative nature of fashion, we begin to suspect that our work is merely shallow trend-following and empty form-pushing.

In the fall of 1991, Nancy Skolos presented the work of Skolos/Wedell to the students at CalArts with a reserve common throughout the profession: the design conglomerates of the 1980s had diminished, out of necessity, to the small offices of the 1990s. With refreshing honesty, Nancy Skolos presented a gorgeous brochure that she admitted had unfortunately failed to increase sales for the client. That it was presented to an audience of designers for its formal qualities says that Skolos/Wedell considered it one of their better (looking) pieces in spite of the fact that it did not "function" in a way that was meaningful for the client who had commissioned it. When asked what was the purpose of graphic design, if not to aid marketing, Nancy replied, "I don't know ... to make the world a better place?"

Alleviating the contradictions of an oppressive and stratified modern society through design was a major impetus behind much of the work and theory of the Bauhaus. However in 1992 America, a graphic designer is most frequently expected to increase profits, not to dissolve class barriers. As the United States bears the weight of deficit budgets, military muscle-flexing, institutional racism, and an impoverished infrastructure, that old Modernist desire for an improved world certainly exists. And it is a noble cause. However, gorgeous graphic design, regardless of its efficacy for the client, may or may not contribute positively to the world as a whole (its content helps determine that answer), but it does enrich the visual vocabulary of the profession. Yet we seem to feel uncomfortable embracing that as a valuable contribution in and of itself.[5]

We take pleasure in style. We thrive on form. The content of our work is for the most part predetermined; we design to indulge our obsession with the visual. For many of us, our *integrity is compromised* by clients who want larger point sizes or a different color palette. We demote to "job" status the projects that fall short of our aesthetic expectations due to budget constraints or client-imposed parameters. This becomes the "bread and butter" work. While potentially functional, it is withheld from slide presentations for purely aesthetic reasons. Meanwhile we seek out paper company promotions or open-minded clients whose projects allow more creative freedom: these are the projects we finesse into the wee hours of the morning.

More importantly, these are the projects upon which our reputations as "good" designers are made. They win the awards, the professional seal-of-approval that guarantees we will be asked to lecture, to show this very work, and will qualify us to judge the work of our peers in the next design competition. That this work is rewarded on formal terms alone exposes our obsession with its surface value. Functionalist ethics no longer apply. How could they, when the work is judged out of context, in split-second time, by criteria that goes no further than immediate impression?

To admit that formal concerns in graphic design are bound to personal style and fashion as much as (if not more than) to client communication, to reveal that our system of professional recognition says one thing (appropriate communication) while acting out another (beautiful, cool, gorgeous), to confess that we revel in expressive artifice might be considered self-defeating when attempting to justify design's relevance to industry. Yet in the internal dialogue of the profession, these acknowledgements are necessary when assessing the forces influential to our work and the unspoken values by which we deem the work "good." Communication, client needs, and content have an indispensable role in what we do, but they tend to dominate most discussions. Few attempts have been made to evaluate what we suspect is an obsession with stylistic fashion, although its prevalence is frequently denounced. To better understand the reciprocal relationship between style and culture and graphic design, it is necessary to examine style's history within Western culture, as well as to analyze its contemporary incarnation as what Neville Brody calls "a voracious animal … consuming itself."[6] Yet we need to do this without losing sight of the aesthetic pleasures, as can happen when deconstructing sex or humor.

TIMELESSNESS VS. TIMELINESS

That which we call typographic style is first and foremost
determined by our way of life and our working conditions.
—Jan Tischold, On Typography, *1952*

Style has been a communicator of cultural values ever since the earliest societal structures gained complexity. In the late Middle Ages when merchant class purchasing power increased and previously exclusive images of wealth and power, clothing and material possessions, could be purchased by non-aristocrats, style became an exchangeable commodity of social status. The democratization of elite images of wealth exploded with the rise of industrialism and mass production throughout the nineteenth century. Imitations of aristocratic style became affordable for the burgeoning middle class. Extravagant fake ornamentation came to replace quality and craftsmanship in conveying the value of material goods. "By the 1830s, the term design was assuming a modern definition, describing the superficial application of decoration to the form and surface of a product. The notion of decoration was becoming more and more distinct from the overall plan of production. This separation of form from substance became a characteristic paradox of nineteenth-century industrialism."[7]

Increasingly, the image gained currency. The rise of photography and chromo-lithography contributed to the growth, power and proliferation of the disembodied image. "Freed from the encumbrances of matter, the look of the visible world could now be easily, and inexpensively, reproduced."[8] As images of style became something one could acquire, their perceived meaning, the signifieds of their original referents, became the real commodities.

As a reaction to, the stylistic free-for-all that painted the face of the Victorian era, the designers of De Stijl, the Bauhaus, Constructivism and others sought to re-instill meaning into form, or rather to create form that held intrinsic meaning; to sweep clean the immoral application of meaningless decorative pretense. Many aligned themselves with engineering, mass production, and socialist politics. The visual embodiment of their revolutionary ideas were, for these designers, fundamental and universal. Concurrently, at the Bauhaus "for most, an endless obsession with pure form, in spite of (or oblivious to) any clear ideology was considered a sufficiently noble endeavor."[9]

Meanwhile, across the Atlantic, the American marketplace presented a different set of criteria for both the motivation and the evaluation of form-making. By the 1930s, design had become an effective tool of commerce and was shaped by the competition of the marketplace and the drive for profit.[10] While American designers were committed in their rhetoric to the rationalist and functionalist foundations of Modernism, "… the U.S. designers lacked … the political and social idealism that inspired their European counter-parts and soon their slogan 'styling follows sales' had replaced the more purist 'form follows function.'"[11]

Corporations utilized planned obsolescence, with unabashed honesty, as a marketing tool to stimulate the shrinking markets of the Depression. Manufacturers were no longer content to control only the means of production. In the search for ever-expanding markets, their influence spread through the shrewd use of advertising and design into the realm of consumption, by promoting a culture of wasteful excess in which the lifespan of material goods became increasingly shorter, diminishing ultimately to one of disposability (a strategy which created many new opportunities for the budding design profession). This "dynamic obsolescence" embodied the ideals of change, progress, and upward mobility; conspicuous consumption posing as the American Dream. "By the early 1920s, the advertising industry had begun to publicly define itself as both 'the destroyer and creator in the process of the ever-evolving new.'"[12]

Many of the avant-garde designers from Europe were thrown into this new arena. While their ideas influenced American design education, their impact was felt primarily through the influence of their styles, lifted and re-contextualized and within the American marketplace. "Agha paints a pessimistic picture of the acceptance of European designers, stating that they were used because they could produce 'Attention Value, Snap, and Wallop; while in their spare time they were allowed to indulge in innocent discussions about the Machine Age, fitness to function, and objectivity in art.'"[13]

NEOMANIA

History is no longer five, ten, fifteen years ago.... History is last week.
—John Weber, in discussion at CalArts, 1992

If we fast-forward to contemporary America, where the image has come to replace not only specific realities but, increasingly, verbal communication as well, (the language of advertising) we see that style has begun to feed on itself, entering into a monologue of self-reference. In the ensuing procession of stylistic simulacra, forms give their original meanings the slip. A type style that originated in an ascetic cloister now signifies both an urban street gang and State power.[14] Increasingly, "... objects in practice become signs and signs objects and a second nature takes the place of the first—the initial layer of perceptible reality."[15] Specific styles refer only loosely to their origins, if at all. And *stylistic change* itself acts as a signifier for progress and evolution: the most recent (regardless) has become synonymous with the best, a legacy of planned obsolescence.[16] While the condition itself is not new, it now moves with unprecedented speed.

Styles are assimilated overnight in the search for the "ever-evolving new." Not only is real history up for grabs, but also each and every new look as it originates, surfaces, and is instantly sucked up, at which point it is deemed "history." Its very existence guarantees its death. "Style is something to be used up. Part of its significance is that it will lose its significance."[17]

We live in an era of sound bytes and hyper-time. The immediacy of television, satellite connections, fax machines, and phone modems has propelled our reality into hyperdrive. These technological advances when combined with the American values of freedom of (preselected) consumptive choice, upward mobility, and progress through rapid turnover, in part a by-product of the consumerist growth strategies of twentieth-century commerce, create an insatiable appetite for the new. "Roland Barthes called this phenomenon *neomania,* a madness for perpetual novelty where 'the new' has become defined strictly as a 'purchased value,' something to buy."[18]

GRAPHIC DESIGN: FEEDING THE FIRE

As graphic designers, we are not necessarily predisposed to chase after fads; those who do are participants in (victims of and party to) a hegemonical social condition whose pressures are compounded by the design establish-ment's system of rhetoric and rewards. Competitions take only a quick glance at the surface of work, and publications most frequently give recognition to those with a unique personal style (and those best at self-promotion) while simultaneously sounding off about appropriate communication and marketing concerns. It is a mixed message that can leave designers unclear about the impetus and impact of their work.

The transformations of April Greiman's work have been followed in the design press and documented in her own book, *Hybrid Images.*[19] Her formal developments grew more out of her personal experience and interests in technology rather than from specific client applications.[20] Greiman's considerable notoriety did not arise because of the legitimacy of intrinsic design solutions she invoked, or because of the function of her work. It was her style.

Recognition has its limitations: a designer's lifespan is getting shorter by the minute. When Jonathan Barnbrook came to visit CalArts in early 1992, he showed work he had done since leaving the Royal College of Art. His portfolio included a call-for-entries for the Designers & Art Directors club in Britain which he produced just two years after his graduation. Barnbrook represents a recent British phenomenon: the student star. It is difficult to imagine the American design community embracing such a young designer. He confessed he had been selected by the D & AD in an attempt to boost their "hipness" ratings, an act propelled by the economic desperation in that country. At the same time, he expressed a real fear and loathing for the Graphic Design Pop Star treadmill—and with good reason. "I'd hate to think I'll be a has-been in ten years ..." That's a realistic fear, considering his almost instantaneous stardom. Prematurely it would seem, once designers are publicly recognized they are perceived by some to be "history": their newness has worn off.

Thankfully, the reign of a small and entrenched design aristocracy is fading. Invigorating new voices are necessary, but the rate at which styles and stylists are being gobbled up and spit out reflects more than just growth within the profession. Its pace is in sync with consumerist culture.

Neville Brody's stylistic overhaul from his early work for *The Face,* hyperactive, bold, and geometric; to his later work for *Arena,* a stripped-down Helvetica and grid-based design, came out of necessity. His early look had such explicit characteristics that the stylistic signifiers that made his work unique were easily consumed. Alternative work feeds the mainstream, its daring diluted through assimilation. To avoid being eaten alive, Brody was forced to revamp the look of his work.

The media overload of daily life propels our visual vocabulary. For many, the spectacular environment is a point of departure. But for those less innovative, or just plain lazy, skinning existing formal styles can be a shortcut to instant relevance. (Witness the proliferation of fat sans serif, tightly kerned—it's everywhere! Very shortly though, its omnipresence will be its demise.[21]) Design annuals feed the problem by reproducing their award-winning contents merely as external shells lacking context, content, audience, or parameters. They foster an environment of superficiality. Without an understanding of the motivation behind the appearance of a piece, and why it is considered successful, it becomes much easier to peel back the surface skin and reapply it elsewhere.[22]

Some designers look to the established stars to foretell the future. When Brody made a presentation at the 1989 AIGA Conference in San Antonio, he spoke about creating original solutions from familiar ingredients. Whether keenly ironic or just plain oblivious, a spectator animated Brody's dilemma by asking aloud, "So what's the new hot typeface for next year?"

Here's the paradox: while an overt personal style is easily skinned, it is also most frequently recognized, rewarded, and published. Since design is not necessarily a lucrative profession, recognition is the primary reward for many; it validates our work in the eyes of our peers and potential clients. At the same time, once noticed, the countdown begins. But if the style in work is subtle, if it requires deciphering, engagement, or (worst of all) time, it may evade imitators; but it risks being overlooked by the rewards system, strengthening the craving for a stylistic "ever-evolving new" and forcing the concerns and interests of the profession to the surface level.

TIME FOR CHANGE?

Surfaces come and go. Meaning is in a constant state of flux. Weingart's approach, his spirit of rebellion, and his use of intuitive decision-making still resonate, in spite of the fact that some would consider his formal vocabulary burnt out. Ideas have more staying power (but are by no means timeless) while forms have an increasingly shorter lifespan.

Design pieces, like style, are ephemeral; and, like Old English, carry meaning via context. Styles and meaning change concomitantly with cultural change (whether or not our ideas, processes, or values also transform). Therefore the personal continuum of each designer, by definition, responds with fluidity. Each new step in the continuum is not *necessarily* better, maybe just different; at once a reply to the work that preceded it and a manifestation of the cultural forces that shape the new environment, however quickly the next step comes along.

The motivation for change is multi-layered: personal growth, exposure to new influences, shifting social and economic contexts are an intrinsic part of the game. However, values like newness and originality, which overlook the fact that all work is derivative in one form or another, misplace our attentions. Novelty for novelty's sake can be a weak but successful ploy for attention and recognition. Style for communication's sake is basically what we do. It is the language we speak. Rapid-fire reaction to, and rip-off of the superficial aspects of style as it is reproduced in annuals and journals seldom goes deeper than the surface. The challenge is to acknowledge the pressures of *neomania* without succumbing to the seduction.

Originally published as "What Is This Affliction That Makes Graphic Designers Crave Perpetual Stylistic Revolution?" in Emigre *no. 24, 1992.*

Endnotes
1. "Girl Says School Violated Her Rights," *Los Angeles Times Valley Edition,* February 8, 1992, P. B3.
2. Vittorio Magnano Lampugnani, "Applied Style vs. Intrinsic Style," *Domus,* February 1992, p. 734.
3. *AIGA Journal,* Volume 9, Number 2, 1991.
4. Ellen Lupton, "Post Script," *Writing/Culture Monograph V: The Bauhaus and Design Theory,* New York: The Herb Lubalin Study Center of Design and Typography, The Cooper Union for the Advancement of Science and Art, p. 33.
5. This condition is exemplified by the current distrust (and ridicule—a weak critique) of personal, academic and experimental "fringe" work, in spite of the use of Template Gothic and multiple-reading strategies appearing in corporate annual reports and other "mainstream" work. (see Steven Heller, "Cult of the Ugly," *Eye,* Number 9, Volume 3, 1993, p. 52–56.)
6. Neville Brody interviewed by Rick Poynor, "Neville Brody," *Eye,* Number 6, Volume 2, 1992, p.8.
7. Stuart Ewen, *All Consuming Images: The Politics of Style in Contemporary Culture,* New York, Harvard Books, 1987, p. 33.
8. Ewen, p. 25.
9. Dan Friedman, "Modernism: Style vs. Ideology," *AIGA Journal,* 1991, p. 6.
10. This was, of course, taking place in Europe as well, only to a lesser degree. In Europe it was not uncommon to have national boards whose sole purpose was to promote good design. Whereas, "in America the very notion of privileging 'aesthetic' principles over considerations of market demand and 'popular' taste tended to be regarded as an expensive indulgence." (Dick Hebdige, *Hiding In The Light,* London: Routledge, 1984, p. 60.)
11. Penny Sparke, *Design in Context,* Secaucus, NJ: Chartwel Books, 1987, p. 49.
12. Ewen, p. 242.
13. Mike Mills quoting M.F. Agha, "Herbert Bayer's Universal Type in its Historical Contexts," *The Bauhaus and Design Theory,* p. 43.
14. Makes sense.
15. Dick Hebdige quoting Lefebvre, 1971, p. 17.

16. Hence the premium on originality as opposed to tradition. To be distinctive, to stand out, to change or re-invent, are predominantly twentieth-century values.

17. Ewen, p. 52.

18. Ewen, p. 51.

19. April Greiman and Eric Martin, *Hybrid Imagery,* New York: Watson-Guptil Publications, 1990.

20. Designers with a singular vision tend to seek out clients for whom their inclinations are most appropriate, be they architects, rock bands, or corporations—the inverse of the industry standard: "In the beginning was the Client, and the Client has this problem, see ..."

21. The very mention of this distinctive style instantly dates this essay.

22. This is not an attempt to define or qualify influence, historical or stylistic quotation, and general fashion trends of which we are all participants.

SECONDHAND CULTURE
by
Sharon Helmer Poggenpohl

In looking back I find three important ideas that have shaped American culture: technological development, the consumer economy, and more recently, the information economy. Before I relate these specifically to visual communication, I would like to locate graphic design for you. Of the design disciplines, graphic design is the least codified, criticized, and historically developed. In "The Legibility of the World: A Project of Graphic Design," the sociologist Abraham Moles explores the primacy of everyday life—so much of society is institutionalized, that "everyday life" is no longer the residue but the primary part. This is where the individual works on a personal project, whether writing a paper, making a meal, or seeking out entertainment. This is where the individual is autonomous.

Visual communication presents "an entire large integrated diagram within the framework of our life and translates the elements of that life into a sort of intelligible discourse. The door, the arrow, the corporate identity, the logotype, the traffic sign, is only the appearance, privileged and standardized, of a 'knowledge through signs' of the world of things, products, and actions. Our existence then becomes more and more symbolic because it is lived more and more inside an ideographic world where we prepare our actions not with objects themselves, but with signs that designate them."[1]

We are constantly adjusting our personal world map based on second-hand information, frequently prepared by a designer. I have no direct experience with Gregor Mendel's pea experiments, I have not been to Patagonia, I have never met Freud or Frost; and yet I know of them—words and images concerning them are part of my world map. Most of what we know is prepared, screened, somehow processed for us.

Moles goes on to discuss graphic design's mode of access to the individual in terms of contingency as people wander through space-time whether the city or a printed page. Visual communication acts as a cultural amplifier. Visual communication "seeks to transform visibility into legibility that is, into that operation of the mind that arranges things in the form of signs into an intelligible whole in order to prepare a strategy for action."[2]

Moles concludes with ten axioms, five of which I want to paraphrase here:

1. The designer is a modest demiurge: He or she takes charge of the daily

environmental pattern in a hedonistic context where the measure of his action is the quality of life.

2. The designer is an environmental engineer, and his fields of action are character-ized by two things, the scale of his perception of the shells in which humans are enclosed, and the types of sensorial aspects that he vouchsafes in his action.

3. In consumer society design is no longer concerned with a particular object, but with the totality of an environment on a given scale.

4. Everyday life is the designer's subject matter. It is what remains when society has institutionalized everything....

5. The function of the designer is to increase the legibility of the world. The world is a labyrinth that must be unravelled, a text that must be deciphered. Each individual scrutinizes it as his life unfolds.[3]

With Moles' context in mind, let me return to technology, consumer and information society.

Attitudes toward technology have swung between extremes over the past forty years. From the mid-sixties to the mid-seventies technology was suspect: On the one hand it was associated with progress, a deeply American value, and a better and more convenient life. On the other hand, it represented dehumanization, loss of jobs to automation, and anxiety over complexity and human decision making. Writers such as Jacques Ellul and Lewis Mumford developed cautionary tales concerning technology, while McLuhan embraced the new media. Today the debate is curiously silent as we begin to confront the latest technological probe—genetic engineering.

The task of visual communication parallels shifts in technology and mass communi-cation. From the mid-forties to the mid-sixties, the picture magazine was a driving force in portraying the development of the physical culture of this country. *Look, Life,* and *Show* magazines developed a mass audience for their graphic presentation of events and products. By the mid-sixties, television was becoming more sophisticated and available as the mass means for communicating lifestyle, products, and entertainment. Today, we are on the edge of another technological shift represented by the computer and interactive media. With each shift graphic design mediates between the ideas, products, and services of the culture and the American public. Today, critical voices reflect on the role of information in the culture. Such writers as Neil Postman in his book *Amusing Ourselves to Death: Public Discourse in the Age of Show Business* or Theodore Roszak's *The Cult of Information* begin to ask difficult questions about the information revolution.

A paradigm does come to mind that puts into relief technological issues. It is typography or more specifically the design of letterforms. The design of letterforms is part of a long humanistic tradition stretching back to the Romans. At least one author[4] attributes the rise of western civilization with its codified laws and spirit of scientific inquiry to the invention of the phonetic alphabet. Letterforms are frequently quite beautiful but they are largely out of the public's awareness.

Let me begin in the forties. Letterforms were designed for an industrial manu-facturing process, either Linotype or Monotype, which cast either lines of type or individual characters in hot metal from a master mold. The development of a type font was a slow and costly design and craft process. The physical nature of the typography was a system—it was difficult to beat the system—a tradition grew up around the system's very real physical constraints.

The development of phototypography in the late fifties simplified the intensive craft and manufacturing aspects of type design and production. Analog letterforms could be developed more quickly and economically using a photomaster to generate a range of sizes. Better inter-letter fit (kerning) was possible and the traditional visual system of font and letterforms were now open to optical/photographic manipulation and distortion. Typographic traditionalists were horrified.

Typographic innovators were thrilled. Now came a flowering of bizarre type faces. Milton Glaser designed Baby Teeth and Houdini and there was Fat Cat, Fat Chance, Fat Face, Bubble, and Buxom to name a few. Amateur typographers came out of the closet and shared their vision. It was a riot of display letterforms.

In the late sixties, the IBM Selectric Composer, a better than ordinary typewriter, was the precursor of the digital revolution in typography. It still had analog letterforms but it also had a more developed character to variable unit space relationship plus an early if limited memory.

At this point some interesting experimentation was going on how to adapt the letterforms to be machine readable. Evans and Epps designed a set of characters that were based on a square grid with no diagonals and no curves. Wim Crowel and Jay Doblin also tackled this task. The concept was to design characters that were machine readable *and* readable (even if strange looking) by ordinary people. We were at a stage when we valued the machine more than our humanistic tradition. The expectation was that we would adapt to what technology could do rather than adapt technology to our needs and values.

The mid-seventies saw the beginnings of the dot matrix and digital typography. Today, typography does not exist in a physical form at all until it is called up on a screen or printout. It exists only as a series of numerical relationships and a set of instructions. The design of letterforms has changed from analog to digital. Type designers today are trying to design appropriate letterforms for the new technology, but while this is in process, old hot metal and photofaces are being digitized often with poor results. The visual values of the typographer are in a state of flux.

A design discipline that relates directly to our consumer society is corporate identity. The identification of objects, brands, and corporate entities is a significant communication strategy in a consumer society. Sampling symbols and logotypes from the forties through the eighties will reveal changing stylistic and communication attitudes that may have interesting parallels in the world of art. Corporate identity is facing a crisis because of the proliferation of symbols and logotypes and the limited and formulaic vocabulary that designers are accustomed to use when addressing these problems.

A design discipline that relates directly to an information society is the design of textbooks and more specifically readers. There is a literacy crisis in this country. That we have mandatory public education for all children is no accident—a democratic free society depends on literacy. A technological society depends on the ability of citizens to learn new skills. I learned to read with Dick and Jane. My youngest son learned to read on the computer. What has happened in the intervening thirty years reflects cultural change in terms of content and form. To quote Kenneth Boulding: "One of the main purposes of national education is to distort the image of time and space in the interests of the nation."[5] The early reader may be both an interesting cultural filter and an interesting design filter.

Before concluding, I would like to make an observation about American graphic design that troubles me. This past year there were three visiting Dutch designers at Rhode

Island School of Design where I teach. Anton Beeke, Robert Oxenaar, and Jan van Toorn all had exhibitions of their work and gave lectures both formally and informally. I was struck by their political engagement with cultural issues, by the challenging "unpretty" aesthetic of their work, by their frankly sexual, unretouched approach to life. In contrast, American designers seem determined to detoxify life to make it "pretty." Perhaps it is a puritanical strain in our character, or Modernist/Post-modernist/utopian imagery run amok, or the pervasive domination of business and its illusions. Something is missing in visual communication—it seems to be in a holding pattern.

In conclusion, one conceptual frame that spans all the design disciplines and is very American is the idea of the future. From the forties to now how has our vision of the future changed? Certainly architecture has its milestones in projecting a future. The development of the NASA logotype and identity program was a systematic look at a communication future. The film *2001* comes to mind as a *tour de force* in visualizing life in space and all the product design that entails. From a mythic standpoint, the role of the computer HAL encapsulated our cultural fears concerning computer technology. Likewise, the more recent film *Blade Runner* with its tale of replicants raises questions about genetic engineering and what it means to be human. Further, *Blade Runner* portrays a malevolent vision of the future of cities. Technology and the future is a topic worth considering.

Originally published in the Society of Typographic Arts Journal, *1988.*

Endnotes
1. *Design Issues:* Vol. III, No. 1. Abraham Moles. "The Legibility of the World: A Project of Graphic Design," p. 44.
2. *Ibid.*, p. 48.
3. *Ibid.*, p. 52–53.
4. *The Alphabet Effect.* Johnathon Logan.
5. *The Image.* Kenneth E. Boulding. Ann Arbor: University of Michigan Press, 1969.

SINCE WHEN DID *USA TODAY* BECOME THE NATIONAL DESIGN IDEAL?

by

Michael Rock

In a recent *New York Times* Sunday magazine article on school textbooks, writer Robert Reinhold described California's new history series as "... filled with colorful charts, graphs, time lines, maps and photographs in a format suggestive of the newspaper *USA Today*." There it is again. Since when did *USA Today* become the national design ideal? Everywhere you look you find *USA Today* used as an analogy to describe a noteworthy design format. Making ideas "accessible" is the operative term for the information age. But too often information is drained of its significance in the name of accessibility.

Some things are designed for reading: scholarly journals, literary reviews, financial pages, and their ilk are fairly impenetrable to the casual page flipper. Other objects like

USA Today, annual reports, fashion magazines, and so on are for looking. (Haven't you heard in the course of a design project someone say, only half in jest, "No one actually reads the copy, just make it look good.") Then there are the gray areas. These include news magazines and textbooks, which imply reading but are increasingly about looking. If you compare *Time* or *Newsweek* or a fifth grade schoolbook of twenty years ago to their present incarnations, the change is remarkable. The headlines are bigger, the captions are bigger, the photographs, charts, and call-outs are all bigger. Something had to go, someone must have decided, and what went was the text.

The trend in typography is clearly towards a destruction of narrative text, with images increasingly responsible for carrying the content. Running copy is being replaced with exaggerated hierarchies, charts, graphs, sidebars, boxes, captions, and call-outs that reduce the "story" to a collection of visualized pseudo-facts. It is the design equivalent of the video sound-bite, with complex ideas boiled down (in the words of Nigel Holmes, *Time's* design director) to "manageable chunks."

HOW TO COMPETE AGAINST TV

The resulting designs often have the look of information, but without real content. Beyond its stylistic implications, this new typographic sensibility represents a change in the consumer's relationship to information, the author's authority, and the significance of the form. There is a fragmentation of communication, with the model of contemporary typography no longer being the linear argument but the simultaneous slogan. For instance, a *Newsweek* story may now open with an image that takes up as much as ninety percent of the spread, with only a small introductory paragraph of text as accompaniment. We are rapidly approaching the critical point where the graphics overtake the meaning.

The rationale behind the accessibility movement is that information is easier to absorb in small pieces. Prodded along by marketing data, publishers and designers feel the need to compete with television and video for consumer attention. We have all heard that newspaper readership is down and that television has surpassed reading as the information source-of-choice for the majority of Americans. In response, publishers seem inclined to apply the TV info-tainment format to newspapers, and magazines. The logic is something along the lines of "TV is fast, vapid, and unbelievably successful. Publications should employ the same techniques as TV."

This perhaps makes sense in mass market magazines like *Entertainment Weekly* or *Spy* or even in corporate annual reports, where the message is not necessarily crucial; those products are not intended to challenge your intellect. When the same stylistic formats are applied to newsmagazines, newspapers, and school books, the implication may be more troubling. The distinction between what is news, opinion, entertainment, and propaganda is blurry enough. The turn toward graphic oversimplification may make the boundaries even more obscure. U.S. Education Secretary T. H. Bell referred to this phenomenon as part of the "dumbing down" of American textbooks that removes all complex information in attempt to capture the reader's attention. But if students are unable to read and to grasp complex subjects, is the problem in the book? Is simplifying the content to fit into "exciting" *USA Today* formats going to solve the problem?

DESIGNING FICTIONAL FACTS

Publications made for looking rather than for reading can suggest entire themes with carefully composed photographs or coded design forms that avoid the kind of supporting evidence demanded in expository writing. (Consider the photograph from *People* of November 1991 showing Clarence and Virginia Thomas curled up on their couch reading the Bible. How can you respond to that image? How can you reason against it?) These formats emphasize the incredible power of the art-directed image, buttressed by the decontextualized quotation, the boldface caption, the "scientific" diagram, and the brightly colored map. Charts and diagrams are certainly useful for offering general, relational explications of an issue but they necessarily shave away the ambiguous, nuanced, or obscure aspects of any idea. The information has been preprocessed, prechewed; it can only lead to one conclusion. And so the design of these pages controls the reading, siphoning off all complexity and presenting a slyly fictional "fact."

At the most fundamental level, the spread of the *USA Today* style represents a destruction of traditional narrative ideals. Narrative implies an author as well as a reader. The reader negotiates the process of the rational argument, checking any specific point against the entire premise. The credibility of the content is measured against the author's authority. The argument set forth is understood to be limited by the perspective inherently implied in the narrative voice. But images and charts seem to not imply an inherent point-of-view. They radiate a kind of false objectivity because the concept of the image-as-opinion is difficult for most people to grasp.

Cultural critics may see this shift toward the fragmented layout as an example of the continuing decline of textual authority, with the author's intention giving way to the reader's interpretation. They may praise this impulse. "Design becomes a provocation to the audience to construct meaning, consider new ideas, and reconsider preconceptions," says Cranbrook's Katherine McCoy. The philosophy of deconstruction may indeed serve as a tool to describe the original move toward fragmentation. But when the concept becomes codified and adopted as mainstream style, when the devices of mass culture adopt "deconstructed" typographic mannerisms, you can be sure it is not done to put greater interpretive power into the hands of the audience.

Fighting to grab one second from the harried, over-informed consumer, the makers of the mass media have concluded that messages must be instantaneous, offering about the same content level as a fifteen-second television commercial. (As Nigel Holmes puts it, "… the dentist may well get through his first appointment sooner than you thought.") If a chart with a picture of Uncle Sam and a Russian bear on a seesaw balanced over an oil barrel can replace several paragraphs of text, all the better. No one has time to think about a rational argument; it takes too long, it's too boring. A sharp image and a few well chosen words can produce the same idea without the nuances but with a kind of prefabricated logic.

LOW-CAL READING

Setting aside the more sinister interpretations of this trend, one could argue that it actually relates to basic shifts in the way typography and design are produced. The Macintosh opened up to designers a vast array of new graphic possibilities, giving them access to what is the equivalent of sophisticated typesetting terminals. Intricate settings, overlapping or run-around type, complex charts and graphs that were once too costly and time consuming to design are now within the scope of even the smallest studio. Similarly, book and magazine publishers have greater digital composition possibilities and more four-color printing forms.

Or maybe the best explanation for the spread of *USA Today* look-alikes is that it is an inevitable extension of the LITE phenomenon. If beer or mayonnaise or individually wrapped slices of American cheese make you fat, then: a) stop eating and drinking so much; or b) remanufacture the products with fewer calories. We are more comfortable with the idea of changing our products than with changing our habits. Maybe publication design is under the same pressure. Maybe we want the "experience" of reading without all that heavy, annoying thinking. Maybe it's LITE design; it tastes great and it's less filling.

Originally published in I.D. *magazine, March/April 1992.*

ON TYPISHNESS: THIS IS MY THEORY. MY THEORY IS WRONG.

by

Karrie Jacobs

The more I see, the less I know. That's how it is with me. I look at ten pieces of graphic design and an idea forms. Above my head is a thought balloon, a glistening ellipsoid of perfection. I look at an eleventh piece of design, and the balloon bursts. Can you picture the Hindenburg in flames over Lakehurst, New Jersey? It happens to me all the time.

I have a theory. Rather, I *had* a theory. I had a theory until I decided that my theory was wrong.

Working on my theory gave me an appetite so I went out for lunch. Afterward I stopped at Rizzoli, the art book store, and looked at picture books. Thumbing through a new book on typography, I came upon a *McCall's* magazine spread from the early 1960s designed by Otto Storch. It illustrated a story about parfaits; layered desserts in elongated, bell-shaped glasses. There was a photo showing several concoctions and in between two of them was the lead paragraph of the story; a block of type shaped just like a parfait glass. Now, I knew about Storch, that he was famous for that sort of thing. I knew that, but it didn't have any significance until I was standing there in Rizzoli, my belly full of chowder, my head full of theory. The Otto Storch spread became the eleventh design.

The ten pieces that preceded Storch, the pieces on which my theory was founded, were a New Music America poster by Appleton Design of Hartford, Connecticut; a pair of Peugeot ads by HDM Advertising of New York City; a letterhead created for the industrial design firm, Design Logic, by David Frej of INFLUX design in Chicago; two catalogs designed by Thirst's Rick and Noni Valicenti, also of Chicago; a pair of annual reports by Samata Associates of Dundee, Illinois. (Are you counting? That's eight, and they're all in the "Communication Graphics" section of the *AIGA Annual*); an ad for a twenty-four hour French greasy spoon, Restaurant Florent, designed by M&Co of New York; and an ad for Sea Breeze Facial Cleansing Gel that I tore from a fashion magazine, designer unknown.

What they have in common is a trait I call "typishness." They all use type as if letterforms were dominoes or tiddly winks, as if lines of copy were pipe cleaners or pick-up sticks. They use type playfully, joyously, exuberantly, with utter abandon. I like typishness. I do. It's a blast. But there's something about it that makes me think that the party is a wake. I think typishness is celebrating the terminal illness of the printed page. At least, that's my theory.

My theory is wrong.

But I'll tell you about it anyway.

If I can't give you truth, at least I can show you a good time. Think about it: when have you ever gotten either from a design annual?

Our relationship is on the rocks. That's my theory. Or maybe it isn't quite so bad. Maybe it's just not a sure thing, a forever thing the way it once was. You, me, and the printed word. We used to be inseparable like Manny, Moe, and Jack; like Peter, Paul, and Mary. We were as right as Orpheus and Eurydice. Actually, we're a lot like Orpheus and Eurydice. Do you know that story? No? Well, let me be your Bullfinch.

In Greek mythology, Orpheus and Eurydice were not married long before tragedy struck. Eurydice, pursued by an amorous shepherd, stepped on a snake in the grass, was bitten, and died. Orpheus traveled to the underworld to rescue her from the dead. He sang his heart out and played his lyre, and he so moved Pluto, Proserpine, and their Furies that they allowed him to lead Eurydice away from death. The one condition was that he not look at her until they'd reemerged in the land of the living. But Orpheus, at the last minute, turned to check on Eurydice—one quick glance—and she vanished like a ghost. Orpheus went to embrace Eurydice, but there was nothing there. She had been spirited back down to the underworld.

I picture this happening much the way text disappears from a monitor when the computer goes down. Where do all those words go? To the underworld, I suppose.

My theory is about Orpheus, Eurydice, and typishness. My theory is that if we attempt to separate the printed word from its paperbound form we will make it disappear. We will turn around to look, and it will be gone. And our foreknowledge of this impending tragedy makes us a little odd about type. Some of us have become stalwart preservationists or formalists while others, those with whom I'm concerned here, have become giddy, perhaps a bit bathetic, and typish. Very, very typish.

My theory, of course, is wrong.

For starters, it's based on the sort of punditry I dismiss out of hand. Personally, I don't believe that books as we know them or magazines or newspapers—the ink and paper versions—are going to be snuffed out by electronic media any time soon. (But I do believe that if and when this comes to pass, graphic artists will be as much an endangered species as writers. We'll be the icemen and the punch-cutters, respectively.) There is, however, a constant hum, as annoying as a 3:00 A.M. mosquito, about the death of the book, the magazine, the newspaper, the annual report, the poster, the leaflet, the postage stamp, the dollar bill. Databases have already been substituted for reference works—*Roget's* is on a floppy, *Webster's* is on the hard drive—and there are predictions that high-definition, bit-mapped monitors will take the place of books, and be every bit as nice.

For instance in the March/April 1989 *Language Technology* (a magazine published in the Netherlands for "wordworkers" who use computers), I read an article called "In the Future, Paper Will be Used for Paper Cups." The author, Avery Jenkins, savors, like so many others have savored before him, "the tantalizing promise of a paperless future."

The technology is getting better and better by the minute, says Jenkins. And Hugh Dubberly, Apple's creative director for computer graphics, wrote in the winter 1989 edition of the *AIGA Journal of Graphic Design:* "Now, I readily admit that computer screens are not great places to read books. Not today, anyway. But screens are improving—even surpassing the quality of laser printers. Last spring at the National Computer Graphic Association convention, you could see a nineteen-inch computer screen with a resolution of 200 dots per inch. Each dot could be any of 256 greys. Type looked like type. Photos looked like they came out of an annual report."

The technology threatens the death of type as we know it. I'm not talking about the progression from hot metal to cool digitization. I'm talking about the end product, symbols on paper. Technology portends the death of books as tangible objects. Whether or not I believe it will happen is beside the point. The potential is real.

Books have died before. In the Middle Ages, the works of antiquity were destroyed or hidden away in monasteries for centuries. Writes historian Peter Gay in the first volume of *The Enlightenment: An Interpretation,* "When Boccaccio visited the great Benedictine library of Monte Cassino, he found it a room without a door with grass growing on the window sills, and the manuscripts, covered with dust, torn and mutilated ... he asked one of the monks how such desecrations could have been permitted and was told that the monks would tear off strips of parchment, to be made into psalters for boys or amulets for women, just to make a little money."

The constant of our time isn't invasion by barbarians, it's rapid technological change. This change both allows and encourages typishness. Computers mean that anybody can be perfect. They also mean that anybody can be willfully imperfect. In the desk-top era, every amateur can conjure precision and so precision becomes an amateur's game. Professionals, then, are obligated to go crazy. This is part of my theory. But if the pundits are right, technological change means that the most advanced output equipment, high-resolution devices like the Scitex or the Linotronic, will be obsolete in no time. Output will be unnecessary. All the wildness and all the perfection will be for naught. Type will be a ghost. We'll turn around, and it will be gone.

Typishness indicates to me that type is being treated the way we treat our prized icons, our endangered icons, the ones we love too much to give up. Type has become a juju. Like the green glass Coke bottle which has made a recent and very calculated reappearance. Like the Horn & Hardart Dino-Mat, a camped-up tribute to the nearly extinct automat. Like ceiling fans. Like muscle cars. Typishness is the swan song of the printed word.

Who is typish? Richard Pandiscio of the *Paper,* a New York downtown arts monthly, is extremely typish. He's been typish for years. In the April 1989 issue, he had columns of type curving to match the figure of actress Joanne Whalley, who plays a seductress in *Scandal.* Helene Silverman was typish during her tenure as art director of *Metropolis* (represented in the Cover Show), and she is currently being typish in the post-literate world of MTV. In a video for a song called "Anna Ng" by a band, They Might Be Giants, she used lyrics moving a bit too quickly to be read, emphasizing the beat. Likewise, Tibor Kalman of M&Co, who is consistently typish in print, was even more so on his firm's video for Talking Heads, which relied heavily on dancing typography. Of course, these are all people from whom typishness is expected.

Look, and you will find typishness at work in surprising places. There are corporate reports by Pat Samata, whose type does everything except line up in columns. There are Peugeot ads from HDM Advertising, which use type in literal, so-dumb-they're-smart sight-gags. One, with the headline "It'll have you believing the world is flat," shows a car driving across a block of copy consisting of shattered letters and bumpy, potholed lines of type.

Look at the advertising in magazines and you'll find type doing the fandango, the mazurka, the limbo. Type follows the contours of a model's face in a cosmetics ad, and it undulates in a department store ad. On television, commercials have become profoundly typish. In some campaigns, the entire concept is built on type. Typewriter type, reversed-out type, flashing type, blinding type, pounding type. Television commercials now have more subtitles than a festival of foreign films.

So, if typishness is the death rattle of the printed word, then what's it doing on television? Hell, I don't know. I *told* you that my theory is wrong.

What happened to me at Rizzoli was that Otto Storch's parfait glasses posed a tough question. They asked, how can contemporary typishness be the last fling of the printed word if Otto Storch was typish in 1960? How could that theory be correct if Bradbury Thompson was typish in 1949? And Lester Beall in 1935? And Ladislav Sutnar in 1941? And Alexander Rodchenko in 1923? How?

How, indeed.

Certainly we are in a period of ostentatious design. Designers have renounced the one-typeface, one-way approach of a decade ago, and they've moved on to type fetish, a fevered romance with letterforms, both perfect and distorted. And technology plays a starring role in many, but not all cases. In fact, some of the most typish designers are also the least enamored of high-technology. But this type frenzy is nothing we haven't experienced before.

The real problem isn't the holes in my particular theory. The problem is the practice of trying to coherently sum up the contents of an annual, trying to draw real conclusions from fragments of a year. It can't be done. Every theory based on a selection of a year's worth of design is bound to be wrong. Every round-up of trends in graphic design is a fiction.

My theory is that today's typishness is a final, nostalgic, heartfelt tribute to a dying medium. My theory is wrong. At least, I hope it's wrong. When I turn around, I want to see something there.

Originally published in the AIGA Annual, *no. 10, 1989.*

THE CURSE OF THE NEW
by
Dugald Stermer

This is a true story, with only the names omitted to protect the trendy and the uncharacteristically self-effacing, respectively. Several years ago, maybe ten, a well-known veteran designer from Los Angeles approached an old pal, a designer turned illustrator based in San Francisco, and said, "Hey, I just saw a bunch of your stuff when I judged the LA Art Directors show; nice." In answer to the obvious question he replied: "Sure, most of them. But how long are you going to keep sliding by on that style before you move along? I won't go for it again." He said it kidding on the square, and it stung, for a while.

Upon considerable reflection, the sting was caused by two factors. The most immediate, and least important, was that it was said not by an envious competitor, but by a respected friend and colleague. If he were asked about the encounter, I'm confident he would say either, "It was just a joke," or "Hell, I say things like that all the time, just to keep my buddies from getting too complacent." And if the work he referred to had been faddish or gimmicky, the remark might have helped to move his friend off the dime. But in that case, why vote to honor it?

That is, however, of little concern. What resonates even today is the assumption that what we do during our working lives is a succession of tricks pulled from a bag filled with stuff of our own, mixed willy-nilly with that we've borrowed from others; and that we grab our gambits and gimmicks based on whatever's hot, or not, at the moment.

This seems to be a post-industrial revolution, twentieth- century notion. Perhaps automobiles, military hardware, and razors are not alone in being designed for sequential obsolescence. It appears that designers and illustrators, along with musicians, painters and performers are expected to continually revise their style and approach in order to survive the dreaded epithet, "dated." For some reason, writers are relatively immune to this judgement. John Updike and Larry McMurty, to name just two Pulitzer recipients, have each written several novels dealing with the same characters and situations—sequels—told in the same voice and point of view. They were all dealt with individually by the critics and audience, alike. No one, to my knowledge, suggested that maybe Updike ought to move off his Rabbit kick and on to something more hip, say, along the lines of *Bright Lights, Big City*.

Before our newer-is-better age, in which newest is best, artists in all fields were, for the most part, allowed the time to develop their skills along with the content of their work; in fact, the two were both parallel and inseparable. It is impossible to imagine Da Vinci painting *The Last Judgement* on the Sistine Chapel Ceiling; equally difficult is visualizing *The Last Supper* as painted by Michelangelo. Try the Brandenburg Concertos as composed by Beethoven instead of Bach; or *The Adventures of Huckleberry Finn* as related by Henry David Thoreau.

The whole point of skill in the arts, it seems to me, is to shorten the distance from the brain (and heart) to the fingertips. As skill develops, so too the ability to communicate the message, uniquely one's own, whether through words, form, movement, shape, or tones. That we are a product of our time and place does not mean that we have to be a slave to them.

The quest is, finally, for integrity in the root meaning; to have our work evolve as closely integrated with ourselves as skill, will, practice, and fortune allows. Some find the road early; others, like me, finally get rolling after what seems like ages of flailing around the field, making it all the more gratifying, like finally being allowed to cease beating your head against a mirror, blindfolded.

The trick—we always knew there had to be one—is in recognizing, for better or worse, that you are finally you.

A LETTER TO THE EDITOR

It was with interest and no little astonishment that I read "The Curse of the New," by Dugald Stermer. Interest because I have been aware of his work for some time, and astonishment in that he comes down squarely in opposition to change, much less progress, in the arts.

While Stermer acknowledges that we are a product of our time, he then implies that we don't necessarily have a role in reflecting contemporary values, tastes, and styles. This flies in the face of most of what passes for Western culture, a tradition of intellectual and artistic evolution which has, for the most part, defined our present as well as our past.

Change is not simply fad or fashion. It is more a function of new technologies, political alignments, scientific discoveries, and many other kinds of upheavals, social and otherwise. Stermer claims, obviously and correctly as far as he goes, that Twain couldn't have written *Walden*, nor Thoreau *Huckleberry Finn*. However, neither could have written much of anything, more accurately, neither's writing would have been read or remembered, if they had had the misfortune to have been born before Gutenberg.

Face it, Stermer, graphic design has and will continue to change, drastically and forever, with the universal use of the computer. And when designers discover the limitless possibilities inherent in cable television, their work will be unrecognizable by today's Luddites. Much of it will no doubt be trendy and finally irrelevant; as long as we applaud the achievements of our colleagues, there will be imitators, resulting in short-lived fads.

We also tend to stumble around for a while as we learn to use new tools, often forcing them to imitate the work of older, more familiar technologies and art forms. Early photographers, such as Julia Cameron, shamelessly copied the composition and subject matter of classical painting, before they began to explore the camera's potential; a process that still continues. The contemporary example is the synthesizer, which is still being employed to approximate—soullessly—orchestral music. To be sure, there are many graphic artists, mostly illustrators, who are desperately attempting to bend the computer to act like a brush or pencil, but this too will pass as more adventurous artists enter the field.

Relax, Stermer, change isn't bad or good. It's just different.
Sincerely,
Dugald Stermer

Originally published (minus the Letter to the Editor) in the AIGA *Journal of Graphic Design, vol. 10, no. 3, 1992.*

CULT OF THE UGLY
by
Steven Heller

"Ask a toad what is beauty.... He will answer that it is a female with two great round eyes coming out of her little head, a large flat mouth, a yellow belly and a brown back." (Voltaire, *Philosophical Dictionary,* 1794). Ask Paul Rand what is beauty and he will answer that "the separation of form and function, of concept and execution, is not likely to produce objects of aesthetic value." (Paul Rand, *A Designer's Art,* 1985). Then ask the same question to the Cranbrook Academy of Art students who created the ad hoc desktop publication *Output* (1992), and to judge by the evidence they might answer that beauty is chaos born of found letters layered on top of random patterns and shapes. Those who value functional simplicity would argue that the Cranbrook students' publication, like a toad's warts, is ugly. The difference is that unlike the toad, the Cranbrook students have deliberately given themselves the warts.

Output is eight unbound pages of blips, type fragments, random words, and other graphic minutiae purposefully given the serendipitous look of a printer's make-ready. The lack of any explanatory précis (and only this end note: "Upcoming Issues From: School of the Art Institute of Chicago [and] University of Texas,") leaves the reader confused as to its purpose or meaning, though its form leads one to presume that it is intended as a design manifesto, another "experiment" in the current plethora of aesthetically questionable graphic output. Given the increase in graduate school programs which provide both a laboratory setting and freedom from professional responsibility, the word experiment has come to justify a multitude of sins.

The value of design experiments should not of course be measured only by what succeeds, since failures are often steps towards new discoveries. Experimentation is the engine of progress, its fuel a mixture of instinct, intelligence, and discipline. But the engine floods when too much instinct and not enough intelligence or discipline is in the mix. This is the case with certain of the graphic design experiments that have emanated from graduate schools in the U.S. and Europe in recent years—work driven by instinct and obscured by theory, with ugliness its foremost byproduct.

How is ugly to be defined in the current Post-modern design climate where existing systems are up for re-evaluation, order is under attack, and the forced collision of disparate forms is the rule? For the moment, let us say that ugly design, as opposed to classical design (where adherence to the golden mean and a preference for balance and harmony serve as the foundation for even the most unconventional compositions) is the layering of unharmonious graphic forms in a way that results in confusing messages. By this definition, *Output* could be considered a prime example of ugliness in the service of fashionable experimentation. Though not intended to function in the commercial world it was distributed to thousands of practicing designers on the American Institute of Graphic Arts and American Center for Design mailing lists, so rather than remain cloistered and protected from criticism as on-campus "research," it is a fair subject for scrutiny. It can legitimately be described as representing the current cult of ugliness.

The layered images, vernacular hybrids, low-resolution reproductions, and cacophonous blends of different types and letters at once challenge prevailing aesthetic beliefs and propose alternative paradigms. Like the output of communications rebels of the past (whether 1920s Futurists or 1960s psychedelic artists), this work demands that the viewer or reader accept non-traditional formats which at best guide the eye for a specific purpose through a range of non-linear "pathways," and at worst result in confusion. But the reasons behind this wave are dubious. Does the current social and cultural condition involve the kind of upheaval to which critical ugliness is a time-honored companion? Or in the wake of earlier, more serious experimentation, has ugliness simply been assimilated into popular culture and become a stylish conceit?

The current wave began in the mid-1970s with the English punk scene, a raw expression of youth frustration manifested through shocking dress, music, and art. Punk's naive graphic language—an aggressive rejection of rational typography that echoes Dada and Futurist work—influenced designers during the late 1970s who seriously tested the limits imposed by Modernist formalism. Punk's violent demeanor surfaced in Swiss, American, Dutch, and French design and spread to the mainstream in the form of a "new wave," or what American punk artist Gary Panter has called "sanitised punk." A key anti-canonical approach later called Swiss Punk—which in comparison with the gridlocked Swiss International Style was menacingly chaotic, though rooted in its own logic—was born in the mecca of rationalism, Basel, during the late 1970s. For the elders who were threatened (and offended) by the onslaught to criticize Swiss Punk as ugly was avoiding the issue. Swiss Punk was attacked not so much because of its appearance as because it symbolized the demise of Modernist hegemony.

Ugly design can be a conscious attempt to create, and define alternative standards. Like war paint, the dissonant styles which many contemporary designers have applied to their visual communications are meant to shock an enemy—complacency—as well as to encourage new reading and viewing patterns. The work of American designer Art Chantry combines the shock-and-educate approach with a concern for appropriateness. For over a decade, Chantry has been creating eye-catching, low-budget graphics for the Seattle punk scene by using found commercial artifacts from industrial merchandise catalogues as key elements in his posters and flyers. While these "unsophisticated" graphics may be horrifying to designers who prefer Shaker functionalism to punk vernacularism, Chantry's design is decidedly functional within its context. Chantry's clever manipulations of found "art" into accessible, though unconventional, compositions prove that using ostensibly ugly forms can result in good design.

Post-modernism inspired a debate in graphic design in the mid-1970s by revealing that many perceptions of art and culture were one-dimensional. Post-modernism urgently questioned certainties laid down by Modernism and rebelled against grand Eurocentric narratives in favor of multiplicity. The result in graphic design was to strip Modernist formality of both its infrastructure and outer covering. The grid was demolished, while neo-classical and contemporary ornament, such as dots, blips and arrows, replaced the tidiness of the canonical approach. As in most artistic revolutions, the previous generation was attacked, while the generations before were curiously rehabilitated. The visual hallmarks of this rebellion, however, were inevitably reduced to stylistic mannerisms which forced even more radical experimentation. Extremism gave rise to fashionable ugliness as a form of nihilistic expression.

In "Ode on a Grecian Urn" (1819), the Romantic poet John Keats wrote the famous lines: "Beauty is truth, truth beauty—that is all/Ye know on earth, and all ye need to know." Yet in today's environment, one standard of beauty is no more the truth than is one standard of ugliness. It is possible that the most convention-busting graphic design by students and alumni of Cranbrook, CalArts, and Rhode Island School of Design, among other hothouses where theoretical constructs are used to justify what the untutored eye might deem ugly, could become the foundation for new standards based on contemporary sensibilities. Certainly, these approaches have attracted many followers throughout the design world.

"Where does beauty begin and where does it end?" wrote John Cage in *Silence* (1961). "Where it ends is where the artist begins." So in order to stretch the perimeters of art and design to any serious extent it becomes necessary to suspend popular notions of beauty so that alternative aesthetic standards can be explored. This concept is essential to an analysis of recent work by the Chicago company Segura, who designed the programme/announcement for the 1993 *How* magazine "Creative Vision" conference and whose work represents the professional wing of the hothouse sensibility. Compared to the artless *Output,* Segura's seemingly anarchic booklet is an artfully engineered attempt to direct the reader through a maze of mundane information. Yet while the work might purport to confront complacency, it often merely obstructs comprehension.

A compilation of variegated visuals, the *How* piece is a veritable primer of cultish extremes at once compelling for its ingenuity yet undermined by its superficiality. Like a glutton, Segura has stuffed itself with all the latest conceits (including some of its own concoction) and has regurgitated them on to the pages. At first the juxtapositions of discordant visual material appear organic, but in fact little is left to chance. The result is a catalogue of disharmony in the service of contemporaneity, an artifact that is already ossifying into a 1990s design style. It is a style that presumes that more is hipper than less, confusion is better than simplicity, fragmentation is smarter than continuity, and that ugliness is its own reward.

But is it possible that the surface might blind one to the inner beauty (i.e. intelligence) of this work? Ralph Waldo Emerson in *The Conduct of Life* (1860) wrote, "The secret of ugliness consists not in irregularity, but in being uninteresting." Given Emerson's measure, it could be argued that design is only ugly when devoid of aesthetic or conceptual forethought—for example, generic restaurant menus, store signs and packages. Perhaps, then, the *How* booklet, which is drowning in forethought, should be "read" on a variety of levels wherein beauty and ugliness are mitigated by context and purpose. Perhaps—but given the excesses in this work, the result can only be described as a catalogue of pretence.

During the late 1940s and 1950s the Modernist mission was to develop design systems that would protect the global (not just corporate) visual environment from blight.

Yet while Modernism smoothed out the rough edges of communications by prescribing a limited number of options, it also created a recipe for mediocrity. If a Modernist design system is followed by rote, the result can be as uninteresting and therefore as ugly—according to Emerson's standard—as any non-designed newsletter or advertisement. So design that aggressively challenges the senses and intellect rather than following the pack should in theory be tolerated, if not encouraged.

For a new generation's ideas of good design—and beauty—to be challenged by its forerunners is, of course, a familiar pattern. Paul Rand, when criticized as one of those "Bauhaus boys" by American type master W. A. Dwiggins in the late 1930s, told an interviewer that he had always respected Dwiggins' work, "so why couldn't he see the value of what we were doing?" Rudy VanderLans, whose clarion call of the "new typography" *Emigre* has been vituperatively criticized by Massimo Vignelli, has not returned the fire, but rather countered that he admirers Vignelli's work despite his own interest in exploring alternatives made possible by new technologies. It could be argued that the language invented by Rand's "Bauhaus boys" challenged contemporary aesthetics in much the same way as VanderLans is doing in *Emigre* today. Indeed VanderLans, and those designers whom *Emigre* celebrates for their inventions—including Cranbrook alumni Edward Fella, Jeffery Keedy, and Allen Hori—are promoting new ways of making and seeing typography. The difference is that Rand's method was based strictly on ideas of balance and harmony which hold up under close scrutiny even today. The new young turks, by contrast, reject such verities in favor of imposed discordance and disharmony, which might be rationalized as personal expression, but not as viable visual communication, and so in the end will be a blip (or tangent) in the continuum of graphic design history.

Edward Fella's work is a good example. Fella began his career as a commercial artist, became a guest critic at Cranbrook and later enrolled as a graduate student, imbuing in other students an appreciation for the naïf (or folk) traditions of commercial culture. He "convincingly deployed highly personal art-based imagery and typography in his design for the public," explains Lorraine Wild in her essay "Transgression and Delight: Graphic Design at Cranbrook" (*Cranbrook Design: the New Discourse,* 1990). He also introduced what Wild describes as "the vernacular, the impure, the incorrect, and all the other forbidden excesses" to his graduate studies. These excesses, such as nineteenth-century fat faces, comical stock printers' cuts, ornamental dingbats, hand scrawls, and out-of-focus photographs, were anathema to the early Modernists, who had battled to expunge such eyesores from public view.

Similar forms had been used prior to the 1980s in a more sanitized way by American designers such as Phil Gips in *Monocle* magazine, Otto Storch in *McCall's* magazine, and Bea Feitler in *Ms.* magazine. For these designers, novelty job printers' typefaces and rules were not just crass curios employed as affectations, but appropriate components of stylish layouts. While they provided an alternative to the cold, systematic typefaces favored by the International Style, they appeared in compositions that were nonetheless clean and accessible. These were not experiments, but "solutions" to design problems.

Two decades later, Fella too re-employed many of the typically ugly novelty typefaces as well as otherwise neutral canonical lefferforms, which he stretched and distorted to achieve purposefully artless effects for use on gallery and exhibition announcements. Unlike Gips' and Feitler's work, these were aggressively unconventional. In *Cranbrook Design: the New Discourse,* Fella's challenges to "normal" expectations of typography are described as ranging from "low parody to high seriousness." But the line that separates parody and seriousness is thin, and the result is ugliness. As a critique of the slick design practiced throughout corporate culture, Fella's work is not without a certain acerbity. As personal research, indeed as personal art, it can be justified, but as a model for commercial practice, this kind of ugliness is a dead end.

"[J]ust maybe, a small independent graduate program is precisely where such daunting research and invention in graphic design should occur," argues Wild. And one would have to agree that given the strictures of the marketplace, it is hard to break meaningful ground while serving a client's needs and wants. Nevertheless, the marketplace can provide important safeguards—Rand, for example, never had the opportunity to experiment outside the business arena and since he was ostensibly self-taught, virtually everything he invented was "on the job." Jeffery Keedy and Allen Hori, both of whom had a modicum of design experience before attending Cranbrook, availed themselves of the luxury of experimenting free of marketplace demands. For them, graduate school was a place to test out ideas that "transgressed" as far as possible from accepted standards. So Wild is correct in her assertion that it is better to do research and development in a dedicated and sympathetic atmosphere. But such an atmosphere can also be polluted by its own freedoms.

The ugly excesses—or Frankenstein's little monsters like *Output*—are often exhibited in public to promulgate "the new design discourse." In fact, they merely further the cause of ambiguity and ugliness. Since graduate school hothouses push their work into the real world, some of what is purely experimental is accepted by neophytes as a viable model, and students, being students, will inevitably misuse it. Who can blame them if their mentors are doing so, too?

Common to all graphic designers practicing in the current wave is the self-indulgence that informs some of the worst experimental fine art. But what ultimately derails much of this work is what critic Dugald Stermer calls "adults making kids' drawings." When Art Chantry uses naive or ugly design elements he transforms them into viable tools. Conversely, Jeffery Keedy's Lushus, a bawdy shove-it-in-your-face novelty typeface, is taken seriously by some and turns up on printed materials (such as the Dutch *Best Book Design* cover) as an affront to, not a parody of, typographic standards. When the layered, vernacular look is practiced in the extreme, whether with forethought or not, it simply contributes to the perpetuation of bad design.

"Rarely has beauty been an end in itself," wrote Paul Rand in *Paul Rand: A Designer's Art*. And it is equally mistaken to treat ugliness as an end in itself. Ugliness is valid, even refreshing, when it is key to an indigenous language representing alternative ideas and cultures. The problem with the cult of ugly graphic design emanating from the major design academies and their alumni is that it has so quickly become a style that appeals to anyone without the intelligence, discipline, or good sense to make something more interesting out of it. While the proponents are following their various muses, their followers are misusing their signature designs and typography as style without substance. Ugliness as a tool, a weapon, even as a code is not a problem when it is a result of form following function. But ugliness as its own virtue—or as a knee-jerk reaction to the status quo—diminishes all design.

Originally published in Eye *magazine, no. 9, vol. 3, September 1993.*

THE OBSCENE TYPOGRAPHY MACHINE
by
Philip B. Meggs

At a recent Washington AIGA meeting, editors from four major design publications held a panel discussion. One of the shills in the audience asked: "Do the design magazines establish design trends, or do you merely follow and report about them?" After all of the editors replied that they weren't too interested in stylistic trends or the latest fashion, one editor commented that the one *real* trend that everyone in the room should watch closely is the increasing importance of computers in graphic design. Most designers who have overcome their computer phobia and learned computer-assisted design have become mesmerized by its possibilities. Text can be poured into columns, PMS matchcolor backgrounds can be changed instantly to try different color combinations, and type size and style can be changed at will. For thousands of organizations with publications budgets too small to afford design and typesetting services, desktop publishing allows a significant upgrade of routine printed material ranging from internal company publications to public-school study guides and church bulletins. But this wonderful new tool that is revolutionizing graphic design has its dark side.

Unfortunately, the ease of computer use puts potent graphic capabilities into the hands of people who are devoid of any aesthetic sense about typography and have little or no understanding of the most basic principles of design. Powerful new software programs including Aldus Freehand and Illustrator 88 give the designer (or moron, as the case may be) the power to flip, rotate, stretch, or bend typography with the click of the mouse button. This permits some of the most obscene type forms ever devised or imagined. Certainly, distortion can be a useful and innovative design tool when handled with sensitivity and intelligence, but we are seeing type distorted in violation of everything that has been learned over the past 500 years about making functional and beautiful letterforms. Newspaper advertisements are a major source of grotesque typographic distortion, as headlines are stretched or condensed to fit with about as much grace as a fat lady squeezing into a too-small girdle.

A principle from perceptual psychology is that when identical rectangles are placed on the page with one in a horizontal position and the other in a vertical position, the horizontal rectangle will appear heavier, even though it is identical to the vertical form. A typeface designer spends hours refining his strokes, shaving horizontal fonts until they appear to have the same thickness as the vertical form.

Everyone who takes an introductory typography class learns that if a letter composed of curved strokes such as an O is the same height as a letter composed of vertical strokes such as an *E,* the *O* will appear too small. Typeface designers optically adjust circular forms, which must extend slightly above the capline and slightly below the baseline to appear correct.

One reason a typeface is considered a masterpiece is because the designer achieved optical harmony in adjusting the size and proportion of the parts—not mathematically, but aesthetically and perceptually. Frederic W. Goudy's Goudy Old Style, Adrian Frutiger's Univers, and John Baskerville's Baskerville: these typefaces are honored as great tools of communication and works of art because a virtuoso designer poured heart, soul, and countless hours of work into creating harmonious relationships between letterforms.

Suddenly in 1988, anyone with a Macintosh or other computer and a $495 software program could wreak havoc on these beautifully crafted forms. Take, for example, Helvetica Medium created by Max Miedinger and Edouard Hoffman thirty years ago. It is a simple operation to grab the corner of the type with the mouse and squeeze it down into a shorter version, or stretch it into taller, condensed versions. In the condensed versions, the horizontal strokes will be stretched wider, while the vertical strokes will maintain their width. The result is grossly misproportioned letterforms. The optical adjustment of the *O* and *S* is exaggerated, making them seem too tall for the other letters. The computer is a dumb robot, totally ignorant of the principles of perception mentioned earlier. We are seeing typography approach this level of obscenity as students, neophytes, and even experienced designers, berserk over the new toy, violate well-drawn letterforms without bringing compensating values of expression or form to their work. Goudy and Baskerville must be spinning in their graves, and Frutiger and Miedinger must be quite depressed to see their artful letters, created as an act of love, destroyed by those who either cannot see or simply do not care.

One impact of this new graphic software relates to what is becoming known as deconstructionist typography whose integrated whole is taken apart. While some of the practitioners of this new typographic movement exhibit great sensitivity and originality, others are merely flitting through the collection of graphic procedures available with the new software. Operations that formerly required painstaking cut-and-paste work, such as setting type in an oval or along a curved baseline, can now be performed instantly by drawing an oval, a circle or a meandering line, typing in the text, then clicking the mouse on the word "Join" in the menu. The oval, circle, or line instantly becomes the baseline of the type. These graphic devices provide a vocabulary of instant clichés, executed as simply as snapping one's fingers. Often, these techniques are used, not for thoughtful communicative or expressive reasons, but simply because they are there. The problem for designers exploring the elastic typography and/or the deconstructionist sensibility on a computer is, "What do you do for an encore?" As with most specialized tools, a computer-graphics program permits one to do a limited number of things very efficiently, but only operates within a fixed range of possibilities. Its innovative graphic techniques will become old and tired very rapidly as more and more people hop on the bandwagon, transforming graphics that originally appeared fresh and innovative into hack work.

Another problem with all this graphic power is that tremendous capability is put into the hands of people who don't know an ampersand from a hole in the ground. A newsletter recently crossed my desk with each column of type line spaced differently, because the novice desktop publisher discovered that the page-layout program would permit automatic leading to fit the column depth. Columns in 10-point Times Roman with no leading were adjacent to other columns set in 10-point Times Roman with about 25 points of leading between the lines. Text columns were justified, producing gaping holes in each line of type due to poor word spacing. He or she was too naive about typography to realize how the inconsistent word spacing destroyed legibility and the tonal quality of the page.

Although equipment manufacturers and software developers have made modest efforts to educate their users about the rudiments of design through little booklets explaining effective page layout or newsletter design, complete with case studies of redesigned publications with notable improvements, a new generation of unschooled graphic designers—editors, public relations agents, secretaries and other do-it-yourself desktop publishers—are totally ignorant of the rudiments of publication design and typography. Adobe, the company that developed the PostScript software that transforms crude bitmapped type on the computer screen into refined high-resolution output, publishes excellent materials. Some software tutorials address design issues, but do it poorly. More must be done. There should be an ethical responsibility on the part of companies that put powerful tools into the hands of uninformed people without educating them about the proper use of these tools.

The obscene typography machine can also be the sublime typography machine. Professional designers can explore new creative possibilities and spend more time developing concepts and designing and less time laboriously executing their work. As this technology becomes available in third-world nations, their efforts toward education and development can take quantum leaps forward as a result of the economy of desktop publishing. The computer-graphics force is now with us, but its dark side must be controlled; otherwise, the obscene typography machine is going to inflict unimagined graphic atrocities upon the public.

Originally published in Print *magazine, September/October 1989.*

FORM
FOLLOWS
FUNCTION

MEANING
by
John J. Rheinfrank and Katherine A. Welker

WHY MEANING?

"All form, no content." As designers all of us are probably familiar with this phrase. Although often said in jest, there might well be some truth behind the words. Non-designers sometimes look at our work and, failing to see beyond the surface, ask us, "Does that color (line, space, illustration, form, texture, shape, etc.) *mean* anything, or is it just there because you think it looks good?" At the same time, as designers, we occasionally look at the work of non-designers and mutter under our breath (again, with a grain of humor), "All content, no form." And, again, there might be some truth behind our teasing. Take, for example, the standard text document which is usually formatted according to guidelines established when typewriters were popular, or products whose physical presence has been shaped by engineering expediency rather than by a thoughtful response to human need.

The underlying issue here is *meaning.* What does the use of a particular color mean on a particular product? How can the meaning inherent in a text document best be expressed through page layout? How can a designed object communicate its meaning in terms of use and in a way that will make sense to a given user in a given situation? What is meaning, with respect to design, anyway?

THE OLD VIEW OF MEANING

Until recently, the primary focus of design was on form—with a tacit recognition that the elements of the form of an object evoke a multitude of associations for the individual who interacts with it. What these associations were, though, was not well understood. The understandings we did have were primarily intuitive and superficial in nature.

As the focus of design shifted to include the experiences of those who use and interact with objects, the whole issue of what objects "mean" to users has moved to the foreground. We are starting to see the form of an object less as the end of the design process and more as the beginning of the user's experience. In designing the form of an object, we want to design it so that we create the user's experience of it as well.

In our search for understanding about what meaning is and how we can build it into objects, we have borrowed insights from other fields. In particular, many of the notions about meaning that have been adopted as a part of product semantics come from semiotics, the study of signs. One of these notions is that meaning is something that is attached to things but separate from them—like our shadows are separate from our bodies, but attached (usually at the feet). Another is that we can understand things and their meanings outside of the real world—that they can have some sort of abstract existence in mental free-fall. Because of these ideas, we expect to find a fairly pure connection between objects and their meanings, one in which the meaning of an object is an almost direct result of its form—again, like the shapes of our shadows are a result of the forms of our bodies. We look for a few mediating circumstances (like the angle of the sun) when we don't quite see a match, but we assume that we can build these circumstances into the equation. We expect that we can still find a connection between objects and their meanings, a connection that is basically independent of real-world situations the objects might be a part of.

In effect, the semiotic triangle says that meaning and form are separate but connected. The triangle can also be extended to capture meaning on different levels or in different contexts. For example, a single object may have meaning in terms of what a person can do with it, the social attitudes surrounding it, or its aesthetic appeal. We may consider as a special case the context that is created by the multitude of other meanings within which one particular meaning is located, and with which it interacts. In looking at meaning this way, we recognize that meaning is dependent on context, but we still make the crucial assumption that meaning can be characterized independently of the situation in which it is created.

Underlying the semiotic perspective itself is an assumption that we have access to some objective reality—that the connections we make between form and meaning are the right connections, that we can identify all of the circumstances that bear on what meaning any given form will have. And as designers we have tended to assume that once we have identified the form that will evoke the appropriate meaning for the user, we simply use it and we will have successfully designed the object's meaning.

We suggest that the assumptions that underlie the semiotic perspective distort our understanding of what meaning is and limit our ability to design objects that are deeply meaningful. In response, we would like to argue that meaning is deeply and exclusively built inside of a context or situation. For example, when an object is placed in a situation, it is meaningful in ways that may or may not have been predicted by its designer. The object may also bring about changes in the situation, changes that are in some sense a part of its meaning. Finally, the meaning of a thing is reinvented by each individual who uses it, and evolves along with the situation of which it is a part.

A NEW VIEW OF MEANING

In design meaning is therefore not so much the arrived-at *sense* of an object (*qua* making meaningful objects), but a plunge into *sense-making* and a discovery of the qualities of objects that collaborate to produce authentic, meaningful situations. For example, the true meaning of a glass vase does not reside in the material that is glass or the form that is the vase, but in the ability of the vase to display flowers against the background of an old wooden bookcase. Situations like these can be described as events in settings (the perceiving of flowers in a physical context) in which objects (the flowers, the vase, the bookcase) appear and contribute to peoples' capacities to create meaning (an impression of a summer field in an indoor office). Objects that appear in situations can be concrete objects like vases or abstract objects like classification schemes. They might also be new classes of objects, like scenarios (vignettes in which imaginary users use imaginary products) which are examples of objects that can help people envision still better objects.

Within this new view of meaning design can be seen as the envisioning and subsequent embodying of objects that act to frame situations. In this sense the most interesting design work will consider the design of the essential situation first, followed by the design of the objects that will create a myriad of experienced situations. For example, think about designing a flower-viewing situation rather than a vase. This requires a shift in the way designers think about designed objects. We must not think of objects as nouns with static meanings, but as verbs with the dynamic capacity to create multiple meanings through the actions they evoke—much as the vase evokes "the display of flowers."

Under this new view objects are seen as acting to register situations. First, we must recognize that people use each other and their environment as resources to socially construct understanding and creativity. People collaborate to grind shared lenses or eyeglasses through which events are filtered, intention is framed, and activity proceeds. With a recognition that sense-making lies behind situatedness, powerful new objects and object types (concrete and abstract) play a crucial role in the construction of a consensual reality. For example, consider the laboratory, which has played an essential role in the formation of scientific practice. As designers we might sit at a drawing board and design a laboratory using the latest in architectural style and fashionable office furniture, yet neutralize or (worse yet) even destroy the basis for advancing scientific practice. However, when our starting point is the (situated) acceleration of scientific practice and its social construction, an entirely new range of objects reveal themselves most of which cannot (and should not) be constructed at our drawing boards, but as part and parcel of the ongoing work of the laboratory and the organizational culture within which it is embedded.

When we consider objects as carriers of information about the external world—especially information about both past and potential experiences—we see their value as creators of meaningful situations. Objects designed through the consideration of meaningful situations have the capacity to express what can be created out of—or even through—them. This approach changes the role of the designer. As designers we do not see ourselves as professionals sitting at drawing boards designing artful or functional objects. We see ourselves as creators of the "clay" from which people can craft powerful objects—and even new object types.

MEANING-*IN-SITU* CAN RESHAPE DESIGN ACTIVITIES

The idea we have been proposing—that designed objects create meaningful situations of use and cannot be considered in isolation from those situations—has historically played a *tacit* role in most design activities. Designers have always been aware that the results of their work have meaning outside of the design studio. What we would like to do now is propose that designers *explicitly consider,* if not actually *design according to,* the situations of use[1] that are shaped by the objects they create. To show how considerations of "how objects create meaning-*in-situ*" can contribute to design activities, we will discuss a spectrum of approaches that integrate meaning-*in-situ* with design.

APPROACHES TO INTEGRATING MEANING-*IN-SITU*
WITH DESIGN ACTIVITY

Sleepwalking

Design does not take place in a vacuum. At the simplest level all designers are subliminally aware that the objects they design will take on meaning outside of their studios. In many cases, however, this subterranean awareness is not brought to the surface in a way that overtly influences the design of objects. Sleepwalking, then, is the design of objects with some recognition that the situation created may be important—but without an understanding of how the designed object might actually produce viable or non-viable situations. The sleepwalking approach can lead to successful design in much the same way that a sleepwalker can navigate successfully through a house. The results are on occasion surprisingly successful, occasionally disastrous, and almost always mysteriously accomplished. Office furniture designed from a sleepwalking approach might include some appropriate innovations, some mistakes, some wonderful surprises, and a large number of simply inappropriate responses.

Complementing

This is perhaps the most common approach to consciously considering the situations objects create and the meanings objects are likely to produce within situations— while designing the objects themselves. Complementing is 1) conscious consideration of the situation an object creates; 2) designing the object in a way that conforms to the situation's functional requirements, structures, and subjective appeal; and 3) ensuring that the object and the situation enrich and shape each other in a way that adds new meaning to both. Complementing is essentially working without altering the existing framework. The results are generally successful, if conservative and unsurprising, responses to existing design problems. Office furniture designed from a complementary approach would be just what you would expect—a set of solid space-creating solutions which would meet the stated user needs and which would create the desired space-situation according to the assumption set that currently frames the work situations.

Expanding

Another related approach to crafting situations through the design of objects is expanding the frame. This approach results in the desired situation and also leads to an expansion of it. In the world of advertising this approach might be called "new and improved." The expanding approach goes beyond the complementing approach, allowing designers to suggest that products might have meanings other than the immediately obvious ones and to create situations other than the immediately obvious ones—without threatening the comfort or efficacy of the status quo. The expanding approach might produce results that would anticipate latent needs: for example, flexible office furniture solutions that could define a number of different spaces in a number of different ways, perhaps supporting collaboration in addition to individual work.

Opposition

This might be the second most common approach to thinking about and reacting to the meanings designed objects create in their intended situations of use. In assuming an opposing stance a designer first recognizes the most appropriate complementary approach and then purposefully designs objects that are inconsistent with it, if not the exact opposite of it. Objects designed through this reverse polarity usually make no sense (create no meaning) in their situations of use. In a few cases this mismatch effect is a desired outcome. When opposition is successful, the result can be a product-situation mismatch that enriches the user's view of both the product and the situation. When opposition is unsuccessful, the result is a dysfunctional, uninterpretable, unusable product. Office furniture designed from an opposing approach would result in something entirely different from what one would expect: for example, no office furniture at all.

Reconceptualization

Reconceptualizing is a shift to an entirely new design plateau based on an entirely new set of assumptions. If a designed object has sufficient substance (meaning) to precipitate the creation of a dramatically different situation, then the new product-situation pair constitutes a radical shift in the structure of the situation—and in the assumptions of the people present in the situation. In effect, the presence of the object in the situation leads to a new view of the situation in the same way that a new conceptual framework shifts our view of the world. In the office furniture industry the introduction of panel systems as a product created situations (individual cubicles, group meeting rooms, etc.) that supported the further use of panel systems. Reconceptualizing can also be done proactively. Design teams can make the decision to design objects that challenge existing situations or that reframe existing situations. In this sense, reconceptualization is taking a possibly unexpected approach in response to newly uncovered needs. For example, a reconceptualized approach to office furniture panels might be thick panels that contain storage and create walls.

Co-design

Co-designing actually spans the last four approaches. Co-design means that the approach to the design challenge is addressed by both the designer and the user, and possibly a number of other players as well. Co-design of meaning-*in-situ* makes the situation the focus of the design activity, in part because users can give designers a sense of how they might experience the situations created by designed objects and designers can give users a sense of the situations inherent in their objects.

> '*When I use a word,' Humpty Dumpty said, in rather a scornful tone,'*
> *it means just what I choose it to mean—neither more nor less.'*
>
> '*The question is,' said Alice, 'whether you can make words mean so many different things.'*
>
> '*The question is,' said Humpty Dumpty, 'which is to be master—that's all.'*
>
> *—Lewis Carroll,* Through the Looking Glass

Originally published in the American Center for Design Journal, *vol. 5, 1990.*

Endnotes

1. There is an intriguing distinction between concrete and abstract situations. In everyday activity people are quite adept at using concrete situations as resources for understanding. There is some indication that the schema of expert practice evolves in the presence of abstract situations.

THE URGE TO MAKE THINGS
by
Leo Lionni

In his brilliant TV series, "The Ascent of Man," Jacob Bronowski theorized that hominization occurred when, for the first time, *Pithecanthropus erectus* picked up a stone and kept it for future use. In that precise moment, Bronowski said, the hominid had been endowed with imagination and the will to make things, graduating, so to speak, with a degree in humanity.

When, some five million years after that ominous event, I was asked what I considered the principal motivation for my work, after a blank moment and unaware of the implications of my answer, I said: "an irresistible urge to make things." I thought, "It's true." Were I forbidden to paint and sculpt and draw, I would be content to make bricks, tiles, or boxes, or any object I could make with my hands.

I was oversimplifying, of course; but later, when I was at work on a sculpture, I recognized that magic moment of pure *making,* when suddenly all interferences vanish, leaving the hands free to perform their assigned task swiftly, lightly, and with deserved arrogance. Modest though this may seem compared to the more popular moments of *inspiration,* for an artist it is, I believe, the happiest, most fulfilling moment of the entire creative process.

Years ago I was given a book on Chinese painting by a scholar-friend who described it as "definitive." That statement alone caused me to approach the book with awe. And I did so right from reading the first words, which I remember verbatim: "When a Chinese painter paints a tree, he becomes a tree." The terse weight of the words and their temple-bell rhythm made of the statement an irrefutable axiom, typically Oriental, not to be questioned. And that was how I perceived that first reading.

A few days later I wanted to quote it, and not remembering the exact wording, I read it once more and automatically I thought: What about an American painter who paints a tree, doesn't he become a tree? Didn't Cézanne become every apple he ever painted? Morandi, his bottles? DeKooning, his paint? Goya, the King of Spain? Didn't Eames become his chair? Is it possible not to fill the form or the things we make with our feelings and our mind?

The best proof that indeed we do is perhaps when we endow inanimate objects with human qualities or faults: An honest structure, a straightforward design, a frivolous detail, a humorous façade, a vulgar painting, a generous plan. When I was four years old, my answer to the question "What do you want to be when you grow up?" was, "The bell of the trolley car." Uninhibited as I was, identification with an inanimate object was spontaneous and immediate (besides, I wanted to be heard).

Obviously, thing-oriented people are more conscious of things than others. Some are obsessed by them to the point of mania. I believe myself to be one of these people. I not only make things such as paintings and sculptures and books, but if I had infinite space, I would collect any object, man-made or not, that I judge aesthetically, functionally, and metaphorically exciting. I could fill warehouses with them.

Even books, word-things that should be judged by their content, fascinate me as objects. I confess that I have many books in my library that I have never read nor had the intention of reading. I want them because their sheer presence represents a yearning, a mood, a love, and yes, an act of self-preservation. When my eyes scan my library, the typefaces of the titles, the textures of the covers, and their imagined weight give me a moment very like the pleasure of reading. Even when I am in the process of creating one of my own books, I cannot wait for it to be finished; less perhaps for seeing the text and illustrations finally in print than for the physical pleasure of holding it in my hands.

This metaphoric power of things gives us, their makers, responsibilities that we cannot escape. Willy-nilly, as a tangible extension of our character, they reflect our attitudes and express our values. The things we make are our gestures. They can indeed be aggressive, modest, elitist, democratic, sexist, gentle, austere, civilized, and just plain silly.

As the complexities of modern urban living proliferate under our very eyes, and the resulting deterioration of values leaves us aghast, the necessity to make clear moral statements through the things we make is important and urgent. Never more than today, when the world and our very lives are in the hands of the makers of words and war—the lawyers and the generals—has it been so important to realize that the things we make bear social and political messages.

To escape from this responsibility through the antics of capricious games of taste and intellectual self-complacency is, in the present circumstances, an unforgivable act of desertion.

Originally published in the AIGA Journal of Graphic Design, *vol. 9, no. 2, 1991.*

DRAWING AND DESIGN: AN IDEA WHOSE TIME HAS COME, AGAIN

by

James McMullan

There is a crucial connection between drawing and design which is much more than the simple ability to explain our design decisions in sketches. Drawing is a physical act which puts us in touch with how we really experience space and form. Design, when you examine its fundamental impulse, is informed reflex. We make shapes, choose intervals, and decide on hierarchies all from deep instincts, which are expressed in the act of drawing. The drawing hand, moving at the will of our purposeful choices and also the subconscious biases in our nervous systems, creates the basic structure upon which all other aesthetic decisions are made.

It might be argued that if drawing is a pipeline to the deep well of our reflexes, then any kind of drawing, no matter how amateurish, provides the same access to these reflexes. This would only be true if we were content with reflexes that were a one-way system, bringing back from the subconscious the same bits of shape and content over and over again, but not susceptible to refinement or expansion. As a matter of fact, in the doodles we make as we talk on the phone, we have a pretty good example of what these subconscious reflexes can produce when left to their own devices. What these doodles reveal is a vocabulary of curls or triangles or blocks, or rudimentary monsters that have some special meaning for us. But it is the interaction of these primal themes with new information which provides the artist with the creative usefulness of the reflexes. The monsters of the deep must be trained so that it is the drawing hand, working with dexterous intelligence, that becomes the dance master of our gestural impulses. It is only through drawing that the personality of the nervous system can creatively encounter the rational invention of the mind. The experienced, subtle movement of the drawing hand is sensuous enough to stay connected to strong gestural impulses; at the same time it is flexible enough to evoke new forms and follow the explorations commanded by the brain. Without drawing there would be no way to meld the world of the rational and the world of the intuitive. Visual invention would have to proceed (as it often unfortunately does) in a step-by-step linear way, or to be circumscribed by a very limited repertoire of shapes.

Drawing brings into balance the literary and graphic aspects of our design. When we draw well, we can use it as a kind of alchemical process to distill word ideas and image ideas down to whatever really works between them. In drawing, the physical act itself provides an intensifying "container" which makes possible a kind of thinking which occurs at no other time. Typically, we advance the drawing half from reason and half from intuition, and the drawing itself provokes still more intuitive and associative responses which in turn provoke more drawing. This fertile interaction between the hand making marks and the mind responding occurs most successfully with artists who draw well—and drawing well inevitably means the ability to evoke the forms you see or remember. The hand must move with enough dexterity to stimulate an interior recall and re-living of the subject as you draw it. This mental voluptuousness makes possible the "knowing" of our subject in a complex way, which would be very difficult to accomplish if we tried to break the subject down into its component parts. Drawing advances our knowledge of what we observe and helps to trigger all our deep-seated memories and associations.

Because so many of the final stages of design are often done by specialist photo-graphers or illustrators, many designers assume that their own rudimentary drawing skills are sufficient to the task. What this point of view misses entirely is that the ability to draw, besides putting us in touch with the rich information of our reflexes, is the great gateway to design invention. Whether or not the designer decides to create the actual image, he or she needs to be able to draw well enough to conceive the project in truly visual terms. The designer needs the ability to turn and refine ideas in the way you see, dramatically illustrated by Picasso in his sketchbooks; to understand how the adjustment of a single line can affect the universe of a drawing, or how the ability to draw a bowl of fruit, for instance, opens up all kinds of other possibilities for abstracting and simplifying that bowl of fruit.

Drawing can connect us to the physical circumstances of our own lives by giving us a way of seeing and internalizing our landscape and, if we can see the objects, people, and places around us, we can also use them as the raw material of our own inventions. Wouldn't it be gratifying to see a stylization of a ballet dancer that felt like it started out as a real experience of dance, and not simply as a photograph or drawing from a research file?

The true language of visual artists is drawing. Designers who learn to speak in this language fluently can move beyond the relatively inexpressive ingenuity of headlines, graphic puns, or style genres. Just as good painting moves us beyond what can be described anecdotally, good design can transport us to that subterranean and only partially rational realm of rhythm, association, dream, color, and light which is unlocked by drawing.

Originally published in the AIGA Journal of Graphic Design, *vol. 8, no. 3, 1990.*

DANCE & PLAY IN VISUAL DESIGN: VISUAL MANIFESTATIONS OF PHYSICAL EXPERIENCE
by
Frances Butler

Visual experience parallels, both theoretically and actually, the actions and responses inherent in the rhythmic structure of dancing and the freely outlined elements of play. Whether the physical experience is that of the eye moving around a page, the hand turning the pages of a book, or the body traveling through a reading environment, time and movement are critical elements in comprehension and in the perceived significance of a text. Time and movement and their interaction with reading establish a dialogue between concentration on a page and the turning of the page that establishes a rhythm which can be either used to emphasize the content or can be made the actual subject of the work at hand (despite the content). There follows a presentation of different varieties of visual materials in which the perception of sequence is exaggerated into its own significance, thereby enlarging the experience of reading.

The traditional book is a formalized sequence of events. Chapters in book design manuals are even titled "The Anatomy of the Book." This rigidity is justified as leading to "clarity through order." The traditional sequence of parts has undergone gradual change, especially due to the impact of photography which has led to an ever-increasing number of books which are principally visual. Typographic elements have changed in scale and placement to incorporate this new emphasis. Page structure, too, has been narrowly outlined by tradition; and the grid system, currently fashionable for integrating text and visual material, carries on the conventional belief in clarity through order. Beyond convention, one starts with the page shape, every point of which can be marked or not marked (see Emil Ruder's *Typography*); the choice of markings establishes or inhibits a rhythmic sequence through subsequent pages.

Increasing density of marks is one kind of interval, this is exploited in Anton Stankowski's *Visible Presentation Of Invisible Processes,* and made explicitly textual in Gerhard

Ruehmn's gradually obscured book pages, where text disappears into ever-larger black shapes. The idea of partially obscured text has been further manipulated by the English artist Tom Phillips in his many versions of *A Humument*. Here significant bits of text are left uncovered in a matrix of speech bubbles. Emil Ruder's yearlong series of covers (1963) for *Typografisches Monatsblatter,* in which a grid gradually darkens, is another example of this stately rhythmic progression.

Change of placement of similar elements through a series of pages, change in scale and proportion, and even repetition of non-changing elements, are effective rhythm generators. Piet Zwart's catalogue for the *Nederlandisches Kabel Fabriek,* 1926, has never been surpassed in the eloquence of its repetition and variation.

Gradual change of proportion through a series of images is the principal device used by Winsor McCay in his beautifully drawn and colored comic strip *Little Nemo in Slumberland* to indicate the deepening dream. Rabbits or raspberries gradually overwhelm the drawings and eventually awaken Little Nemo when their relative size can no longer be contained. Massin indicated change in oral and aural volume and proportion by enlarging or reducing the scale of the text type in relation to the human figures in his version of Ionesco's *La Chantatrice Chauve,* and Ron Johnson's poem in black and white *Io and the Ox-Eyed Daisies* successfully presents wordscale and color change as the principal vehicle for meaning.

All of these devices are examples of a metaphoric running line which propels the reader through a sequence of pages, encouraging the turning of the page. There are other compositions which bring the reader to a halt and emphasize the connection between elements within a page, a process which begins when the reader realizes that the composition includes too many finite parts to be adequately comprehended at one glance and begins to follow a trail of foci to the understanding of the visual syntax. Sometimes this linear process is given explicit and orderly form as in the nineteenth-century children's board games based on spirals, often coiled snakes. In maps too, one traces an actual line which makes the linkage between events or places clear, especially in the diagrammatic maps of transportation systems like the London Underground. And the primary trail of reading order, (for Latin alphabet users the pattern is left to right) can be used consciously as well, as is shown by Ian Hamilton Finlay's transparent poem about waves breaking on the rocks. On the left side of the glass the word "waves" is silkscreened many times, moving and breaking up into the right side of the glass which is dominated by the printed word "rock."

Sometimes the connection between visual incidents is not made explicit and the reader must try to trap these incidents into a syntax. Much contemporary graphic design has essentially a reader-sequencing structure. This is true of many Japanese posters, especially the early work of Tadanori Yokoo and now the poster work of the Los Angeles *slash-and-spritz* school. The contemporary Japanese posters continue a style of seventeenth to nineteenth-century woodcut book prints, where the text flows around the image in a manner that closely parallels the loose structure of language in some Japanese poetic styles. (See the *Illustrated History of the Kagoshima War,* 1877, cited in *Design Quarterly* No. 55, 1962.) Early European woodcut folk broadsides often exhibit this unstructured mix of words and image, and the fact that such widely disparate peoples made their way happily through these conglomerations argues against the necessity for order to achieve clarity, which is so often promulgated in typographic theory.

The comic strip on the other hand represents a very closely controlled sequence of text and images. Eventually comic strip story units were joined together with the same visual links used in film editing. The eye is led to a point on the edge of the frame in one unit, and is carried from that point into the next unit. These connections are sometimes exaggerated in comic strips as in the Flash Gordon comics of the thirties, or the Barbarella comics of the 1960s.

Returning from sequence limited to the roving eye to that which leads from page to page, some books are designed so that the page must be turned in order to see the full image. The nineteenth-century Japanese catalogue, *Koshu Jissu,* a presentation of many wonderful things, shows some of them wrapped around the edges of several pages. In Tom Raworth's *Logbook* I used this idea, carrying the image around the edges with the added complication of sometimes presenting the text which elucidates the image on the page after the picture. For example, in the two double-page spreads which illustrate the passage, "The river Medway has overflown its banks near Tonbridge, this would imply that the infinitive was to overfly," the first double-page spread shows a woman sighting down a rifle and the second spread shows both the text and the man who was "overflying" until shot down.

Another variety of experimental page turning involves descending through the book. Jiri Kolar, the Czech artist, made a book with holes of decreasing size cut out of the pages through which one peers down to the last page. MaryAnn Hayden printed *Two Cross Seizings* on opaque and semi-transparent rice papers so that changing layers of type and imagery are visible at each page opening. Poltroon Press used the transparency of rice paper also, printing in *Confracti Mundi Rudera* a poem about fog on the inside of a Japanese folded page. Actual transparency has often been exploited by book makers or by concrete poets like Dieter Rot and Hansjorg Mayer who printed poems on concentric plastic cylinders.

The flip book is another example of lateral reading. Holbrook Teter and Michael Myers of Zephyrus Image produced a wonderful gestural comment on the poet Charles Olson in *Folgers,* and Alastair Johnston made use of this flippant idea in *A Partial Primer for Pedestrians* in which flashing red "DO WA"s gradually change to green "WA"s. A related idea is the tear-apart book. *Stroke Order,* another Poltroon book, is perforated so that squares can be removed and the text changed. Raymond Queneau, in his Pataphysical books, slits each page into single sentences which can be easily torn out to change the text. These books really can't be reversed.

The play element of book openings is celebrated in special unfolding or unwinding procedures. Scrolls are now made principally for their physical properties, either for play or for ritual. Other book makers and binders have produced books in which the quality of the paper or the nature of its unfolding are as much a part of the meaning of the book as the text. Claire Van Vliet of Janus Press has collaborated with Twinrocker paper mill to make an unfolding book which gradually reveals dissipating colored clouds in the handmade paper. Both Kathryn Clark and Peggy Prentice of Twinrocker have made paper books in which the manipulation of the book structure is the subject—including irregular page sizes, highly tactile paper surfaces, and housings made in clay by Marjorie Levy. Heidi Kyle, a book binder, has commented on the folding of book pages into signatures with some very elaborately folded books including insetted fans of Chinese-lantern-style pleating between the pages. These books, like all of those emphasizing the unfolding of pages, change shape as the book is opened. A further style of book which allows for changing shape is the "fifty-two pickup" book, separate pages of which can be rearranged vertically or horizontally to infinity. Robert Grenier's book *Sentences* is one example of this style, and a smaller exercise is Sylvia Salazar Simpson's *Eggs Verbal*. The final comment on changing book shape is that made by Zephyrus Image in their little pleated book of accordion pictures, titled *Accordion to Saint Luke*.

A final category where the rhythm of reading is as important as the text are those projects in which realization is delayed by time or space. Jigsaw puzzles are the most obvious example of delayed revelation, although the precise appearance of an image can also delay understanding of what it represents. A puzzle I designed, *The Beast in the Jungle,* includes paired tigers, one rendered in checkerboards, so that it does not immediately look tigerish. *Airwaves,* another project involving delayed realization, presents a string of hands, each holding a card. The cards contain the letters for "Airwaves" on one side, and "not waving" on the other, and they refer to a poem by Stevie Smith in which the refrain runs, "I was too far out she said, and not waving but drowning." And as one moves to read the cards, stretched on taut wire, the slight air movements cause the hands to wave.

Movement from one unit to another interjects space into the understanding of visual sequence, and there are certainly many conceptual art projects which explore this. We also participate in extended spatial reading when we follow freeway signs or move through airports, or when we used to come across the Burma Shave signs, or on a more intimate scale when we read the older painted signs on buildings in which the letters are lined up vertically. I once produced a large scale project called "space printing" which was an investigation of many different definitions and conventions about space notations. This project had one part which can be cited for an appropriately good-humored and ephemeral ending to this compendium of reading experiences which incorporate mental and physical games into a procedure usually considered stationary and dignified. One of the many barriers in that project had a very pale printing of white cloudy dots on many layers of sheer blue fabric so that the accumulated white showed up enough to make a word visible—a picture of skywriting. This was presented as an example of the category "Temporary Space Printing"—the only other example of which is the large but fading grin of the Cheshire Cat in *Alice's Adventures in Wonderland*.

Originally published in the Society of Typographic Arts Journal, *vol. 2, no. 2, Spring 1981.*

SEX, LIES,
AND
STEREOTYPES

PROPAGANDA AND PERSUASION[1]
by
Dugald Stermer

Propaganda and Persuasion; a nice alliterative title, but as the two words are redundant—at least for our purposes—let's dump the second one. Propaganda, then, from *Congregatio de Propaganda Fide,* established by Pope Gregory XV and translated as Society for the Propagation of the Faith; spreading the Word among the unwashed. *Webster's Unabridged* defines the word as "the spreading of ideas, information, or rumor for the purpose of helping or injuring an institution, a cause or a person," and "a public action having such an effect." If we insert "products or services" in place of "a cause or a person" in *Webster's* definition, that pretty much describes what designers do, at least what clients pay us to do. In current but loaded terminology, propaganda is what our perceived enemies do; we, on the other hand, inform and educate.

Enough etymology; let's see what designers chose as propaganda that worked on them. And a warning: it is not a particularly pretty sight.

The hodge-podge of images you are herewith assaulted by is a portion of the unedited—but admittedly augmented—result of a request made to many conferees. About a month ago I sent a note to everyone who had registered for this conference, asking each for a single image, in slide form, that has had a "singular impact on your life." I was scrupulous not to place this within any context—such as business, personal, political, or religious—because I felt that it would be more effective if each of us defined "singular impact" for ourselves.

But I did telegraph one punch; the letter mentioned that these slides would be used within a propaganda framework, wrapped inside the larger theme of "dangerous ideas." It might still be argued that had the request come from other than a professional organization, the result might have been different—but not by much.

Whatever the quibbles, this collection is an astonishing reflection of our concerns and attitudes; especially so, considering that nowhere near the 500 recipients of the letter responded—itself a telling reaction. It should also be added that I couldn't help salting the presentation with about twenty slides of my own.

This is propaganda at work, for better or worse. From the Catholics to the Commune, the intent has always been to "have a singular impact" on others. And the just demonstrated fact is that when five hundred designers were asked to come up with a piece of effective propaganda, only a couple were actually designed by designers; and those were obviously picked because of their merit as design and not the impact of the message they conveyed.

To some degree, all of this was expected. It is clear that most of what shapes our opinions, attitudes, and behavior is accidental and random—unless you happen to believe in predestination. For example, no single image, or collection of images, did nearly as much to withdraw public support for the war in Vietnam as did the single photograph of the naked girl running from napalm. The situation was happening with appalling frequency at the time, but not until it was captured so eloquently on film did anyone take much notice; then, of course, the public became outraged.

The other face of war, victory, exemplified by the famous Iwo Jima flag-raising photograph, had an equally stunning but opposite reception; this time it increased our determination to win the war in the Pacific during World War II. This was propaganda in the literal sense as the event was restaged to obtain just that effect. Since you are clearly too young to have been much affected by the picture, I snuck it in.

No one thought to send in the Sistine Chapel ceiling nor any detail therefrom. I received but two pieces of religious imagery, regardless of deity or dogma. Yet never, ever, has so much money, art, and energy been expended at the altar of propaganda as by the missionaries.

Far more surprising, even disquieting, is that there was not a single slide of the one image designed by a real designer in the twentieth century, used to the fullest by the client, which had worldwide impact to the extent that the symbol is instantly and universally recognized, and yet remains in the context for which it was created—even though the Third Reich has, along with Hitler, long since expired.

It's astounding, come to think of it, that although the swastika has emerged and re-emerged for centuries in civilizations throughout the world, it is unlikely that for many generations to come it will have any other meaning but that associated with Nazism.

More interesting omissions: You saw no peace symbols (surely that must have affected somebody), red crosses, nuclear bomb mushroom clouds (except one that I snuck in), nor any of our craft's award-winners such as Bert Steinhauser's rat advertisement, or some of the George Lois/Carl Fischer *Esquire* covers of the 1960s, nor any of the cause posters and ads done by Glaser, Chwast, Sorel, and Davis in the East; and Marget Larsen, Howard Gossage, and Jerry Mander on the West Coast. These all had content, were designed for maximum impact, and some of them even succeeded in changing minds, raising money—whatever their intent—but they are remembered by us, if at all, for their design qualities and not for their messages.

Several factors are at work here: The first and most compelling is that most if not all of the images that have materially affected our lives are directly related to all-too-real events, things, and people. A designer simply cannot compete with childbirth, marriage, war, or any other intensely personal experience when it comes to shaping our attitudes, emotions, and opinions.

Another element is less obvious and somewhat more manageable. When we are asked to produce work of a propaganda nature—meaning that which addresses ideas and opinions as opposed to products and services—it is normally accompanied by little or no money in the hands of a client group with even less idea of how they want to pitch their message, and said message running counter to established commerce, government, and public opinion; in short, a BB gun against a tank, with you as the marksman.

At such a time, it is little wonder that given so few rewards for so much effort, and with such long odds against any kind of victory for our client; our thoughts turn, however unbidden, to irrelevancies like creative autonomy, design competitions, and the possibility of awards. Then too, the messages being presented in issue-oriented material are often far more complex than those we encounter in traditional advertising. For example, when flogging toothpaste, we can safely assume that our audience has knowledge of its existence and its benefits and even has some personal contact with it. Our job is simplified in that we just have to convince them to try our stuff.

But trying to build opposition to the war in Vietnam, say, back in 1964, was considerably more problematic. First we had to spread the news that there was a country named Vietnam, far, far away in Southeast Asia; next, that there was a civil war raging over there; third, that the U.S. was beginning to get seriously involved in that war; and fourth, that this is probably a very bad idea for the following reasons, etc.... etc....

Not, you will observe, a fitting discussion for a snappy poster, a visual pun, or a Doyle Dane Bernbach one-liner. Also, the opposition wrapped itself in the American flag and claimed patriotism and freedom for its own. But this is nothing new or unique; nearly all public service communications, with the exception of those taken on by the Ad Council and those favoring motherhood over baby raping, are by their nature underdogs; your friends become those who don't care one way or the other about the cause, for at least they don't actually shun you.

Nevertheless, BB guns were and are being sporadically fired, by, among others, some of you here today, and a number of memorable and moving images are being created. But none of them is likely to have the singular impact of children fleeing war, even in grainy black and white. You just cannot beat reality in the battle for hearts and minds.

Originally published in the AIGA Journal of Graphic Design, *vol. 7, no. 4, 1990.*

Endnotes
1. Adapted from a speech given at the AIGA conference in San Antonio in 1988.

GUERRILLA GRAPHICS
by
Steven Heller

It may seem a trivial question in the wake of America's "victory" in the Gulf, but this is a propitious time to ask: "What has graphic design done to change the world?" Desert Storm provided a textbook example of how a nation, indeed the world, could be caught up in a tornado-like propaganda effort that successfully swept aside virtually any attempt at dissent. U.S. Government control was so effective that otherwise rational people were sucked into the patriotic vortex. Few dissenters were heard in the media, least of all graphic designers as a group, and I know of only two who could muster the presence of mind and personal resources to print anti-war posters which they then distributed themselves. While this does not imply that graphic designers could have altered war policy, it does mean that few even tried.

Designer response was disappointing, but not at all surprising. For the last decade, as a profession, graphic designers have been either shamefully remiss or inexcusably ineffective about plying their craft for social or political betterment. While traditionally, graphic designers in America have tended to lean toward the liberal side of the political seesaw, in recent years one would be hard pressed to find visual confirmation of this in either the design annuals or on the street. Evidence of designer concern is found in the form of well-meaning but woefully masturbatory poster exhibitions and portfolios organized on general humanistic themes such as peace, human rights, and the environment. Getting several hundred international practitioners to design and produce their own posters may be a show of solidarity, and might occasionally produce something of symbolic value, but many of the designers invited are far more interested in throwing together another good portfolio piece.

Thematic shows which posit social relevance as a design problem are doomed to failure. When designers and illustrators have nothing to say about a subject they say it obtrusively. Themes like war and peace, the environment and the economy are simply too enormous for anyone to make sense of, let alone try to solve in one graphic image. Once we've acknowledged that designers have certain inherent limitations as message bearers, the question which must be asked is: "Can graphic designers actually do something to change the world?" The answer is "yes," if one disregards the fact that there are very limited outlets for this kind of work, and accepts the fact that being socially responsible means taking the initiative oneself, dealing rationally with issues, and having a commitment to a specific cause.

The designer's power comes directly from the design medium itself and will have positive effects only if that medium is used efficiently. Sue Coe provides a good example of what one might call "surgical propaganda": the art of effectively targeting a problem area. Though trained in England and best known in the United States as an editorial illustrator, her unique talents have been remarkably under-utilized by most editors and art directors, who are afraid of her strong, polemical voice. Indeed, it is the work of imitators who reproduce Coe's style without her content, which is more frequently published. Coe is therefore forced to find alternative outlets for political expression. In small press journals and books, print and painting exhibitions, she has focused on one critical area: animal abuse. Her lurid images of slaughterhouses, rendered in pencil, gouache, and oil, expose commercial killing centres to be as hideous as any human death camp. However, the purpose of Coe's work is not just to provoke public outrage, but to influence new legislation, and she will be satisfied if she can in any way help to alleviate the inhumane treatment of domesticated animals. In fact new animal protection statutes to U.S. Government food production restrictions are now pending, in part owing to Sue Coe's efforts.

Although lately the hermetically sealed fine art world has become more hospitable to social and political activity, mainstream graphic designers have not, in fact, created anything like a critical mass of socially relevant propaganda. Nevertheless, in recent years there has been interesting guerrilla activity in the form of strategically lobbed graphic barrages from anonymous individuals and design collectives such as Gran Fury, the graphic arm of the AIDS activist group Act Up. These guerrillas have produced an arsenal of inexpensive graphic pieces which, more often than not, are then illegally hung or pasted on lampposts, mailboxes, hoardings, and walls. The design is functionally transparent, printed on small presses or photocopiers, on cheap paper, and is usually left unsigned. The difference between many of the purposeful, professionally designed pieces and their amateurishly produced counterparts comes down to effectiveness. A professionally designed flier will occasionally have more authority, if not visual appeal, than a more casually produced one.

In addition to bringing a certain design clarity to social and political messages, the guerrillas have also had an effect on mainstream design. An increasing number of American designers are now taking a more active role in their communities by doing *pro bono* work. But *pro bono* work must not be viewed merely as conscience-soothing "charity work," but rather as a commitment. The occasional good deed is unlikely to change very much at all. What designers must do is take the initiative, select their own causes to champion, and be prepared to devote themselves to carrying out work in the cause's best interest, not their own, over a long period of time. Graphic designers might not have the power to earn millions for a cause or regularly change legislation, but they can make some changes in the world if only an effort is made.

Originally published in Eye *magazine, no. 4, vol. 1, 1991.*

DISPOSABILITY, GRAPHIC DESIGN, STYLE, AND WASTE
by
Karrie Jacobs

Several months ago, this woman who makes her living as a recycling consult-ant called me and interviewed me for a report she was doing for the Environ-mental Protection Agency. It was about how to make recycled materials commercially viable. I had written an article about package design and garbage (*Metropolis* 12/88), and I had interviewed her. She read the article, which led her to believe that I would know the answer to certain questions. She sent me a list of them in the mail and then called me up to get my response.

Here's a sample question: "Do you believe that advertising is predictive of, determining of, or merely reactive to emerging trends and values in culture?"

I wasn't even sure whether this was a multiple choice question or an essay question.

More confounding though was her telephone interview technique. She was talking to me on a speakerphone which made it sound as if she were under a mattress.

Which, Lord knows, she might have been.

And she was recording my responses not with a tape recorder, not with a pen and notepad, but with a typewriter. It sounded like an IBM Selectric to me. So she'd ask an impossible question, I would start to say something into that uncomfortable electronic dead zone that speakerphones create, and then there would be this roar of typewriter noise. I would do my best to answer, trying to ignore the clatter, trying to be incisive or thoughtful or at least smart.

I'm pretty sure that nothing I said made even the slightest bit of sense.

And I found myself trying to answer the following question: "Do you believe that a universal symbol or logo for 'environmental-friendly' or 'recycle-friendly' items would be considered a desirable feature by industries whose products would qualify to bear it?"

Of course, the short answer is yes. Emphatically yes, because corporations want to seem like they are doing the right thing. It moves products. It makes for press-release fodder.

I chose to give the long answer. I felt compelled to explain why most universal symbols or logos that get affixed to things are a bad idea. I began to explain to her, or to the dead air between her telephone speaker and her Selectric, that universal symbols—the UPC for one—tend to make unlike objects look more alike and that I personally saw this, this creeping homogeneity, as something that was every bit as threatening to our quality of life, if not the survival of the species, as the garbage crisis.

At some point, I realized that, while I was still talking, the Selectric was silent.

She wasn't the right audience for an analysis of the graphic integrity of all those symbols in which arrows go around in circles.

You might be.

You might he exactly the right audience to address this point to. You're supposed to care about this kind of thing.

The problem is that all of these symbols that various industries have cooked up to mean that their container is either recyclable or made from recycled materials or that they sincerely wished it was—and there are a lot of them—all of them are really, really ugly.

The best one—which is also the most common one—comes from the Container Corporation of America. You've seen it countless times and probably never given it much thought. It's three arrows, each given a half-twist chasing each other in a kind of rounded triangular configuration, the snake biting its own tail. The recycling consultant says the three arrows represent the cyclical aspects of an interdependent system. She thinks its a good symbol.

And it is. Conventional wisdom has it that a strong, recognizable logo is a good logo. It's just not a very interesting one.

One of the things that I think happens is that designers, faced with creating graphics to express social or political messages either take the safe touchy-feely route or, more often, make their symbols look corporate. Maybe to make the message, whatever it may be, seem more palatable to the mainstream. Maybe because that's what style dictates. Maybe it makes perfect sense. But the recycling symbol is a corporate icon representing a corporate solution to a social problem.

The funny thing is that recycling, if you take it as far as it can go, is, in our consumer culture, a very radical idea. It's inherently anti-consumption. It's about not buying. Maybe the new environmental movement needs some new symbols, ones that don't look like they came from a corporate identity firm, ones that are as radical as the changes that need to occur.

I have this theory that there's no such thing as a dangerous idea, that it's hard to get a satisfying visceral response from anyone based on an idea.

You want to get someone mad, break their car window and steal the tape deck. But say something or write something, even something that undermines the very foundations of someone's life or career, and they just shrug.

Ideas have been degraded into a commodity known as Information, and like other commodities—Smith Brothers Cough Drops, Isotoner Gloves, Lipton's Cup o' Soup—nobody pays them any real attention.

When the Ayatollah Khomeini decreed that Salman Rushdie should die because of some words he'd written, in a novel no less, it was, in a way, refreshing. Writers find it flattering when their ideas command attention.

Of course, among religious fundamentalists ideas are still dangerous because ideas—albeit a narrow and proscribed set of ideas—structure their lives.

But how about among graphic designers?

I thought, what would be considered dangerous within the context of graphic design? What would make a graphic designer angry?

I'm talking about a class of people who, for the most part, don't even get pissed off when you accuse them of plagiarism. Accuse a writer of plagiarizing, and you get your face broken. But a graphic designer will say, "Yeah. I stole it. So what?"

I *know* how to make an art director tense. You just go, "Oh, by the way, did anyone tell you there was a sidebar?" Or you say, "You didn't use that photograph, did you?" Or you say, "Did you mean for that to be just the tiniest bit crooked?"

But that won't generate real anger, just heat rash. And those aren't really ideas, just selections from the Editor's Phrase Book. But how about this:

Everything you do is garbage.

There's an idea.

I thought it might be fun to get up in front of 1,000 graphic designers and say that. I thought it might even be dangerous.

Everything you do is garbage.

Has a nice ring, doesn't it?

The thing is that I mean it.

And I mean it in two ways. There's garbage, and there's garbage.

First of all, with the possible exception of books—okay, and record jackets—everything you design is destined to be thrown away. And pretty quickly too.

Why do you think they call it ephemera?

Graphic design is the design of highly disposable items: newspapers, magazines, annual reports, packaging, promotional materials, capabilities brochures, posters. It all winds up in the garbage.

Forty-one percent (by weight) of what the people at the Environmental Protection Agency like to call the MSW Stream—meaning the Municipal Solid Waste Stream—consists of paper and paperboard. Eighty percent of that winds up in landfill.

Think about what's in your own personal landfill, the garbage can at your office, the garbage can at home. It's all stuff somebody designed. Okay, a lot of it is the stuff you yourself designed and botched, crumpled up and threw away. But someone designed that "I Love New York and the Lady, too" coffee cup. My own garbage can is full of press kits that somebody designed the hell out of.

Literally, everything you do is garbage or at least is potential garbage. After all, one man's portfolio piece is another man's debris.

This by the way, is also true of everything I do, although I'd like to think that people actually send away for those black binders and keep every issue of *Metropolis* for posterity.

For a time, my one stated ambition in life was to work for a publication that wasn't on newsprint so that my stories wouldn't come off on my hands, and so I would never again see someone wearing one of my articles as a rainbonnet.

The second way in which everything you do is garbage has to do with another type of disposability.

Style is the most disposable thing there is.

Graphic design is largely used as a way of giving things style. It's about cloaking magazines, products, corporations, events, whatever in newness.

Think about the work you do. How many times does someone call you up and say: "We want to hire you to make our publication or our identity exactly the same as it's always been." I'm not saying this doesn't happen. But design is mostly about the new.

The assumption is that when a designer is called in a lot of things are going to be thrown away.

Granted, sometimes you're asked to manufacture oldness, to do graphics that supply a make-believe history to a new product. But even that oldness is a form of newness.

I think there's an undeniable relationship between style and garbage. I think if you look at the evolution of style you will learn a tremendous amount about where garbage comes from.

One book I look at when I want to think about style is called *Package Design: The Force of Visual Selling*. It's by Ladislav Sutnar, and it was published in 1953 when packaging was just making the transition from something to put things in to an advertising medium, from substance to style.

This book is a compendium of beautiful packaging. Every package Sutnar shows is so simple; not simplistic or simplified, but simple.

It's tempting to call the designs of this era naive. But I don't think so. Not these designs. It would be, I think, incorrect to call Paul Rand's Bab-o cleanser container naive. It had a kind of knowing beatnik look. It would be a mistake also to call the old Joy dishwashing package naive. It was done by Donald Deskey associates in 1948. And Lester Beall's wrapper for McGavin's Brown Bread wasn't naive either. The main differences between those old packages and the ones we have today is style. Even the difference in the materials is related as much to style as to technology.

Technology is a style.

The oozing, hyper-real, four-color photography was once expensive and impractical. Instead the packages relied on more elemental graphic tools like wonderfully wrought type, geometric forms, and illustration.

Sutnar wrote: "From its point of sale, your package will be brought home, where it will enter the intimacy of a household. Here, removed from the context of marketing, it will be seen as never before. For it will be looked at closely, handled, used from day to day by its final possessor. As an object of unique personal possession, whether stored in a freezer or, more visibly, placed on a shelf or perhaps on milady's dressing table, your package now invokes new demands: it must embody visual delight, to the pleasure and flattery of its possessor."

I don't know about you, but I've never been pleased or flattered by a Lean Cuisine package.

When discussing what happens to a package after it leaves the store, designers today sometimes concern themselves with function—there are new kinds of toothpaste caps and detergent box closures—but they don't have much to say about the package as an individual aesthetic object. They're mostly concerned with the impact their design has in a crowd.

The scene on the supermarket shelf is like the scene outside a fashionable New York City club on a Saturday night. Desperate people dressed as stylishly as they know how to dress, looking as attractive as they know how to look, stand in a crowd trying to catch the eye of the all-powerful doorman or doorwoman. They wave their hands to get noticed, trying to get across the idea that they are good enough, beautiful enough, and cool enough to be granted permission to pay their money and come inside.

Of course, it's impossible to look or be cool under such circumstances.

The supermarket becomes a cavalcade of desperate new looks, new shapes, new materials, new ways of apportioning food, new microwavable substances. All of it is about catching your eye. All of it is about catching your interest. All of it is about that instant in which you decide to grab something off the shelf and put it in your cart.

Under such circumstances, it's impossible for design to be cool in any respect.

When I was writing about package design and garbage, I would go for walks in supermarkets. Because the logic of supermarkets—once your inside the door—is so compelling, because the packages, in the crowded, visually dynamic context of the store, seem so wonderful, I would find myself thinking: "How could anything be wrong with this? This is heaven."

But when I would stop and examine an individual package, instead of considering it as a part of the panorama, I would be amazed by how little thought was given to either aesthetics or common sense. One of the worst offenders is the awkwardly shaped squeezable Heinz ketchup bottle. It's made from a hodge-podge of plastics which makes it tough to recycle (particularly compared to glass), and it will never biodegrade. But on top of that, it's also really unattractive compared to its graceful, bevel-edged glass counterpart.

You know, there's just this overripe, overwrought, overeager quality to so much of the packaging. It's a style. It's supposed to make routine household goods—ketchup for instance—seem new. Desirable. Alluring. Sexy.

And it's this willingness to be suckered by fake newness again and again that's gotten us into trouble on the MSW stream. Sutnar, whose own work showed a fascination with repeating patterns and random geometric phenomena, must have loved the hell out of those swirly caramel candies. In his book he shows six cellophane-wrapped boxes of caramel Gyros, all lined up so you can see the cross section of the candies. You know, these are the kind of candy that looks like a jelly roll with a layer of brown caramel and white sugary stuff rolled up together.

I was looking at the picture of those candy spirals the other day and started thinking that they might make a better symbol for recyclable or made from recycled materials than those bad, boring arrows. They're kind of organically shaped and soft edged and have a very nice, primitive quality to them.

In fact, about a year ago, when I was researching my article on garbage, I spoke with a woman named Mierle Ukeles. She has a unique station in life. She's the artist in residence of the New York City Department of Sanitation. She's turning a new garbage transfer station—where garbage trucks dump their loads into barges—into a museum where people can go and see what happens to the things they throw away.

Mierle uses the spiral as a motif in her work. In Flow City, as her garbage museum will be called, visitors will walk down a ramp through a spiral collage of recyclable materials.

Going around and around on the floor, wall, and ceiling will be a snaking trail of aluminum cans, plastics, and glass. She explained to me that the spiral is the metaphor she uses for the recycling process. It represents, she said, "a philosophical attitude that creation is not the end point, that responsibility doesn't stop with the first shape, that responsibility runs constant."

Last year, a little before the presidential elections, I was sitting in this croissant joint in lower Manhattan talking with Mierle. She was telling me about how she became a garbage artist.

It started when she had a baby.

Motherhood demonstrated to her the importance of maintenance. She began to think of a city's sanitation workers and other civil servants, all the people who make the infrastructure work, as being to the city as a mother is to an infant. Both maintenance workers and mothers are involved in the process of bringing nourishment and taking away waste.

Ukeles realized that in our society maintenance is undervalued. In a society driven by newness, keeping the old well-maintained and intact—whether it's a highway overpass or a toaster oven—is troublesome and unimportant. Bridges collapse and toaster ovens get thrown away and replaced with new toaster ovens. And it's this obsession with the new, something which is fed by every medium we come into contact with, that gets us into trouble.

My question, one that I don't really know the answer to, is how important is newness?

How important is stylistic change?

I'm not talking economically. I'm talking personally, intellectually, emotionally.

Is it a matter of life and death?

It might be. Honestly. In certain ways, style is the most important thing that there is.

During a panel discussion in New York last year, Neville Brody likened style to a skin cancer. The implication, I guess, is that style is something that, if left unchecked, will spread and eventually kill off the substance that lives beneath the surface. I can see that. I mean style is kind of a glut on the market right now. Everybody's got some.

But without style, would Neville be here? Would any of us be here? I know I wouldn't.

This used to be a content country, but now it's a style country. Perhaps the appropriate name for the age we live in is not the information age, but the style age.

Maybe I'll write a book and call it *Style Anxiety*.

I've been thinking a lot about style. About what it is and how important it is. I find it hard to separate style from content.

Granted that when there is no content, only style, it's pretty obvious. And when there is not style, only content, that's glaring as well. But when they're both present, it's hard to tell where one ends and the other begins.

Style and content: Are buildings that are deconstructed outside also deconstructed inside? Will Herman Miller be doing deconstructed office furniture systems? Will Otis be doing deconstructed elevators?

Would *Emigre* magazine work if it had the same content and a different style, if it looked like, say, *Spy?* Would *Spy* work if it had the same content but looked like, say,

USA Today? Would *USA Today* work if it had the same content and looked like, say, *Emigre?*

What if the *USA Today* weather map was done up in *Emigre* graphics?

I'd like that a lot.

Does the changing style of a company's annual report—you know, dreamy illustration one year, social realism the next, headshots the year after—does that have any relationship with how the corporation actually does its business?

Would New York's World Financial Center seem like a different place if the Duffy Group did their ads instead of Drenttel Doyle, if they were all charming woodcuts instead of pseudo-fun configurations of type?

We burn our way through a lot of style; you could fuel a resources recovery plant— you know, trash to energy—on discarded style.

Recently I went someplace where they had no style. I went down to Orlando, Florida and visited EPCOT Center's Future World.

It was a business trip.

You may have forgotten that the word EPCOT is an acronym: Experimental Prototype City of Tomorrow. Walt Disney originally thought it would be an actual city with people living there. Somebody must have realized after Disney died that a city with inhabitants would be too messy, too difficult to control. Too full of styles.

At Disney World what they have instead of style is discipline. They are very good at control there. One unusual thing that they do is control the path your eyes take. Not only do they make sure you park in exactly the right parking space but they make sure that you walk into pavilions the way they want you to, and as you ride on one of the many people movers, the cars swivel to make sure you are always facing the exhibits at the optimum angle.

At EPCOT there are Kodak-sponsored Picture Spots, signs that say: "This location recommended by top photographers to help you tell the story of your visit in pictures."

Picture Spots could only be necessary in a place without style.

The future that is displayed at EPCOT is sponsored by General Motors, Exxon, Kodak and other corporations so it is all corporate Modernist in appearance and attitude. This is the 1970s version of the future. Unlike a World's Fair, this Future World has the distinct disadvantage of being permanent, which means it seems more like the past every day.

Unlike the past, the way you might experience it at Colonial Williamsburg or Henry Ford's Deerfield Village, the future is not supposed to feel so, so preserved.

This static quality to EPCOT is another earmark of the absence of style. If it had style, there would be change.

At EPCOT , they're still showing a movie at the Exxon energy pavilion bragging about supertankers docking at the beautiful port of Valdez. Some things do change at Walt Disney World. There are new attractions. EPCOT is getting a new pavilion this month, one that will bring Post-modernism to Future World.

"Would it be appropriate," the PR woman asked the architect who was about to give me a tour of the Wonders of Life, as the new pavilion is called, "to describe the color scheme as turquoise and magenta?"

The architect, an "imagineer" in Disney talk, replied, "Yes, I think so."

Inside the gold geodesic Wonders of Life dome, it is all Post-modern colors. There are pediments, arches, and references to vernacular style. It's Memphis. It's MTV. It's Pee-Wee. The cliches of 1980s design are all there.

I suppose this is a form of recycling. We are just about done with Post-modernism. We are throwing it away, and Disney World has picked it up and reused it, fit it into their vision of the future. If you're not encumbered with a strong sense of style, wearing hand-me-downs isn't a problem.

And speaking of Post-modernism, I visited the new Michael Graves designed hotels which are still under construction on a site near EPCOT. The Swan and the Dolphin, as they're called, are fairly rectilinear brick buildings, ornamented with giant copper green swans, clamshells, and urns, and painted with sea-green waves. Disney World doesn't refer to this style of architecture as Post-modern. They call it Entertainment Architecture. And here, I think they have done a superior job of phrasemaking. It's a much truer way of describing the style.

Entertainment architecture. They have a way with words there. The garbage cans all say "waste please."

I left EPCOT and the Orlando area, where every place you could eat, drink, be entertained, or sleep seemed to be part of a chain, with an appreciation for the importance of style in our lives.

Everything you do is garbage.

And you know what, maybe I've got this whole thing backward. Maybe the important idea isn't that stylistic change begets garbage. Maybe it's that garbage allows stylistic change to occur.

We all generate a lot of garbage. It's our by-product and our product.

Generating stylistic garbage is part of the creative process. It gives us breathing room.

Generating real garbage is also part of the creative process. And this garbage is beginning to deny us breathing room.

And garbage is a hot topic …

Garbage. Our problem with garbage, our obsession with garbage. Our fucked-up love-hate affair with garbage.

So we are obligated to think about garbage. That might mean something very simple, like getting clients to use recycled paper stock for their publications. Creating a market for recycled products is as important as bundling paper and putting it on the curb.

We are obligated to think about garbage not just because we are so intimately involved with the disposable, but because it is now the style to be environmentally concerned. And we are style-conscious people.

Environmentalism has been a style before. We've been through that. We've worn our ecology flags on our denim sleeves. Now it's a style again.

So maybe the most important thing we can do is figure out a way to use the style of graphic design to make the new environmentalism more than just a style.

Originally published in the AIGA Journal of Graphic Design, *vol. 7, no. 4, 1990.*

CAN DESIGN BE SOCIALLY RESPONSIBLE?

by
Michael Rock

Responsibility is the design buzz word of the nineties, there's no escaping it. Pick up a design magazine you're you're sure to find it pop up somewhere. Big-shots, settling back after weeding through the morass of entries from some design fashion contest, find time to lament the lack of social commitment in the work they just finished awarding. Professors scramble to inject some political content into their typography assignments. The AIGA even devoted an entire conference to the theme, giving all the regulars a chance to gather and explain how their work has been pro-active all along.

Somehow it seems to be about ninety percent pure spin. With all the talk about social responsibility, do we really understand the complexity of the problem as it pertains to design? The issue of responsibility in a profession involved in the modulation of information is daunting. There is an implicit *power* involved in graphic design that is derived from an involvement with image production, and all power carries with it responsibility. But to date, we have not sufficiently addressed this aspect of the question. Is social responsibility a function of the content, the form, the audience, the client and/or the designer?

According to conventional wisdom it comes down to two basic issues: 1) Don't work for cigarette manufacturers or for companies that produce neutron bombs and nerve gas; and 2) be sensitive to the impact of the materials you specify for your clients. Eight color metallic ink on coated paper is a bad; soy pigment on recycled stock is good. But this elementary reading of the surface problem tends to obscure the more important issues underneath.

In the era of the mega-corporation the delineation between companies is increasingly vague. If you refuse work from the bomb company, will you work for the bank that finances it? What about the art museum it funds? Or the cable TV station it owns? If the designer is an advocate for the client, whose will and message is paramount? There is a confusion here between social and personal responsibility. The designer, like any professional, must examine the implication of any activity or client relationship in light of his/her own position. These are points of individual conscience and integrity rather than social responsibility.

As for the ecological issue, no one comes out against the environment and as the "printed on recycled paper" tag becomes ever more fashionable convincing clients to go the green or environment-friendly route becomes progressively easier. Of course, the end result of a liberal environmental plan is positive whatever the corporate motivation to adopt it may have been. While specifying less noxious materials may be the start—although the exact composition of recycled products is shrouded in controversy and often the term is pure marketing hype—the connection between design and waste may not be so easily remedied.

Perhaps the most significant environmental impact designers could instigate would be convincing their clients not to produce half the useless printed materials they are being commissioned to create or to propose solutions that are significantly reduced in size and complexity. As this is tantamount to encouraging real estate developers to promote open-space legislation, there's not much chance of it happening to any great extent. The profit-minded practitioner is not going to argue to eliminate a project that will lead to a big fee. Enlightened self-interest aside, the laws of capitalist consumption insure this will not be a wide spread phenomenon. To really address this issue, designers will have to redefine how they bill for projects to break the correlation between the bulk of the final product and the design fee.

The designer's social responsibility is a responsibility for creating meaningful forms. Designers may control the conduit through which information passes yet often s/he is unaware of the basic function of the very images being transmitted. The socially responsible designer should be conscious of the cultural effect of all products that pass through the studio, not all of which have great significance. Designers have their hand in such a wide array of projects—from maps to clothing catalogues—that it would be absurd to say that there was a single identifiable social position in the work. Projects may range from the absolutely essential to the downright deceitful. Without evoking some preassigned, politically correct standards, is a working definition of socially responsible content possible?

Dilemmas of personal conscience and environmental sensitivity aside, our preoccupation should be with the facets of graphic design that are directly related to society and our function within it. While we may have abandoned a purely pragmatic description of design, the basic social role—that of mediating, organizing, translating, and creating access to information—remains intact. So is responsibility a function of the form, the content, the materials, or the client? The idea of acceptable form is dubious; ecologically sensitive materials go without saying; content is too broad as to be definable; and the client situation is murky.

It seems that forgoing some standard acceptable content, the issue will be judged on a case by case basis. Most designers are able to juggle several seemingly contradictory accounts at the same time, each having specific value. Some see certain projects as means to fund other more vital, and less lucrative, activities.

Professional design expertise is expensive; only the most profitable companies are able to afford access to sophisticated communication consultation (and we *should* be concerned about this nexus of money, power, and communication). Yet interestingly many designers do their most effective, evocative work for their non-paying accounts. The point of taking on political work or *pro bono* projects is to use the tools of graphic design to help an organization fully access the audience that needs the services or information it offers. *Pro bono* work most often supports groups that service the segments of society that could benefit from—and are routinely excluded from—the information culture. The unfortunate reality is that many designers see the donation of service as an opportunity for a creative liberty they never realize with their paying clients (perhaps they feel empowered and self righteous through their charity) rather than focusing on solving the real communication problem at hand.

A definitive definition of social responsibility may elude us. Perhaps the best we can hope for is a recognition of the complex issues involved in communication. In the time when the access to real information among the disadvantaged seems in increasing peril and where power and money control most of the means of producing and dispersing it, the goal of developing simple and effective mass audience communication seems especially relevant. Clarity may once again become an important social concern, not by fiat but because the content is too vital and important to obscure. Message may indeed rise up over style, but style will be recognized for the important cultural values it transmits. Perhaps the most socially *irresponsible* work is the over-designed, over-produced, typographic stunts that serve no real function, speak only to other designers and the cultural elite, and through opulence and uselessness revel in a level of conspicuous consumption that glorifies financial excess.

Originally published as "Responsibility: Buzzword of the Nineties," in the AIGA Journal of Graphic Design, *vol. 10, no. 1, 1992.*

RED, WHITE, AND BLAND
by
Nicholas Backlund

Think back for a moment to the 1988 U.S. presidential campaign. What images spring most readily to mind? Is it Michael Dukakis astride an M1 assault tank? Is it an endless stream of murderous convicts passing through a revolving door? Or is it George Bush, paterfamilias, on the lawn of his Kennebunkport estate? Can you recall one great poster, brochure, campaign button, or bumper sticker? For that matter, can you conjure up even one single campaign image that was not aired on television? The chances are that you cannot, and this is no accident.

Each American political campaign brings with it the earnest assertions of hopeful candidates, the squandering of huge sums of money, and a visual wasteland of poorly designed campaign materials. In an arena where image is equated with substance, design is curiously absent. So pervasive is the mediocrity of contemporary political propaganda that the material put out by opposing camps is often indistinguishable. More disheartening still is that the level of graphic standards too often reflects the level of serious content.

Recent years have seen European political parties, most notably in England, France, and Italy, enlisting the aid of professional designers and large design consultancies to sharpen their images in the eyes of the electorate. Admittedly there are cultural and historic reasons why certain European parties might be more apt to turn to designers than their American counterparts, and one could reasonably argue that developing a sophisticated corporate image for a political party is a cynical act of pangloss intended to fool gullible voters. Elections, of course, are never won or lost on the standards of a party's graphic design. But design is a form of communication, and communication is, or should be, essential to politics. In America, while the Democrats and Republicans enlist advertising agencies and consultants of every stripe to assist them in campaigning, they do not turn to designers. In fact, judging from a selection of printed matter put out by both the Republicans and the Democrats, there seems to be a pervasive ethic of anti-design.

But what does design have to do with politics, especially in America? In politics, as in anything else, graphic design is used to convey information and, hopefully, sway opinion. As the level of political discourse in the United States continues to erode, voters, inevitably, are becoming frustrated with the empty words and half-truths that are the hallmark of political expediency. Among the root causes of the public's disenchantment are the methods used by politicians, and the parties to which they belong, to communicate with the public.

On a national level, what do the two major parties tell us about themselves, and how do they tell us? There are general attributes associated with each party that are used to broadly define its identity. The Republicans tell us they are pro-family, strong on defense and fiscally conservative, for example. The Democrats tell us they are socially progressive, support civil rights, and favor economic justice. How the two parties translate these ideas into visual ciphers offers a revealing look at how they view themselves and the electorate.

The responsibility for coordinating the party image on a general level falls to the two committees, the Republican National Committee and the Democratic National Committee. These two organizations perform a variety of tasks to further the interests of their respective parties and to get their candidates elected. While most of their efforts involve research, strategy, policy development and, especially, fund-raising; they are also charged with promoting a coherent party image, be it Republican or Democrat.

In America, party image is more closely tied to policy stances than it is to specific visual identities. The sheer number of candidates, the size of the country and the range of positions taken by members of the same party largely prevent all Republicans, say, from adopting a universal "Republican identity." But both national committees do provide their candidates with a sort of generic umbrella identity that serves more to wrap them in the colors of the flag than to identify them as either a Republican or a Democrat.

On the most basic level, party affiliations are signified by, the two parties' logos. Although originally derived from specific historical circumstances that lent them significance, they are today no more meaningful than the branding that distinguishes two types of toothpaste.

The official logotype of the GOP and the Republican, National Committee is the elephant. Following the election of 1874, which the Republicans handily won, the cartoonist Thomas Nast portrayed the Republican vote as a fierce, marauding elephant trampling the Democratic planks of Inflation, Repudiation, and Tammany Reform. The Democrats, in Nast's cartoon, are represented by two geese, squawking and flapping their wings, helpless in the face of the elephant's might.

Nast's cartoon was a concise visual representation of Republican electoral dominance. By succinctly conveying the power of the Republicans, Nast's elephant became a natural, readymade symbol for the party. If practically no one today remembers the genesis of the logo, it is no wonder. The marauding beast has been transformed into a docile proxy for the flag. His strong, muscular back is now a benign blue hump emblazoned with three white stars. His furrowed brow and sharp tusks are gone, replaced by a soft red silhouette. He now resembles nothing so much as patriotic zoo signage.

The Democrats, of course, have the donkey. The origin of the Democratic donkey is more obscure, and its meaning less flattering to the party that it has come to symbolize, than is Nast's elephant. The Democrats were first linked with an ass, or donkey in a lithograph of unknown authorship that appeared in 1837. Entitled "The Modern Balaam and His Ass," the cartoon depicts Andrew Jackson astride a donkey, whipping it furiously with a stick that represents his veto.

"The Modern Balaam" is a reference to an Old Testament figure who came to represent the archetypal false prophet. It is the donkey however, that quickly became linked with the Democratic party in the public eye. Although Nast was not the originator of the Democratic donkey, as is often asserted, he did use the donkey to satirize the Democrats after 1837. And, perhaps figuring that it's easier to join them than to fight them, the Democratic party itself finally appropriated the donkey as its national symbol.

The Democratic National Committee recently adopted a new logo, a stylized flame in gold and black or, alternately, in red and blue, to symbolize the Democratic Party. Glenn Hoffman, direct mail coordinator for the DNC, says he is uncertain of the original reasoning behind the switch. Presumably, the device refers to the flame of liberty or to John F. Kennedy's legacy. Whatever the meaning of the new logo, it has proven to be unpopular with candidates. "The donkey has been associated with the Democratic party for over a hundred years," Hoffman says, "and state and local candidates will almost always use it instead of the flame." Considering that the stylized flame closely resembles the logos of both the French National Front and the Italian Social Movement—both far right parties—this is perhaps not surprising.

Whether it's an elephant, a donkey, or a flame, logos operate on only the simplest level. They serve as quick identifiers on bumper stickers, for example, to let people know to which party a candidate belongs. They no longer have any real meaning beyond the generic label "Democrat" or "Republican." Shaping the larger identity of the parties falls to the advertising, media, and communications departments within each of the national committees.

A distinction should be made between the graphics associated with individual political campaigns and the parties in general. Generally, candidates will hire independent advertising agencies and media consultants to develop the promotional materials for their campaigns, while relying on the national committees for policy advice, strategy, polling results and the like. The national committees promote presidential candidates or those running for key offices and provide, if asked, "political communications" services to those candidates.

More typical of the committees' role in shaping party image is the work of their in-house publications departments. Each national committee publishes all sorts of material ranging from newsletters and magazines to brochures targeting various voter groups or espousing party doctrine on specific issues. These publications are intended to reinforce the party line in the minds of its constituents, alert them to upcoming elections and, of course, soak them for cash.

This political junk mail is really the only form of mass communication that the national parties have with their members on a regular basis. Given the enormous amount of time, money, and energy that is spent on partisan television advertisements, one might reasonably assume that comparable effort might be spent on more traditional media. A spot check at the two national committees suggests otherwise.

Of either party, the Republican National Committee has the most sophisticated in-house graphic design capabilities. Marcia Brown, director of graphic services for the RNC, oversees fifteen designers and production assistants who are responsible for designing and producing the printed material the party sends out. Brown's department is fully equipped for desktop publishing and the RNC houses a print shop complete with its own Linotronic.

"Basically," Brown says, "we design brochures promoting generic Republican propaganda for any project coordinated at the national level aimed at a Republican audience." Recent examples of this propaganda include a pamphlet geared to Asian voters, one touting the Republican's record on crime, one explaining the difference between Republicans and Democrats to women voters, and one designed to bring African-Americans into the GOP fold.

Raising questions of design at the RNC, such as "How do you try to convey Republican values visually," brings an awkward silence. As far as can be deduced from the materials published, there is no concept of design at work at all. The printed material is composed of a jumble of clumsy typefaces that spell out bombastic one-liners.

One reason for the poor quality of the brochures lies in the RNC's assessment of its audience and their notion of design. "Your average person doesn't think of the Republican Party as being associated with glitzy, contemporary graphic presentations," Brown says. "People don't look at us that way, so we are very simple and just get the message out." It is not uncommon for non-designers to associate the idea of graphic design with glitz and flash. It does seem incongruous, however, that one of the most sophisticated political organizations in the world would publish material that looks so terrible, with the purported intention of strengthening its cause.

"We are selling a product, in a sense," Brown says, "but people don't look at a political product as being extravagant like a soft drink commercial. I don't think they would trust it." This notion that people somehow regard "political products" as being immune to the same type of promotion as beverages is echoed by the RNC's director of communications, Ernie Mills. "Going for a more flamboyant look, for us, would be inappropriate," he says. "We tend to take a more, well, conservative approach."

At the RNC, there is no all-embracing concept that directs the visual promotion of the party. Under a previous director, Mills says, the publications and media departments were merged in an effort to "produce a unified and consistent message for the public." Following that director's departure, however, the two departments were separated. Now, Mills says, the inclination is to bring them together again.

But what is the unified and consistent message that the RNC wants to create and how do they convey it visually? "There is really no grand scheme behind our approach to design," Mills says, "and we don't have any one person who is responsible for the look of our design." If there is an overriding concept behind the RNC's approach to graphic propaganda it is, says Mills, "to be fairly straightforward and fairly elegant with a look of quality and value."

Neither Mills nor Brown, it should be pointed out, is a designer. Brown has an advertising and public relations background and Mills was previously involved in desktop publishing and journalism. In Brown's own words, most of her staff is composed of "technicians," a factor which is surely partly responsible for the look of the material her department produces. But as Mills readily admits: "If it looks too glitzy or expensive, people will question what we spend our money on. Our job is to get Republicans elected, not win design awards." Mills' audience, presumably, does not question the millions of dollars spent on glitzy televised political advertising.

Whatever the shortcomings of the design department at the RNC, it is still light-years ahead of the Democratic National Committee. The DNC does not even have a graphic services department. What it does have is a division that creates all of the DNC's direct mail advertising and a quarterly newsletter.

Unlike the RNC's generic Republican propaganda, the DNC's direct mail is "almost entirely geared towards fund-raising," says its direct mail coordinator, Glenn Hoffman. While the Republicans produce poor graphics in service to their cause, at least they produce them. Apart from the newsletter, the Democrats' efforts seem geared exclusively towards increasing revenues. This being the case, there are few examples of how they interpolate their ideals into graphic statements on the national level.

The DNC, however, does have an concept that determines the look of its graphics, such as they are. "If we have an in-house style," says Hoffman, "I'd have to characterize it as 'Presidential,' because obviously we're trying to get a Democrat elected to the White House." For the purposes of his direct mail campaigns, the Presidential look is fostered through the use of ivory or grey paper stock. This concept, Hoffman says, is especially evident during presidential elections when "the White House becomes our *de facto* logo."

If the Democrats' visual identity has been superseded by the dictates of direct mail solicitation formulas, it's merely a reflection of their priorities, and it is certainly no sin to place other priorities above a cogent visual identity. It would be wrong, however, to assume that the influence of either national committee on the shape of American political graphics ends with the materials that they themselves produce. Each national committee houses a vast repository of information and resources to assist candidates to best position themselves—strategically, politically, and visually—in the eyes of the electorate.

An example of how the national committees can affect the tone and substance of political discourse on even a local level can be seen in a campaign guide issued by the Republican National Committee to candidates running in state legislative and local elections. Along with useful advice on such matters as fundraising, grass roots organizing, campaign planning and the like, is a section devoted to "Campaign Communications." Campaign communications, the manual explains, involves how a candidate transmits his or her message to the public, whether through speeches, printed materials, graphics or "earned media coverage."

The manual urges candidates to "consider these 'tongue-in-cheek' guidelines for successful campaign communications: 'Truth is what the people believe'; 'People are susceptible to flattery'; 'People are greedy.'" While the manual's unflinchingly cynical view of human nature is to be admired for its candor, the practical effect of this advice is a debasement of the notion of true "communication." The manual then goes on to discuss the role of issues in a political campaign: "It has been said that issues are the 'Catch-22' of politics; we know that very few people vote solely on the issues, yet candidates are still expected to talk about them and have opinions on them." It may seem surprising that political candidates are expected to have opinions, but the real use of issues seems to be as, in the manual's words, "a vehicle for building a candidate's name recognition and image." Once a candidate has established an image, the manual offers some straightforward advice on how to represent that image graphically. It explains that the design of campaign graphics should be the essence of simplicity, focusing the viewer's eye first on the candidate's last name, second on the office for which he or she is running and thirdly on the candidate's first name.

The manual describes the successful use of graphic design in a political campaign in terms familiar to anyone who has suffered through the relentless bombardment of advertising during an election. "In political graphic art, repetition helps transform the message into an identifiable entity." The manual also counsels against the use of shadow-effect and three-dimensional typography—sound advice which, incidentally, is consistently ignored by the RNC's own in-house graphics department—and adds helpfully that "if you need to pay a graphic artist to create [a logo] design, you'll only have to pay for the logo once."

Even if the advice contained in the manual is useful in a practical sense, it is also disingenuous, lacking in ethical considerations and pusillanimous with regard to graphic design. But on the most utilitarian level, the advice is certainly time-tested and proven effective. Although it does not encourage candidates to lie or be dishonest, it does suggest that a campaign can emphasize a candidate's form over his or her content and still be successful. The realities of getting elected are becoming increasingly dispassionate and it is understandable, if not exactly laudatory, that candidates feel forced to use and manipulate the tools at their disposal.

The prospect of designers becoming a force in political campaigns, to the degree that advertising agencies, media advisers, and image consultants are currently, is dim at best. Yet some of the most forceful graphic art in the past has been created in the service of politics. One need only think of El Lissitzsky, James Montgomery Flagg, or the legions of artists hired by the government during World War II to begin to imagine the potential of design to sharpen political debate.

Not only would the aesthetics of political communications improve dramatically, but the designer's talents of distillation and forceful presentation might even help to rouse an apathetic electorate. Instead of the vapid negativity of televised advertisements, which strike quickly and offer no chance for reflection, perhaps the use of designers could give rise to a new visual vocabulary of politics. And this work needn't be tame or "nice," but could be extraordinarily powerful. Some real visual bite could be added to the thrust and parry of partisan politicking.

There is no evidence to suggest that politicians will soon move away from the craven patriotic boosterism of red, white, and blue visual platitudes. But even safe symbols like red, white, and blue bunting can become political liabilities if not designed properly, as the Democrats discovered after their 1988 convention. In a calculated effort to make the hues of the American tricolor that draped the stage come across more vibrantly on television, they were altered, which then opened the Democrats up to accusations of practicing "pastel patriotism."

Even in the cynical, calculating world of contemporary politics, the thoughtful use of designers could go a long way toward raising the level of public political discourse above empty symbolism to embrace the substantial issues that are, or should be, the stuff of politics. Designers can't save politics from its own culture, but they do represent an under-used and much needed political commodity.

Originally published in I.D. *magazine, March/April 1991.*

THE BOAT
by
Paula Scher

Dear Paula:[1]
Thumbing through the latest AIGA annual, we ran across the picture of Pentagram's partners gathered together on a boat on the Thames and we couldn't help noticing that you were the only woman in the group. And then we recalled that the art department at CBS Records wasn't exactly a bastion of feminism, either.

How would you feel about writing 1000 or so words for us on the subject of breaking into and working for the boys' clubs? (I know it's not an original topic, but you always provide an original point of view.) Has your experience in the male-dominated Pentagram of the early nineties been different from working in the male-dominated CBS Records of the early eighties and before? Have you ever suffered tokenism? At the Chicago AIGA Conference last year, Cheryl Heller remarked that being the lone woman among male professionals brought an element of surprise that worked to her advantage. She could easily soar above the low expectations of her colleagues and clients. Has this been your experience? Does your status as a woman executive bring more responsibility in terms of mentoring other women both within and beyond your workplace? Do you consider yourself a role model? Has role-modeling been thrust upon you? Please let me know.

Sincerely,
Julie Lasky
Managing Editor

DEAR JULIE:

I've long resisted the notion of writing a "woman's issue" piece, or what it's like to be the only woman blah-blah. I'm genuinely uncomfortable with the subject because I have conflicting feelings about it. I'd have to have been an ostrich not to have experienced the painful excluvisity of corporate boys' clubs, glass ceilings, and financial exploitation. I can sing along with any woman's group about the sexist-insensitive-noncommunicative-emotionally-inept nature of men and add a few two-syllable adjectives of my own for good measure. But my confusion comes not in the worthy politicizing of women's issues, but in their valid application to a life in graphic design.

Every time I give a presentation to a design group, I'm asked what it's like to be a woman blah-blah. As I'm invited to give the presentation, I'm told that women will really want to hear about being a woman blah-blah. I estimate that sixty percent of the calls I receive to speak or judge are related to woman blah-blah. They go like this: "Hello, can you judge the annual Peoria Hang Tag competition, please say yes because we need a female juror." How I envy my male partners who are invited to speak based on their achievements and prestige as opposed to their sex. I cannot separate my own achievements from being a woman blah-blah.

On the other hand, the tokenism has had its advantages. I've been able to attain a visibility that *might* have been harder to come by if I were male. The visibility may be helpful professionally, but it's always clouded in a veil of "women's issues." How ironic that the grand attempt in the graphics community to promote women designers (me in this case) serves to undermine and diminish achievement.

The thing of it is, I never set out to be the only woman blah-blah. I set out to be a designer. I set out to be designer who could design all kinds of things well, with the hope that those things that I designed well would lead me to even more things to design. I set out as a designer, not thinking that being a woman had much to do with anything. What mattered was the work. After all, designers produce tangible products. You can *see* the results. There is physical evidence of success or failure. I believed that good work brought more good work and that money, while dictated by marketplace, could mushroom, to a degree, in relationship to good work and reputation. I've held these beliefs for twenty years. I've *had* to, or I would not have been able to continue to work. The ability to continually produce work, make professional changes, take advantage of business opportunities as they arise, and create the opportunities yourself when they don't arise is absolutely key to the growth and development of a designer, male or female.

I don't believe that pursuing this course while happening to be a woman is particularly special, nor do I believe there should be a special standard for women. I haven't "broken" into boys' clubs. I am merely following the path of a life in design at a time when doors are opening for women, not merely because they are women, but because they are successfully following that path.

Which brings me to the photograph of the Pentagram partners on the boat. It is interesting how one photographic image can perfectly encapsulate my feelings. You said you couldn't help noticing that I was the only woman on the boat. I was less interested in the fact that I was the only woman; I already knew that. I was struck more by the pure visual physicality of the situation—not the oddity of the sex, but the strangeness in scale. There I am, halfway down the side of the boat in between rugged David Hillman and James Biber, who is twice my size. Kit Hinrichs, who is actually sitting behind James Biber, has a head that is half again as large as mine. And Colin Forbes, who stands with John McConnel and Lowell Williams, way in the back, appears much larger than me. I look like a person who was actually standing far beyond Lowell Williams, and was then stripped into the middle of the photograph but not blown up in proportion to the new position.

The photograph made me look at my own professional situation, and those of other women today, as a matter of strange scale. I'm in the picture, but I'm not blown up in proportion to the new position. (If the photograph had pictured the same number of men and women, the scale wouldn't be strange, I'd just be short.)

I saw a similar thing in the *New York Times* several weeks ago. There was Donna Shalala standing next to Bill Clinton and Al Gore and some male senators and newly appointed Cabinet members and she was not blown up in proportion to her new position. The same week in the *New York Times,* I read about how women's groups were upset with Clinton for not appointing enough women to cabinet posts and Clinton railed against the quotas. All of this served to diminish the wonderful accomplishments of the excellent women who were appointed. One woman in the group. Two women in the group. Their individuality is lost and all one sees is the strangeness of scale.

I'm physically odd at Pentagram, the way I'm physically odd at corporate meetings with clients who happen to be men. I'm physically odd to women who work for men in groups and view me as out of scale to the men in those groups.

I joined Pentagram the way I set out to design. I had had a business with one male partner for seven years. We had been split for one year and I continued running the business myself. I was offered the opportunity to join Pentagram and I took it because I wanted to design things well and get more new things to design. There's no more to it than that. No crusade, no breaking down back room doors. I took some personal risk to take advantage of a new business opportunity, with the price being the daily discomfort of being out of scale.

I can't equate Pentagram and CBS Records. Pentagram is a group of very intelligent, talented, and relatively sensitive men who design well and want to get more new things to design. I may be out of scale at Pentagram, but I was out of sync at CBS Records. That's much worse than being out of scale. One doesn't have to be a woman to be put of sync. All that requires is for one to have a completely different set of values than the larger group. Being out of scale can be uncomfortable. Being out of sync is dangerous. Women need to learn the difference.

It seems to me from your letter, especially in reference to Cheryl Heller's talk, that you are looking for some sort of *modus operandi* for surviving in male-dominated working situations. There isn't one. Men are different. Situations are different. And women are different. The only thing that is a constant for me is my relationship to my work. When I find myself in a professional situation that is purely about politics or personalities and not about the effectiveness of design, I tend to fail.

Which brings me back to my ambiguous feelings about women's issues in relationship to design. A profession that has been long dominated by men is changing. There are simply more women. There are more women who are terrific designers, more women running their own businesses, more women corporate executives, more women changing the scale of things and appearing out of scale in the process.

There are also more underpaid women, more women juggling careers and motherhood, more women who feel squeezed out in a bad economy, more women going to art school and going nowhere afterwards, and more women who are resentful because of their lack of success "because they are women."

There are more women in design groups, more women's panels, more women mentoring women, more women who want to mentor them, more women looking for women's role models, and more women who don't like other women's success.

I don't know what my responsibility is in all this. I'm not sure I have one as it relates to women in general. There are things I've done naturally through relationships that existed by chance. I felt supportive of the terrific women designers at CBS Records because they were my friends. I have encouraged talented students, male and female, equally. I've supported those people I know and cared about who want to design well and get more things to design. It is not a planned activity, or a duty: it is simply part of a life in design.

I don't want to be anyone's "role model." I dislike the term because it diminishes my life by implying that I'm playing some kind of role for other people's benefit. It places my entire life out of scale.

This takes me back to the picture on the boat, where I'm confronted with my own image within a group. The boat ride on the Thames was really lovely. There was a good lunch, terrific conversation, and all in all the most pleasant part of a partner's meeting. I don't remember feeling like an oddity on that boat. But in the photo there is that strangeness of scale. Women's issues in design are focused on scale. We count the numbers, look at the statistics, and demand change, and all the while change is occurring. Change doesn't come in one great thump. It comes one by one by one by one, and it looks kind of funny. And then it doesn't.

Sincerely,

Paula Scher

Partner, Pentagram Design, Inc.

Originally published in Print *magazine, March/April 1993.*

Endnotes

1. These letters were exchanged between Julie Lasky, managing editor of *Print,* and Paula Scher. Lasky's letter has been edited for brevity; Scher's is reproduced in it's entirety.

I WANT TO SEX YOU UP: FABIEN BARON AND THE PURSUIT OF THE SEXY
by
Michael Rock

If Marky Mark can't fondle his jones in Times Square, where can he? There's probably more masturbation-per-square-foot there than any place else on earth. It seems appropriate that the hard-bodied teen idol, known to ignite twelve-year-old passion by dropping his Calvins and *holding on,* should tower over this citadel of onanism.

Marky in Calvins is just the latest in a series of controversial images from art director Fabien Baron. Baron cornered the sex-image market last year with the concurrent release of three highly visible projects: the new *Harper's Bazaar, MadonnaSex,* and the revamped campaign for Calvin Klein. And while he denies a secret desire to lord over a dynasty of bus shelters and shopping mall posters, the French-born designer has made his mark expropriating sexual symbols from the edges of urban culture and dropping them squarely on mainstream America.

Baron offers mall-dom a diluted sexuality, softening homoerotic or cultural references with pop stars and supermodels. So Marky Mark, the all-white rapper in all-white drawers supplies the homogenized version of black culture for the mall-rat contingent. Rapper LL Cool J proffers this bit of cultural analysis of crotch grabbing: "I guess it has a lot to do with male power. The black man doesn't have economic power, but he still has the power of procreation, the power to create, so the black man, he's grabbing for that last bit of power that he has." Mark helps himself to the style and combines it with his New Kids on the Block brother mass-market appeal. In a recent *Voice* article, Lisa Jones rightfully points out that Mark co-opts the black style for suburban consumption. "The straddle, the dance moves, the baggy pants, the drawers showing, the jay bigger than yours, we've seen it all before." Replace Mark with a forty-foot black man in Times Square "and the *Times* might run an anxious editorial on billboards that promote urban violence."

The Calvin Klein ad is actually the second famous crotch-grabbing image from Fabien Baron and photographer Herb Ritts. The original—a shot of Madonna rampant—graced the last of the three issues of *Interview* magazine Baron designed. While *Interview* wasn't enamored with his direction, apparently Madonna was enough to hire Baron & Baron, the studio he shares with his wife Sciascia, to design that short lived phenomena, the *Sex* book. The critics lambasting the *Sex* book for its lack of true eroticism—an hilarious display of mostly male writers breathlessly proclaiming their disinterest in Madonna's naked body—missed the graphic erotica wrapped up in Baron's packaging: slick mylar bag, icy aluminum cover, luscious printing, extravagant typography. *Sex* was a print designer's indulgent fantasy, all surface hedonism and empty pornographic production values.

Sex—the act not the book—is a big part of Baron's signature. Most of his design has been centered around the style industries: magazines like *GQ, Italian Vogue, Interview, New York Woman* as well as Barney's, Kikit, and Issay Miyake. Although his images may raise the hackles of diverse groups, from family values crusaders to feminist critics, sitting in his office at *Harper's* on a dreary New York morning, he seems blithely unperturbed by the public reactions. "People are still very reserved about sexuality in America. They can't accept that this is just fun and that's it ... which is better for advertising because you need a little controversy to make a good commercial."

That commitment to the aesthetics of controversy attracted the publicity-loving Calvin Klein, a man well known for a few overtly sexual ads of his own. "Calvin likes a certain sexiness and the fact that sexiness is controversial is helpful. He's looking for a certain image of sex and so am I." Klein turned to Baron for help with his floundering corporate image that suddenly seemed hopelessly dated. The monumental Bruce Weber images that brought Calvin Klein so much attention in the eighties were played out. Baron helped develop the new CK line in an attempt to bridge to a younger market and Marky Mark became the newest of Calvin Klein's marketing gods.

That link between promotion and sexuality is the underlying key to Baron's success. "Sexiness," the adjective of choice for both Klein and Baron, is transformed into a talismanic mantra; an elusive quality determined and mass-produced by a small group of men—fashion designers, art directors and photographers—for a broad audience of women. (Women still comprise a disproportionate percentage of consumers.) The mass female audience is the palette on which images of male fantasy are ultimately projected; the distinct product of a world imagined by men.

"It is impossible to look at modern advertising ..." wrote Raymond Williams "without realizing that the material object being sold is never enough." Fantasy is devised through large institutional strategies, coupled with saleable products. The structures that determine the content of fashion images are more or less invisible. To a great extent, images of women are directed by men. Inevitably women relate to images of women through the lens of masculine desire. Baron puts it more bluntly: "There's nobody better than the man to know how a woman looks best."

Art direction and fashion photography are all-male games in popular imagination. The swank photographer in his swinging digs has been a staple of popular culture, typified by Fred Astaire's portrayal of Richard Avedon in *Funny Face,* Antonioni's *Blow Up,* and countless other movies, novels, and articles. Avedon and art director Alexey Brodovich, the quintessential male fashion team, are credited with the invention of the modern fashion magazine—ironically the *Harper's Bazaar* of the thirties and forties— supplying the visual style to editor Carmel Snow's vision of the new American woman. (*Harper's* current editor, Liz Tiberis, compares Baron favorably to Brodovich, a comparison Baron rejects: "I'm not influenced by anyone …")

Fashion photography has the cachet of a solo profession of freewheeling, guns-for-hire existing outside of the societal and sexual mores of the businessman and the husband. That fantasy taps into some deep heterosexual male forms; the playboy, the suave womanizer, the maverick with his stable of beautiful women, ignoring the huge influence of gay culture on the profession. The mythic photographer holds an uncontested position of power over the women that work for him. An impassive voyeur, he's paid top dollar to stage his elaborate fantasies. These expensive tableaux are decorated with women bought and paid for, performing on command, enacting a specific image of the elusive "sexiness." Photographer Helmut Newton's remark: "If a photographer says he is not a voyeur, he's an idiot" is especially resonant in regards to the art director. Concealed in the shadows, he gets the pictures in the end. The ultimate fetishist, he pays the bills, orders the scenes, determines the action, but never participates in active production.

The presence of photographer and art director is implicit in the fashion spread. The details of the image are indices of male taste. The art director imbues the model with meaning, applies significance to the purchased bodies. *Sex*—the book—is the ultimate example of the phenomena, a veritable catalogue of effects. Madonna's body serves as the site for a whole range of visual discursive operations. She is constructed by the photo-grapher/art director into a collection of feminine roles. Who ever said Madonna is a feminist role model?

Baron notes that it is the photographer, not the woman, that has the power to give meaning. "Something that is actually vulgar can be very sophisticated—it depends on the way that it is handled. You see a lot of that in the work of Stephen Meisel. It's vulgarity. A woman you would actually see on the street, you love her because she is vulgar, she is disgusting—but the way he makes his picture of her, the way he handles the whole thing, is sophisticated. The elegance is a function of the photograph. Everything is a fine line."

Baron's remark indicates the degree to which control of production equals control of meaning, of the complex codes of fashion, and the arbitration of taste. Advertising images, among which fashion photography must be included, are the ultimate extension of the art director's influence. The control over the action of the models in the photograph is transferred to the wider control over the female consumer. The ad directs the taste and behavior of a mass audience. This primary hegemony of men as producers (of products and images) over women as consumers is evident in legendary ad-man David Oglivy's observation, "the consumer isn't a moron; she's your wife …"

"Its simple," Baron assures me. "I prefer looking at a sexy girl than to an un-sexy girl. And I think that most people prefer looking at a sexy girl than an un-sexy girl." (While you may find that simplicity unsettling, I think most fashion images are created with exactly this logic.)

"But aren't you in charge of defining what a 'sexy girl' is?"

"Yes. Sure...."

And herein lies the crux of the issue. Sexual images both derive from and influence the same set of cultural codes. The fascinating thing about sexual statements as fashion statements is how smoothly the style industry is able to absorb images of resistance and reapply them in support of dominant culture.

Why is it, he wonders, that everyone gets up and arms about Marky Mark when there's a hundred stores selling hard-core pornography right at his feet? "Look, I don't like watching Channel 35 (the cable pornography channel in New York). It is such bad taste. But there is that and normalcy and there is nothing in between. There's family life and Channel 35 and everything in between seems to be a problem." But its that hypocritical societal dichotomy between an imaginary unified family life on one side and a depraved subculture on the other that supplies the power to suggestive advertising that invests the mundane products of domesticity—like clothes—with sexual ambivalence.

Baron reasons fashion is inherently about sex and eroticism no matter how you picture it. "You might not see boobs but you think its not sexual?" Advertising underwear is a particularly loaded situation, notes critic Valerie Steele, in that it "is widely perceived as being among the most erotic forms of clothing because of its intimate associations with the naked sexual body (a person wearing underwear is simultaneously dressed and undressed) and its connotations of undress as a prelude to sexual intimacy." It is the ad's job to attach issues of sexual satisfaction to the consumption of a product while obliterating other aspects like material production, cost, and need. The inclusion of other issues of violence, power, fear, or even of "deviance" like multiple partner intercourse or homo-sexuality, only serves to tap into deeper layers of sexual confusion. An object of both masculine and feminine desire, Marky Mark holding his penis in his skin tight Calvins, ensures that nexus between product and gratification is impossible to overlook.

Since sexually explicit advertising is so common the issue has become the differentiation of products within the field of sexual imagery. This aspect of constructing slight but significant differences between women and men though elaborate photographic constructions, mirrors the advertising directors creation of identity amongst marginally differentiated products. Thus the difference between Marky Mark and Vanilla Ice parallels the difference between Coke and Pepsi, or Calvin and the Gap. It all comes down to sexual desire spliced onto product desire. And how can sexual desire be better represented than by the teenage rock star, hormones raging, surrounded by beautiful women, enlightening us with observations like: "I've had lipstick stains on my underwear a few times ..."?

The fashion image fits rather neatly into what writer Malcolm Cowley termed the Theory of Convolutions. A first level of convolution implies you anticipate an audience's reaction and modify your behavior accordingly. If you anticipate a reaction, but know your audience knows you anticipate their reaction, and so do the opposite, you have a second level of convolution, and so on. And so while the effects of gender stereotyping are rigorously debated, we see the advent of a slew of retro-bombshell pictures of Madonna or Brigette Bardot-replicant Claudia Schiffer that directly counter a new feminist sensibility. The trick is to fly in the face of convention, skirt the edge of social propriety, generate controversy.

Baron staunchly defends the use of overt sexuality to sell products. "Everybody is doing it in all different ways and I don't think there is anything wrong with thinking that way. That's what men and women are about. Sexuality is a part of life and I don't think if should be put outside, on any level, in advertising, in your work, anywhere. The media doesn't help the situation. The advertisers feed off sexuality to create controversy and push their company and the media is feeding off the agencies and the ads ... its a vicious circle." But it's just that cycle that furthers Baron's considerable reputation.

Is there really anything new here? Is it charitable to even call stirring up a little suburban ire with a few racy pictures controversial? A teen idol in underwear—especially in New York where the scene around the bus shelter is sure to out-do the image on it any day—controversial? We've all seen these pictures before, they're the common fodder of advertising. While some critics have been generous enough to see in them the dawn of some new era of tolerance or sexual liberation, I find it difficult to see vague homoerotic imagery as the sign of any great shift in national puritanism when the lesbian scene, the orgy, the striking dominatrix, the "primitive" with the uncontrollable sex drive, the Lolita, and so on, have been time-honored codes of male pornography. It seems to me to be just another example of the world of taste constructed for and by men.

Despite—or perhaps because of—the innumerable pages of analysis sexually explicit advertising inspires, new images continue to be produced at a happy clip. The all-consuming nature of advertising ensures success grows proportionately with outrage as evidenced by Benetton, Camel, Guess?, et al. Fashion advertising is way up there in the levels of convolution. The convolution game can be extended infinitely notes Cowley, just "so long as one is less interested in what one says than in one's ability to outwit an audience."

Originally published as "Fabien Baron, or Sex and a Singular Art Director" in I.D. *magazine, May/ June 1993.*

FLOGGING UNDERWEAR:
THE NEW RAUNCHINESS
OF AMERICAN ADVERTISING
by
Andrew Sullivan

Colgate-Palmolive's TV commercial for New Fab detergent opens with a frame of a naked man on the edge of a bed, squeezing into a pair of jeans. In a parody of a stripper sequence, the camera follows the belt-line up the legs, moves round to the back as he buckles his crotch, and then circles toward the abdomen as he pulls on a snug white T-shirt. The stripper music heats up until, suddenly, a cascade of liquid softener gushes into a Fab detergent container. The guy finishes his routine with a quick pelvic thrust to the music.

A companion commercial for Fab liquid shows two bare male legs getting out of bed in the morning, and being clothed with a pair of yellow sweat-pants. The climax is a strong, silent pull on the groin-level drawstring, and a shot of the man's grinning face.

Of all the new ads focusing on sexuality, Fab's is one of the most innocent. The mood is coy and amiable. Still, a male stripper, even in reverse (the ad's message is that the clothes are so soft you can't wait to put them on), is a long way from conventional detergent ads showing "kids with crap on their T-shirts," as Daniel O'Hearn put it. O'Hearn is the account director at FCB/Leber Katz, the agency that developed the Fab campaign.

While public concern has focused on movies and rock lyrics, and despite the widespread impression that the peak of permissiveness has passed, the art form that probably affects and reflects our culture more than any other—advertising—has become amazingly raunchy. Fashion advertising has been infected with a brazen new elitism, sexism, and objectification of the flesh. Abuse of women, homosexual erotica, and the milder forms of sadomasochism are now commonplace marketing techniques, directed at the average American household. Products as everyday as salami, chemicals, and pianos are being sold with a sexual explicitness once reserved for paying customers, of soft-core pornography. The ADS virus, once restricted to light-risk publications such as *GQ, Vanity Fair,* and *Vogue,* is now breaking out in the general circulation.

The Fab campaign illustrates how acceptable it now is to present the male body—almost always implicitly young, unmarried, and available—as a selling point to wives and mothers. Take a similar but less innocuous TV ad for Levi's jeans. Here, there's an excuse for the raunchiness—jeans are legitimately sold on the basis of increasing your attractiveness to the opposite (or increasingly to the same) sex. Nevertheless, the ad reveals the new parameters of public taste. An attractive man wanders into a laundromat and slowly takes off all his clothes. This isn't a striptease, you understand, despite the assembled throng of transfixed women. He just has to wash all his clothes and, poor guy, forgot to bring any spares. Twenty-five seconds into the act, we get to the jeans. He throws them in with a couple of rocks: stone-washing eighties-style. It's both an erotic and self-consciously witty statement. According to Barbara Lippert, advertising critic for *Adweek,* women are wreaking their sexual revenge: "They want to see men reduced to the bimbos that women are always portrayed as. It's post-feminist fallout."

Male eroticism is the most unprecedented aspect of the new advertising culture. Nude or seminude men are now part of the advertising campaigns of, among others, BMW, Saks Fifth Avenue, Calvin Klein, and the French Socialist Party. Until now, only women were portrayed as passive sex objects. What's interesting is not so much the sudden objectification—even feminization—of male sexuality, but the question why men are buying products sold with male sex. Previous campaigns for men's clothes, perfume, aftershave, underwear, all emphasized women, usually in suggestive or submissive positions. The implicit and readily understandable sales line was that the products would bring you greater success with the opposite sex. Today's male advertising, in contrast, is remarkably bimbo-free—female bimbos, that is.

Of course, it's hard to sell men's underwear without showing a man in his underwear. But an ad for the fashion underwear company Hom shows a subtle change. The figure is not a Jockey model, arms crossed, hair tousled, in a locker room. He's a pouting, sexually ambiguous model, dressed in briefs and undershirt, his right arm lifted above him, his left hand drawing his undershirt away from his crotch to reveal his abdomen, while groping languidly toward his (just visible) left nipple. The discreet implication is that he doesn't smoke Marlboro.

Who are these ads meant for? James Devens, president of Hom, claims no subtlety of targeting: "We don't specify any particular audience … we'll sell to men, women, children, and animals." Pressed, he claims his market is primarily women, since even today women still buy most men's underwear. If women are the market, it says something interesting about the male sexuality they now want to buy: passive, introspective, and sexually ambiguous. But are women really the market? The only magazine to run the Hom ad so far is *Men's Look,* a male fashion magazine. Devens explains, "We don't place them in women's magazines, because they're too expensive." That's clearly disingenuous. This is gay advertising: the marketing that dare not speak its name.

But the new Madison Avenue sexuality is not essentially gay, although a large chunk of its market may be. Its central characteristics are its introspection and separation from social context. Fathers, sons, and businessmen have not disappeared from contemporary advertising imagery, but they have been supplemented by someone else: the single male figure, existing in a sexually charged social void with perfect, Nautilus-chiseled contours. He exists alone, his body a work of obvious labor in the gym, his lifestyle apparently affluent but beyond that unspecified. The famous Calvin Klein underwear ad began the genre. Last year's Soloflex exercise equipment print ads captured perfectly the way in which the eighties fitness ethic and the new sexuality overlap. The muscleman was not some Charles Atlas figure but a young, gymnastic, sweaty boy—emanating sexuality, yet implicitly directing most of it at himself. A current ad for Calvin Klein's Obsession for Men perfume shows a young, attractive man—hair slicked back, suit pressed, and in love in the way only an eighties man can be: he's staring straight into a mirror.

In a notorious picture spread for Guess Jeans, the homoeroticism is lesbian. Two denim-clad girls provocatively intertwine in fields, their clothes buttoned and unbuttoned in various places. By last spring the campaign had moved on to violence and even sadism. Two young girls, in what is claimed to be a reference to the 1956 movie *Baby Doll,* are joined by a man in a black coat, hat, and mustache. In several shots he seizes one girl by the chin, embraces the other at the end of a pier, and, by his appearance and expression, is obviously pushing the girls into some sort of coerced sexual activity. The girls seem to be attracted by the prospect. Last fall's Guess Jeans ad featured an elderly, balding, Mafioso-type man, with sunglasses. In scenes that conjure up the atmosphere of an expensive hotel, he kisses and abuses young women in various states of undress. One is pushed back onto a dining table as her godfather molests her. Another is thrown over a stone fountain, with the Mafioso's sickening power-lust grin blessing the scene. Yet another girl, wearing a tight-fitting black leotard, is kneeling down in front of the man, his face out of view, her eyes inches from his groin, in a picture of fearful pre-fellatial submission.

Typical of this genre of ads, the product itself is barely on view. In eight pages of photos featuring eleven models, only two are wearing denim. One is the girl-slave about to minister to her Mafia-master, the other is the same girl crouching in his lap, her eyes staring with indifference toward us, his aging lips reaching for the bottom of her neck. Do women buy jeans marketed with this message? Guess Jeans refuses to talk about the campaign or its success, but industry experts say the company is thriving. Jacob Jacoby, a professor of business at New York University, explains the logic: "The aim is first to generate attention. How you do it doesn't matter. Research suggests that over time, people separate the source of the material from the content of the message so all you recall in the end is the label, Guess Jeans." Sadomasochism as attention-grabber.

The Guess Jeans campaign is also typical in its simple colors: black-and-white photography overlaid with lipstick-red lettering. It's a technique used not only to stand out from the colorful, glossy crowd, but also because the simplicity of the colors impresses itself instantly on the receptive mind. Blue and red—the favorite colors for much of this advertising—are also used for airport landing strips and were common in the 1930s for totalitarian propaganda. Professor Marshall Blonsky, the editor of *On Signs,* chillingly describes the method as "simple color for simple ideas."

Perhaps the best adjective to describe the ethic of the whole power-sex genre of advertisement is: fascist. Calvin Klein's Obsession for Men is a fine example. The leading print ad of the campaign shows four naked men and two naked women draped over a Nuremberg-style obelisk. Each looks intently, almost painfully, into the middle distance, as if stricken with an acute case of hemorrhoids. They bask in a green-filtered sun, their leaden muscular legs angled over their groins as a languid, careless afterthought. The homoeroticism is mild (presumably two of the men will have to keep themselves company), but the complete lack of emotion—let alone passion—is the real point. None of these models cares about anything, nor do they represent anything recognizably human or humane. Their bodies are as objectified as the obelisk they stand on. Their minds are absent. They have no motivation no possible reason for being there, no thought to express, no communication to convey. They do not even look at one another. But they sell smell.

The narcissism of these nautilized Aryans carries over into more mundane advertising. The aesthetic of fascist-realist torsos photographed either in sepia, black-and-white, or some color filter to give that added "it's-1934-in-Bavaria" touch are now commonplace in fashion magazines, and in the new proto-fascist magazines, *University Man, Men's Fitness,* and all the Joe Wieder muscle/fitness publications. Print advertisements for Sisley, a label of the international Italian fashion company Benetton, specialize in caricatures of WASP Aryanism, set in Germanic landscapes. Young couples with cropped, blond hair are pictured striding into woods, carrying sheep on their shoulders, striding up alpine streams, or trudging through the *Schwarzwald.*

The Polo Ralph Lauren Autumn Collection features an arch world of pre-*Anschluss* aristocracy. Black-and-white tableaux depict elegant Aryan landowners at country-house retreats, sipping champagne in faded tuxedos. The print ads for Toni Gard, a French fashion company, recreate in black-and-white a studied orchard lunch party in a French chateau, servants at hand, styling gel at the ready. Not that the label is exactly foisted upon the potential consumer. Several page spreads go by without the name of the company or designer appearing at all, and those clothes that do feature them are obscured by the sepulchral soft-lens. What is important is the ambience, the creation of a mood. In this case, Nuremberg.

The new ad aesthetic would be easier to defend if it were based on any genuine artistic innovation or creativity. But the photographers of these images—Bruce Weber for Lauren and Obsession print campaigns, Wayne Maser for Guess Jeans, for example—are parasites on the genuine age of artistic fashion photography. The era of Richard Avedon and Irving Penn, working for *Harper's Bazaar* and *Vogue* in the late 1940s to the early 1960s, established much of the lighting techniques, dramatic composition, and figure painting that today's photographers imitate. Even the explicitness of today's eroticism is not new in the field of fashion photography, although it has never appeared in popular American publications before now. Helmut Newton's work for the French *Vogue* in the 1970s—some of it depicting explicit sadomasochism and bestiality—went much further than the soft-core pornography of Obsession.

Today's commercial photo-art is not only unoriginal, it also lacks the fundamental quality of great fashion photography: its connection between human personality and clothes. Avedon and Penn were both essentially portraitists. Few of today's photographers are. "What typifies the new generation is their denial of individuality. You simply can't imagine a Bruce Weber portrait. It's too human a conception" is how Adam Gopnik, a writer on the relationship between popular culture and light art, puts it.

He's right. The central feature of today's ads is the dehumanized uniformity of the bodies they display, a relentless elitism of the flesh. Take Jovan Musk's controversial TV commercial produced by Adrian Lyne, who was also responsible for the original Diet Pepsi campaign and for *Fatal Attraction*. With an opening shot of the question "What is sexy?" it flashes twenty-nine spots in thirty seconds, hypnotically choreographed to a pulsating rhythm. We cannot know the people involved. They clearly have no history nor any relationship that we might have time or interest to contemplate. We see a man spraying a woman with a hose; a woman dancing frantically in front of a backlight; three hands clasping each other on a bronzed thigh; a wet-kiss in a shower. They are all mini-seconds of stylish erotica—arousing, but in an instant, distracting, almost thoughtless way.

The growing sophistication of American advertising (Jovan's previous campaign featured the juvenile slogan "It may not put more women in your life but it'll put more life into your women") reflects increasing influence of European taste—and European ownership—in the American advertising industry. But the calculated sexuality also reflects increased desperation to break through the clutter of competing ads. A Swedish agency, Hall and Cederquist, was hired to design a campaign for a small sneakers company, Travel Fox. To make an impact against competitors such as Nike and Reebok, with something like twenty to thirty times Travel Fox's budget, the campaign focused on sex. A print ad, whose only information about its sneakers was that they were made of leather, featured various permutations of two intertwined nude bodies, just sexually distinguishable, each sporting a pair of Travel Fox sneakers—and nothing else. One ad shows them in the missionary position; another has her bare buttocks firmly placed on his shoulders. Sales in the New York area, where the campaign was concentrated, tripled in a year. The company spent one million dollars in 1986 on the campaign, out of total sales of five million dollars. In other words, twenty cents of every dollar you pay for your Travel Fox sneakers goes to convincing you that they're sexy.

The sneaker campaign also reveals the importance of simplicity. Mood advertising—with little information about the product but plenty of apparently tangential associations—is increasingly regarded as the most effective way of conveying a message. This is partly an attempt to rise above the clutter of information with something clear and visual. Written information is a disadvantage. A study by Jacob Jacoby found that around twenty percent of all advertising copy is misconstrued. (The bad news is, that figure is even higher for editorial material.) The solution? Cut the copy, crank up the copulation.

Fancy theories can't disguise the basic point, though, which is sex. A recent glossy brochure promises "Warmth. Power. Passion. Response." It is selling a piano. A TV ad features a bare-chested man lathering himself in a shower to advertise Liquid Drano. ICI Chemicals boasts about its share of the world fibers market with a photograph shot at ground level looking up three women's pantyhoses. Schick's razors feature a woman singing, "I got a man with a slow hand."

The latest ad for Round The Clock Pantyhose features a tuxedo-clad man returning home to open his mail. One item is a poster. He unpacks it, looks at it for a moment, smiles, and pins it to the wall. Never taking his gaze away, he takes off his tie, drops his suspenders, and falls back into bed. Then he switches off the light. Then we see what he's looking at: a rear view of a woman's legs in pantyhose. The question is: What's he going to do next? It takes an effort to recall that this is an ad for stockings for women, not safe sex for men. Still, preliminary figures show sales are up thirty per cent.

Perhaps the explosion of fantasy and eroticism in advertising isn't a consequence of increasing decadence at all. More likely it is a symptom of increased restraint and monogamy in the period of safe sex. The instant nature of advertising, its uniquely close relationship to the market it attracts, and its ubiquity in every medium make it the leading public art form of the late twentieth century. Now that government has abandoned its traditional role as the cultural and moral guardian of public culture, the ad industry has taken over. We no longer build statues; we mount billboards. The result is a public culture more sensitive to the demands of the faceless, but hardly passionless, many than ever before. Unlike elite, officially sponsored art, advertising has to mirror public taste—middle-class taste—or go out of business. And what the public wants, apparently, is this.

Originally published in The New Republic, *January 18, 1988; and* Print *magazine, May/June 1988. Reprinted by permission of* The New Republic © *1988, The New Republic, Inc.*

IN THE END, IT'S EDUCATION

WHY DESIGNERS CAN'T THINK

by

Michael Bierut

Graphic designers are lucky. As structurers of the world's communications, we get to vicariously partake of as as many fields of interest as we have clients. In a single day, a designer can talk about real estate with one client, cancer cures with another, and forklift trucks with a third. Imagine how tedious it must be for a fireman who has nothing to do all day but worry about fires.

The men and women who invented graphic design in America were largely self-taught; they didn't have the opportunity to go to fully-developed specialized design schools, because none existed. Yet somehow these people managed to prosper without four years of Typography, Visual Problem Solving and Advanced Aesthetics. What they lacked in formal training they made up for with insatiable curiosity not only about art and design, but culture, science, politics, and history.

Today, most professionals will admit to alarm about the huge and ever-growing number of programs in graphic design. Each year, more and more high school seniors decide that they have a bright future in "graphics," often without much of an idea what graphics is. This swelling tide of eighteen-year-old, would-be designers is swallowed up thirstily by more and more programs in graphic design at art schools, community colleges, and universities. Five years later, out they come, ready to take their places as professional designers, working for what everybody cheerfully hopes will be an infinitely expanding pool of clients.

There are many ways to teach graphic design, and almost any curriculum will defy neat cubbyholing. Nevertheless, American programs seem to fall into two broad categories: process schools and portfolio schools. Or, if you prefer, "Swiss" schools and "slick" schools.

Process schools favor a form-driven problem solving approach. The first assignments are simple exercises: drawing letterforms, "translating" three dimensional objects into idealized high-contrast images, and basic still-life photography. In the intermediate stages, the formal exercises are combined in different ways: relate the drawing of a flute to the hand-drawn letter *N*, combine the letter *N* with a photograph of a ballet slipper. In the final stage, these combinations are turned into "real" graphic design: Letter *N* plus flute drawing plus ballet slipper photo plus 42 pt. Univers equals, voilà, a poster for Rudolph Nureyev. Of course, if the advanced student gets an assignment to design a poster for, say, an exhibition on Thomas Edison, he or she is tempted to (literally) revert to form: combine the letter *E*, drawing of a movie camera, photo of a light bulb, etc. One way or another, the process schools trace their lineage back to the advanced program of the *Kunstgewerbeshule* in Basel, Switzerland. Sometimes the instructors experienced the program only second or third hand, having themselves studied with someone who studied with someone in Basel.

The Swiss-style process schools seem to have thrived largely as a reaction against the perceived "slickness" of the portfolio schools. While the former have been around in force for only the past fifteen years or so, the latter are native American institutions with roots in the 1950s.

While the unspoken goal of the process school is to duplicate the idealized black-and-white boot camp regimen of far-off Switzerland, the portfolio school has a completely different, more admittedly mercenary, aim: to provide students with polished "books" that will get them good jobs upon graduation. The problem-solving mode is conceptual, with a bias for appealing, memorable, populist imagery. The product, not process, is king. Now, portfolio schools will rebut this by pointing to the copious tissue layouts that often supplement the awesomely slick work in their graduate's portfolios. None the less, at the end of the line of tissues is always a beautifully propped photograph of an immaculate mock-up of a perfume bottle. Seldom will portfolio schools encourage students to spend six months on a twenty part structural analysis of the semiotics of a Campbell's soup label as an end in itself. Unlike the full-time teachers of process schools, the portfolio schools are staffed largely by working professionals who teach part time, who are impatient with idle exercises that don't relate to the "real world."

However politely the two camps behave when they participate in discussions on design education, the fact is, they hate each other. To the portfolio schools, the "Swiss" method is hermetic, arcane, and meaningless to the general public. To the process schools, the "slick" method is distastefully commercial, shallow, and derivative.

Oddly, though, the best-trained graduates of either camp are equally sought after by employers. East Coast corporate identity firms love the process school graduates; anyone who's spent six months combining a letterform and a ballet shoe won't mind being mired in a fat standards manual for three years. On the other hand, package design firms are happy to get the portfolio school graduates: not only do they have a real passion for tighter-than-tight comps, but they can generate hundreds of stylistically diverse alternatives to show indecisive clients.

What, then, is wrong with graphic design education? If there's a smorgasbord of pedagogical approaches, and employers who can find use for different kinds of training, who suffers? The answer is not in how schools are different, but how they're the same.

Both process schools and portfolio schools have something in common: whether the project is the esoteric Nureyev poster or the Bloomingdales-ready perfume bottle comp, what's valued is the way graphic design looks, not what it means. Programs will pay lip service to meaning in design with references to "semiotics" (Swiss) or "conceptual problem solving" (slick), but these nuances are applied in a cultural vacuum. In many programs, if not most, it's possible to study graphic design for four years without any meaningful exposure to the fine arts, world literature, science, history, politics or any of the other disciplines that unite us in a common culture.

Well, so what? What does a graphic designer need with this other stuff? Employers want trained designers, not writers and economists.

Perhaps the deficiencies in the typical design education aren't handicaps at first. The new graduate doesn't need to know economics any more than a plumber does; like a tradesman, he or she needs skills that are, for the most part, technical.

But five or ten years down the road, how can a designer plan an annual report without some knowledge of economics? Lay out a book without an interest in, if not a passion for, literature? Design a logo for a high-tech company without some familiarity with science?

Obviously, they can and do. Some designers fill in their educational gaps as they go along; some just fake it. But most of the mediocre design today comes from designers who are faithfully doing as they were taught in school: they worship at the altar of the visual.

The pioneering design work of the forties and fifties continues to interest and excite us while work from the intervening years looks more and more dated and irrelevant. Without the benefit of intensive specialized programs, the pioneers of our profession, by necessity, became well-rounded intellectually. Their work draws its power from deep in the culture of their times.

Modern design education, on the other hand, is essentially value-free: every problem has a purely visual solution that exists outside any cultural context. Some of the most tragic victims of this attitude hail not from the world of high culture, but low. Witness the case of a soft-drink manufacturer that pays a respected design firm a lot of money to "update" a classic logo. The product of American design education responds: "Clean up an old logo? You bet," and goes right to it. In a vacuum that excludes popular as well as high culture, the meaning of the mark in its culture is disregarded. Why not just say no? The option isn't considered.

Our clients usually are not other designers; they sell real estate, cure cancer, make forklift trucks. Nor are there many designers in the audiences our work eventually finds. They must be touched with communication that is genuinely resonant, not self-referential. To find the language for that, one must look beyond Manfred Maier's *Principles of Design* or the last *Communication Arts Design Annual*.

Nowadays, the passion of design educators seems to be technology; they fear that computer illiteracy will handicap their graduates. But it's the broader kind of illiteracy that's more profoundly troubling. Until educators find a way to expose their students to a meaningful range of culture, graduates will continue to speak in languages that only their classmates understand. And designers, more and more, will end up talking to themselves.

Originally published in ADC Statements *(American Center for Design Journal), vol. 3, issue 2, Spring 1988.*

A CLOCKWORK MAGENTA AND ORANGE

by

D. L. Ogde

A time in the near future. The graphics industry had collapsed. Most type-setters, graphic trade shops, printers, and design firms had been forced to close, killed by a combination of amazing improvements in technology, the appearance of thousands of design "Kits" (named after the wealthy designer who had created and copyrighted them all, Kit Hinrichs), and an incredible inability by all to persuade clients that so-called "good" design, typesetting, and printing had any real value at all.

First to feel the squeeze were the typesetters. Finding themselves in competition with hundreds of thousands of personal computers, they initially tried to save themselves by becoming "service bureaus," merely providing a printout service to those who wished higher resolution than was available on their own laser printers.

This tactic worked for a few years, but, inevitably, laser-printed resolution improved to the point where it was "good enough." At the same time, of course, designers who had their own laser printers began to rationalize that the rough, jagged letterforms they were gaffing out of these printers were actually more desirable, since they were "warmer" and closer to the early linotype impressions they remembered fondly.

The next to go were the design firms. For years designers had been engaging in Talmudic-like debates about the nature of design and the role of the designer. The opposing sides divided themselves into two camps, "good" designers and "bad" designers. At various times the "good" designers were bad and the "bad" designers were good. Clients, not knowing which was which, ignored both.

Armed with their desktop publishing technology and their "Kits," more and more corporations, institutions, and agencies brought their work in-house. Coincidentally, the government had just created a new program that made it much easier to create in-house graphics departments; the Pixel-Oriented Operator Program—POOP for short. This program forced thousands of poets, Ph.Ds, and English teachers to learn specialized computer graphics tasks.

These people, who eventually came to be called "para-graphs," were hired by the thousands, at minimum-wage salaries, to staff the in-house graphics departments.

With the competition for projects getting stiffer, the technology enabling them to turn out work faster and faster and the demand for "good" design getting lower and lower, those design firms which were still functioning began to compete with each other even more furiously, cutting their prices to the bone. Eventually, with the help of their ever-improving computers, they found themselves in the uncomfortable position of doing all their clients' work in practically no time at all and getting paid nothing to do it.

Following the typesetters and design firms into the ranks of the unemployed were the trade shops and printers. When it became possible to go by satellite directly from a desktop computer to a printing press anywhere in the world, without the need for a single human being to be involved in the entire process, the trade shops disappeared. Later, after low-quality printing became not only acceptable, but actually desirable, traditional printing technology was replaced by small, high-speed, digitized, web-fed color-copiers. All major printers closed their doors, never to reopen.

Hundreds of thousands of typesetters, printers, pre-press specialists, and graphic designers found themselves on the streets. Many formed into gangs of "rowdy-goudys," naming themselves by their colors … magenta, orange, fuchsia, and mauve. The graphic designers all wore black and preferred to call themselves "brodies" in memory of their martyred hero, Neville Brody, the young British designer who, in protest to mankind's irresponsible use of serif type, impaled himself on a tall ascender in the middle of Piccadilly Circus.

These gangs could usually be found carrying cans of spray paint and airbrushes, looking for unprotected and helpless magazines to kidnap and abuse … filling in counters, retouching photographs, adding serifs to sans-serif letterforms. The situation seemed hopeless.

But, as often happens, history has a way of repeating itself. An unknown computer virus, later identified as the "Black Dot Plague," began to show up in computers everywhere. In only a few short years, every computer in the world had developed a complete inability to spell out anything but the strange word "steviejobswashere."

By that time, since everyone in the world except the "brodies" had completely lost the ability to spell, compute, draw, or, for that matter, handle any hand instruments at all, these gangs suddenly found themselves very much in demand.

Graphic design eventually became the most expensive and well-paid profession in the world, and graphic designers became the richest and most powerful people on earth, controlling all corporations, institutions, agencies, and associations, thus assuring the salvation of our environment, all animal life, ethics, and the human race itself.

Originally published in the AIGA Journal of Graphic Design*, vol. 4, no. 1, 1986.*

TWO MYTHS ABOUT DESIGN EDUCATION
by
Gordon Salchow

I have discussed education with many designers and instructors during my numerous years as a design educator. This experience has led me to the realization that there are several seldom-challenged assumptions concerning education in our profession.

I offer herein my own perspective on two of the most persistent of these assumptions. These two "myth" categories may be the most important since they are central to a school's attitudes regarding its curriculum and faculty.

Myth number one: That schools should avoid their own "look" and provide a broad education.

A diverse faculty outlook which inspires distinctively different student portfolios sounds liberal but often signals faculty squabbles, a flabby department, and confused students. A portfolio is the most tangible evidence of a graduate's experience but its glib uniqueness is less important than is its demonstration of the doer's comprehension concerning visual form, communication, design methodology, and basic skills. Such acumen promises purposeful work and creative potential.

Schools should seek, rather than feel embarrassed about, a unified philosophy, even though some innocent practitioners will complain about the singular character of a school's design. If the ideology has substance, the graduates will be confident enough to grow from it in individual ways. This is not to say that colleges should seek a "style," although we may so label that which emerges from considered tailoring. The graduates who are not motivated beyond what was learned in school are better off following sensible organizational and investigative premises than in groping for inventive visualizations. The purpose of graphic design is effective and aesthetically satisfying public communication rather than personal expression, although we applaud and nurture creativity in any profession. Since a series of interpretations is necessarily ingrained in the design process, personality is naturally expressed. An individual's artistry blossoms from knowledge and intensity as opposed to masturbatory indulgence. Schools can provide a rational basis so that their alumni are able (free) to interpret, control, experiment, and communicate and, yes, express.

Time limitations require faculties to select and prioritize curricular inclusions. This means that every design topic cannot be covered. Critics will always see the obvious vocational concerns which are important to their particular concentration as a vital gap. Indeed, there will be some lessons each of us deem important which must be delayed until post-school employment. Schools should, therefore, clearly identify and exploit their special potential so that their limitations are, as in any noble design process, transformed into advantages. Each institution cannot provide the most comprehensive encounter but each can offer a wholesome atmosphere and legitimate insight pertaining to design theory. Designers, or others, who cannot distinguish personality, fluency, and potential within a defined framework; and complain about portfolio sameness or assignment restrictiveness, are like the idiots who suggest that all men of another race look alike. They are revealing their own narrowness. We should not attempt to give the provincial employer everything he expects of an applicant if it contradicts the needs of our students, society, and the profession. Assignments must be correct in relation to educational rather than employment goals.

A school should not be criticized because the work of its students resembles that of their classmates. There are several advantages with shared class assignments and this means that peer portfolios will include the same projects. Additionally, project interpretations have been influenced by the one faculty member as well as colleague responses and the peculiar twists which rightfully evolve during investigation and critiques. The subtle distinctions, within licit perimeters, should be appreciated as more revealing and less banal than conspicuous portfolio unlikeness. The constancy provides reviewers with a superior footing upon which to make judgments concerning the school as well as its individual graduates.

I have come to believe that a most important foundation is quality rather than variety. I would choose an omelet from a great restaurant over the cafeteria's Beef Wellington any day. If I can distinguish the subtleties of a superb omelet, my appreciation for every other food is heightened. Few schools expose students to a genuine understanding of, and appreciation for, real excellence. Americans are fascinated by variety and often interpret this as complexity rather than recognizing that true complexity involves the depth of our understanding. Renaissance personages may evolve out of a rare individual's stature and wonderment, but the imposition of a temporal jack-of-all-trades mentality on under-graduates produces anarchy as opposed to profound understanding and execution. After students have encountered depth, they become increasingly more confident and intrigued by the complex challenges of alternatives.

It would be addle-brained to divorce the terms "liberal" and "education" but smorgasbords do not provide balanced diets for the undergraduate majority. Students need a foundation of those design subjects which are perpetual so that, five or ten years hence, they will master the unanticipated challenges and tools. It is silly to think primarily about liberalization of education by diversification within a department rather than determining and embracing ways to benefit from activities, courses, and experts outside, before, during, and after formal education. We should recognize that a degree represents one fraction of a person's education and acculturation. We do a disservice if we try audaciously to provide *the* education rather than that part of it which we should be expert at and which is the core for our students. In addition to theory, this includes familiarity with procedures and methods plus a sense of the joy of discovery. If a graduate feels secure in his comprehension of the essence of one fertile pursuit, he will more freely extend himself in diverse directions and the context it provides gives him a basis for rational judgment and planning.

It could be argued that four years of a liberal college education should precede any kind of concentration but, in contrast with an eighteen-year-old's sophistication concerning the non-visual aspects of life, we have a great deal of fundamental knowledge to transmit and inspire. Considering this naïveté and the complexity of perception, it might be unjust to further delay visual scholarship. I will add my belief that an ideal design education is particularly viable in a comprehensive university because the nature of our work feeds on a university's academic breadth, although independent art schools do have their own advantages.

Myth number two: That practicing designers are the best design educators.

We feel guilty when our principal time commitment is in the classroom rather than on the board, so we claim to be designers who teach instead of design educators. Once we so align with practitioners, we are obliged to take most seriously what is said about education by the busiest practitioners rather than by the most industrious teachers. One such practitioner might be someone who turns out credible, even inspirational design work, though this might not prepare him to understand the special duties in education. Another practitioner might be someone who grinds out graphic looking imagery for client wishes rather than public need. Either type can become, along with the naively educated instructors who never even had the experience of a plebeian design practice, one of the wretched instructors who perpetuate mediocrity. Inferior comprehension and effort is less tolerable in education than in practice because it is so inflationary in this context. The superficial education which is too common in our profession allows virtually anyone to get a degree, while the number and variety of job opportunities assures most of an eventual livelihood. These "designers" and trusting academicians may assume that this combination of "education" and "success" qualifies someone to teach or advise, as it might in law or medicine.

Part-time teachers often deal dogmatically with the classroom as play-acting the "real world." They function as though this "real world" were more important than their time with students. Education feeds our future but this does not mean that it should be seen as an imitation of what follows. Every experience enunciates its own unique values and perimeters while preparing us for future actions. A professor whose career priority is his studio work is often disinclined to teach a meticulous theory in favor of more seclusive considerations. He tends to ignore the benefits of dovetailing his assignments with those of previous, concurrent, and future courses taught by others. This may be the result of disdain for colleagues, insecurity, or an unwillingness to devote the additional effort needed for team plotting. He may present overly complicated projects which intrigue him and this results in student insecurity or false confidence rather than objectivity and optimism. Education should pigeonhole knowledge, inspiration, and skills in relation to syntactic, semantic, and pragmatic methodologies. Practitioners may mistake training for education by emphasizing "practicality," sexy assignments, fashionable techniques, and/or the novelty of the product's façade. Their schedules are likely to require that student/teacher contact occurs largely through group critiques where preferences are stated, as opposed to careful in-class reasoning of a problem-exploring process. The inevitable studio emergencies delay or cancel student and planning sessions while client expectations are favored, partially because of the financial incentive.

Serious educators realize that a professional's excitement comes from within and involves discipline, rather than depending on the romantic breadth of a particular assignment. Faculty verve and environmental reinforcement have a great deal to do with the development of this poise by a student majority.

Of course, faculty must design and/or engage in serious research while teaching, but the quality of this parallel activity is more important than is the quantity. Excellent, over-worked designers are the most terrific educators only when they take it seriously, are secure within the profession, and respect the compatible but honest differences between education and practice. Then, instead of complaining about the dissimilarities, they conscientiously capitalize on them while building bridges.

Many good designers are not good teachers because they are not able to verbalize the logical but intricate aspects of a design entanglement. Such designers are probably the products of simplistic programs in this or an allied field. Graphic design has few credible ways to foster educational or professional standards. This is not the case in other fields of communication/expression such as literature, dance, or music. There is universal acknowledgment of their theoretical and structural underpinnings as a prerequisite to composition, performance, or teaching.

By the way, I have never met an intelligent design educator who is not also a fine (if slow because of his deliberateness) designer, and unwilling to abandon practice. My stance, then, is that good designers are not always good teachers but good teachers are always good designers. This is because extended intimacy with higher education rigorously clarifies and nourishes individual professional insight.

Student (and faculty) contact with design stars can be magical. It is wonderful for the mature student but is an inefficient primary diet for undergraduates where eminent egos can be disruptively independent. Undergraduate programs must attract and retain a resident faculty of energetic, talented, and thoughtful individuals who respect each other, the students, and the department's plan. Ideally, a school maintains a critical balance of committed full-time and adjunct faculty who are complimented by inspirational visitors from practice and other schools. The less endowed schools should train for the support jobs in design rather than graduating Sunday painters who, five years hence, may occupy positions which allow them to make inferior design judgments and probably inflict their frustrations on the vulnerable idealism of beginners, which perpetuates pseudo-design fluff.

Those who have been soundly educated and have demonstrated their ability, most likely through published design, but choose to devote their main attention to educating others in the classroom and/or through proper research are the true torchbearers. They are needed to clarify, convey, and expand the body of knowledge pertaining to design for communication and to help establish a more consistent standard. Those who command the design process primarily through applied design are in the indispensable position of nourishing higher education via encouragement and example. Superior work is the design community's purest form of scholarship and contribution. It is most effectively addressed by proficient practicing designers and design educators who acknowledge and support each other's appropriately different requirements and methods. Just as educators should engage in practice on its territory, so must practitioners encounter formal education on its terms. Each will still contribute his valuable perspective to the other pursuit. This personifies our consistent confrontation with "unity and contrast."

Originally published in Print *magazine, November/December 1981.*

BACK TO SHOW AND TELL

by

Paula Scher

A year ago I relived an experience I had in my ninth grade Algebra II class. The occasion was a seminar on graphic design education at the Maryland Institute of Art where some practicing designers and design educators shared a common stage. The premise was sound: to generate debate between these factions. However, what resulted was disappointing. Instead of meaningful discussion and clear explanation, the design educators gave pompous presentations on the structure and curriculum of their schools, supported by pedantic visuals and charts. They spoke in jargon I've never used professionally, and didn't understand. These lectures were so abstruse that I hadn't a clue as to what was going on in their schools. I wondered if the students did either.

The "Algebra II" syndrome (a compulsion to hum sixties rock and roll and make spit balls) is my reaction whenever theoretics (theoretics as an end in itself) are applied to design. At Maryland my feelings were compounded. The first was one of shame. That's what happens when I'm bombarded with incomprehensible language. Boredom follows shame: I tune out and squirm in my seat. Then I realize I'm really angry. Boredom is anger. I'm angry in this case because the speaker is supposed to be talking about graphic design, not quantum physics.

"Semiotics" was one of the favorite words bandied about the Maryland session. In fact, some of the educators took great pride in the fact that their schools were breaking new ground in this area. If so, why couldn't any of them make the idea understandable? At the risk of losing anyone who has read this far, the following is a dictionary definition of semiotics: "A general philosophical theory of signs and symbols that deals especially with their function in artificially constructed natural language and comprises syntactics, semantics and pragmatics."

How does it really apply to graphic design? I thought it would be fun to call seven of my favorite "award" winning designers and ask them to define semiotics. Four said they didn't know (one of them didn't want to know); two said that it may have something to do with symbols; and one said she knew but didn't want to answer. If one asks the same designers how a symbol "works," they'll give articulate answers and use good examples to illustrate their points.

It's not just the exclusionary language that bothers me, but the process of making more complex the difficult act of explaining graphic design principles to would-be designers. Obviously my reaction is based on a personal teaching style that might be termed extended apprenticeship. Call it what you will—a style, method or philosophy—it is a hands-on process that has produced tangible results.

In 1982, I was asked to teach graphic design to seniors at the School of Visual Arts, New York. The media department has a loosely prescribed curriculum, with an emphasis on doing—there are few, if any theoretical courses. The school hires working designers who represent a broad range of experiences and approaches. Hence the instructors are completely responsible for course content, and are encouraged to teach what they know best. The students have a certain choice in what they take. After the foundation year they audit classes to see whether they feel comfortable with the approach being taught.

When I first saw the work by the students entering my class, I thought that they were unprepared to enter the job market unless radical improvement occurred over the year. No amount of theoretical instruction would help. Therefore, I created a series of complex assignments which were extensively critiqued. The challenge was to pinpoint what was wrong and show how it could be made better. My method was to use simple language and strong visual examples to illustrate my point. In effect, I became the client. But I also became a graphic fascist, disallowing typefaces, reordering elements, dictating style and content. The students were forced to design and redesign, yet in the process of following these directives they made their own discoveries which had surprising results.

The approach I instinctively used was the old apprentice method. Do what I do, and watch it come out your way. This method requires total commitment. Here the teacher must "give it all away" (style, conceits, tricks) or the premise won't work. It's sometimes threatening. It can be intimidating to watch as a student easily accomplishes something it took me fifteen years to master. But in the end, and in a relatively short amount of time, some potentially good professionals emerged.

At the Maryland Institute seminar one educator presented a chart showing the spiraling growth of students as they absorbed the design theories of successive courses, culminating in graduation—meaning the students were qualified to enter the profession. What hogwash! There was no mention of talent. All the theory in the world cannot replace talent. Talented students can overcome any form of education unless they've been bored out of the profession.

I abhor the charade at the Maryland session. These academicians, I believe, have created "design speak" to give credence to the profession because they're embarrassed that it was once called commercial art. Is it necessary to indoctrinate students with jargon just to compensate for a sense of professional inferiority?

My point comes down to this: Designers learn by doing. They can learn faster when someone gives them a way to do it. When they learn how, they can understand it. And when they understand it they can teach somebody else.

Originally published in the AIGA Journal of Graphic Design, *vol. 4, no. 1, 1986.*

GRAPHIC DESIGN EDUCATION: STRUGGLING THROUGH THOSE AWKWARD TEENAGE YEARS

by

DK Holland

Many who attended the first American Institute of Graphic Arts (AIGA) National Conference in Boston in 1985, remember the heated diatribe by graphic designer Bob Gill, on the state of graphic design education targeted toward graphic designers/educators Katharine McCoy from Cranbrook, Ken Hiebert from the Philadelphia College of Art, and Tom Ockerse from Rhode Island School of Design. Design education was covered with cobwebs, stuck in the theory rut and Gill was telling these educators to "get real" or "get out."

Then came a hurricane named Gloria and shut down the conference. Soon after came a tornado called Apple Computers which revolutionized our industry. Like it or not, design education found itself in the eye of the storm.

The Graphic Design Education Association (GDEA) formed about a year later. A handful of educators got together in Washington one afternoon to discuss teaching budgets and gripe about their deans and quickly turned their energies to forming a very positive agenda that covered everything. Everything that Bob Gill was talking about and then some; concerns like pedagogical research (pedagogy is the art and science of teaching), future roles of technology, accreditation standards, and defining standards of excellence through model curricula. This courageous group of people, currently lead by Robert O. Swinehart, designer and educator from Carnegie Mellon, has since dedicated years to understanding where design education has gone wrong and how to right it. Their vehicles include white papers, symposia, round-table discussions and awards to outstanding educators. Their numbers are small but growing.

The mission statement reads, "GDEA is a national advocacy organization that exists to develop exemplary programs, communications, research, evaluation and recourses for the advancement of graphic design education." They are forging alliances with publishers like Van Nostrand and organizations like the AIGA. They have established the Master Teacher Award which recognizes the contributions of distinguished teachers in field of design education. Rob Roy Kelly, Ken Hiebert, and Bradbury Thompson were three of the first to be honored.

NOBODY KNOWS WHAT WE DO BUT EVERYONE WANTS TO BE JUST LIKE US

Too few people know what graphic design is. *The Occupational Outlook Handbook,* which is the official publication of the Department of Labor, says: "Graphic designers draw or paint illustrations to advertise a product or event. They also draw commercial logos such as corporate symbols or letterheads." And under the category "graphic and fine artists" it says: "A large portion of artists are graphic artists who illustrate and design the flood of magazines, newspaper and TV advertisements, as well as catalogs, brochures, instruction manuals, technical literature, book and record jackets, textiles and other items requiring visual appeal. The field is also called commercial art, graphic art or design." The handbook also states that the most important factor is the portfolio and that no training is necessary to succeed in this area. In order to be considered a profession, a field must require a four year degree of its professionals. We require but a portfolio, at least in the eyes of the government. Therefore we have the same status as floral designers and window dressers.

Design educators, including those involved in the GDEA, are finding that graphic designers should know a lot more than just graphic design in order to contribute well and appropriately in their jobs. "Students get shortchanged if they don't have at least two years of high-quality liberal arts courses. An education focusing almost exclusively on studio courses fails to provide students with the mental discipline and information framework to realize their full potential both in daily life and in their profession," said Alan Siegel, chairman and CEO of Siegel & Gale.

Indeed, there is a vast array of programs available to budding talents in the United States. In fact, that may be part of the problem. While there are about 50,000 architects (either registered or on their way to being registered) in the U.S., there are only 94 schools. While there are 19,000 professional interior designers in professional organizations, there are 185 schools teaching interior design. While there are 700,000 licensed attorneys, there are only 175 law schools. There are 7,000 members of the AIGA and almost 1,000 graphic design programs. Perhaps more good schools but fewer programs would be a key to controlling the flood of students entering the work force. This is what many educators believe, including Kathy McCoy who has come to the forefront of the design education movement.

"We have a huge number of schools, and that number is growing daily, with rapidly growing enrollments. There is a tidal wave of college students interested in graphic design. University art departments are eager to begin graphic design programs in order to build their enrollments, whether they are prepared or not," McCoy said. "These departments are openly using graphic design programs as cash cows to support fine arts programs suffering from shrinking enrollments. As a result, entrenched fine arts faculty are teaching graphic design in many university design programs. These same fine artists generally see graphic design as simply the commercial application of fine art principles and typically hold highly negative attitudes toward design."

One option to control the quality of designers would be to certify designers who graduate from certain accredited design schools while grandfathering most graphic designers who are currently working in the profession. Another option is to raise the accepted standard for graphic design from within and let nature take its course (no pun intended). This may already be happening. "Desktop publishing strikes at the low end of what design is all about. Many non-designers will be able to produce what we now refer to as design but, in fact, is merely styling of typography," Sharon Helmer Poggenpohl, designer and educator, observed. "Design is becoming more important. The designer will be asked, more and more, for ideas. This means being intellectually challenged to contribute in a much different way. There is more interdisciplinary interaction today; with designers in collaboration with other professionals. That's why I think it's very important for schools to get involved in interdisciplinary discussions and activities where they must define and defend their position and consider others' points of view. I find that prospect very exciting.

"Many schools have 'do-as-the-teacher-does' programs where the students imitate the teacher," Sharon Poggenpohl continued, "Design education must become more transformative; teachers should connect with students, with their experiences and cultures. Teachers must give them a more expansive view. I don't think the master/ apprentice relationship is appropriate for the designer."

ARE THE BLIND LEADING THE PARTIALLY SIGHTED?

Although some of the better schools require, as part of their teacher's credentials, a Master of Fine Arts degree many more schools do not even require a four year degree. Nor is there any assurance that teachers can write or have a solid liberal arts background to share with their students. And the bottom line in all cases is that teachers are not taught how to teach design. Shouldn't the standard for teachers be at least as high as that which we expect of their graduates?

In addition, many failed designers turn to teaching to supplement their income. They may not be successful designers but does that prohibit them from becoming successful instructors? We must be careful in understanding the motivation of those who apply to teach by better defining what makes a good teacher. "The ideal design educator knows history, is a thoughtful critic both visually and conceptually, and is able to frame learning experiences in design in exciting and provocative ways. These are essential qualities. It's entirely possible that an average designer can get across a design concept to a class brilliantly. In fact, accomplished practitioners are often best at running a workshop or as an invited guest. They may not be terrific teachers," Sharon Poggenpohl remarked. "Instructors have long grimaced when they hear the phrase, 'Those who can't do, teach.' It's really not fair. There are many teachers who teach for the love of education and because they are good. The only way to tell if a teacher is performing well is to observe the class over a long period and to assess the student's actual design performance."

Don Ariev, chairman of the Graduate Communications/Packaging Design Department at Pratt Institute, observed that we are light years ahead of Asian schools. Ariev has toured many Asian countries including Japan, China, and Hong Kong. Pratt has a very large Asian enrollment, especially in its graduate departments. "Throughout Asia, and particularly in Korea, design students are taught to strongly emulate, even imitate the work of their instructors (what we in the U.S. would consider infringement). Technical competence and diligence are stressed. Many of these students have great difficulty adapting to our education process that encourages innovation and creativity." Ariev said that after graduation, incentive is limited in Asia as well. "Employment in Japan, for instance, is highly regimented. Promotion is based strictly on seniority. Individual initiative or unusual capabilities are not factors in advancement. From my travels, I've noted that employment in Japan is often 'for life' and the new company employee undergoes an extensive training period. It's a sort of combination orientation, education, and brainwashing program. As a result, their colleges need not educate them." Many of Pratt's Asian graduates return to their homelands to teach, American-style.

THE UNDERGRADUATE PROGRAMS

Students who are considering applying to a design school attend national career day fairs which are held annually in every major city, usually hosted by a major university. Each design school has a table and students bring their portfolios. Some schools have a policy allowing them to admit students on the spot. While others, like Carnegie Mellon, require more from their applicants and have done away with the traditional portfolio. They look to the Scholastic Aptitude Tests and a traditional or nontraditional demonstration of visual sensitivities as primary indicators of the student's ability to meet design's challenges.

THE GRADUATE SCHOOLS

Graduate school is supposed to be the in-depth study of a particular subject. Some critics of graduate schools will tell you they are made up of career change students. In other words, a microbiologist with a Bachelor of Science degree decides to get his masters degree in design and switch careers. So he or she spends two years studying design and enters the profession with a Masters but with two years less education in design than someone entering with a Bachelor of Arts degree. "There are good programs that will accept career change students. They simply add a year on to the program for the student to catch up," said Sharon Poggenpohl. "But I have my doubts as to whether those students will make the transition to designer successfully."

Pratt graduate students are sought after by head hunters and corporations. Don Ariev said, "I would estimate that less than ten percent of the students enrolled in my graduate program at Pratt are seeking an entirely new career. And even those few students who are, are making a career 'shift' rather than a radical change. Of the 160 students enrolled in Graduate Communications, off the top of my head, I know that we have a stage-set designer, interior designer and architect. All of our students are interested in incorporating their undergraduate design education and their work experience and thus raise their graphic design abilities to a 'master' level."

CONTINUING EDUCATION

Many established, accomplished practitioners find themselves taking continuing education programs, especially in computer graphics. Things are changing too rapidly to expect that "learning on the job" is good enough or fast enough. Design schools are doing a booming business in this area.

WHEN WE GROW UP WILL WE BE IN BUSINESS?

Besides the traditional typography, color and design courses that are part of a design curricula, it is high time educators looked at designers as potential business people. A good number of business schools have started to include design courses, as they relate to business needs, in their curricula but too few schools teach business in design.

"It's not that we don't care about business, we just have so much to cover that's more pressing at this time," Bob Swinehart responded when asked why business education is not mentioned in GDEA's materials. But if not now, when? Business means ethics, as well as marketing, business practice and planning.

Since design has for many years been linked with fine art perhaps one residual effect is the disdain for business. Yet no one can deny that most of design is linked to the business world in one way or another. A general understanding of business is of paramount importance. I teach Ethics and Business Practice at Pratt in the graduate department. I have many guest speakers, designers who are practitioners, perhaps twelve a semester, about three at a time. I find that, although there are many similar gut reactions to situations we discuss, there is very little common knowledge regarding ethics and business practice.

Business practice and ethics must be debated heavily before we can say there is a clear understanding. So this forum is very important to replicate in schools and design offices. And yet, in many businesses there is a great deal of common knowledge—lawyer to lawyer, architect to architect. This is another reason graphic designers are not yet considered professionals.

Professional organizations, like the AIGA and the American Center for Design can expose students to business through seminars, workshops, publications, and mentor or intern programs. In an age marked by rapid change, this can be a very good way for students to get real life experience.

The AIGA is considered the premier organization for graphic design in the United States and it is led by practitioners. In fact, until recently, it was run primarily by very famous practitioners. This frustrated many educators who felt unwelcome at the AIGA because their agendas and philosophies differed with those in power. Nevertheless, the AIGA has worked hard, over the years, to provide the community with information and guidance regarding education and is to be commended. And the communication barriers have eroded as the necessity to affect design education became more and more apparent. In fact, a National Endowment for the Arts grant was received recently to prepare a 160-page education guide which will soon be available through the AIGA. This illustrated document is intended to show students, considering graphic design as a career, what design is all about.

Other efforts by the AIGA to connect with the education community include the election of Bob Swinehart to the national board. In addition, three Faculty Teaching Assistance Grants are being awarded to teachers "in recognition of innovative project proposals or courses that address significant creativity, and provide a resource for educators interested in effective learning." Gordon Salchow, who teaches at the University of Cincinnati, is on the national board as vice president of education. AIGA has been proactive in understanding why design is an overwhelming white middle-class field. The AIGA has also joined a minorities mentoring program through the High School of Art and Design in New York City.

In the area of business practice and ethics, the AIGA has also created a package of materials including a video of an eye-opening unrehearsed panel moderated by Fred W. Friendly of Columbia University. Included on the eighteen person panel were Milton Glaser, Joe Duffy, and Dan Friedman. Also available is a game called "Where Do You Draw the Line?" Both of these teaching tools were designed to help create a non-threatening forum for the group discussion of ethical and business practice issues. The game has a seventy-two page teacher's guide that accompanies it. The assumption in developing the video and game was that ethics and business practices are brand new areas of knowledge for the teacher as well as the student. In fact, there are almost no books on the subject for designers.

PREACHING TO THE UNCONVERTED

One hundred thousand is an estimate (no one knows for sure) of the number of people who consider themselves to be graphic designers in the United States today. Yet only 7,000 designers are members of the AIGA. There are almost 1,000 college level design programs and less than 150 educators in the GDEA. Education is in a state of chaos and the AIGA and GDEA must use creativity to get the ear of professionals, teachers, students, parents, and employers of graphic designers in order to correct its evolutionary course. Students, teachers, parents, and employers will start to demand more when they "get it." The institutions will be forced to respond or fold. A new standard will emerge.

Milton Glaser once noted that change occurs through the popularization of knowledge. As Glaser remarked, "The movie *Spellbound* showed the public something of what Freud was about. They didn't understand Freud in any depth from the movie, but they understood that there was something named Freud. Popularization frequently distorts the meaning of ideas, but in many cases it is the only way new ideas can enter the general culture."

Perhaps AIGA, GDEA, and the schools themselves have been preaching to the unconverted in a language they can't assimilate. Many in our audience are intimidated or simply bored with academic jargon, theories, and bureaucracy. Perhaps they all need to add a little entertainment value to the equation. Whatever they do, they must capture the imagination of the professional and academic worlds alike. This is what Bob Gill was saying back in 1985. Dust off those cobwebs; get relevant.

PROFESSION, HEAL THYSELF

We are communicators. This makes us the ideal people to solve this communication problem. Design practitioners need to become a part of the communication solution and think through all the literature produced by the AIGA/GDEA and the schools. In each situation, we might start by redefining the problem, as Gill would say, "by emphasizing that part of the problem which communicates something that is unique." What will emerge are solutions that truly captivate and communicate.

Originally published in Communication Arts *magazine, September/October 1992.*

BIOGRAPHIES

NICHOLAS BACKLUND writes about design for *I.D.* and other publications.

JONATHAN BARNBROOK is a designer and typographer, working from England.

MICHAEL BIERUT is a partner in the New York office of the international design consultancy Pentagram.

ANNE BURDICK is a graphic designer and contributor to *Emigre* and *Eye* magazines.

FRANCES BUTLER is a professor in the Department of Environmental Design at the University of California, Davis.

CHUCK BYRNE teaches design at San Jose State University, and is a contributing editor to *Print* magazine.

IVAN CHERMAYEFF is a partner of Chermayeff & Geismar Associates, New York.

RUDOLF DE HARAK has been a designer and photographer for over thirty-five years, and was professor of design at Cooper Union.

MICHAEL DOOLEY is the senior art director at the Los Angeles *Times*, and a contributor to *Print* and *Emigre* magazines.

WILLIAM DRENTTEL is a partner of Drenttel Doyle Partners, New York, and a publisher of poetry and fiction.

DAN FRIEDMAN is an artist whose subject is design and culture. He is the author of *Dan Friedman: Radical Modernism*.

MILTON GLASER is president of Milton Glaser, Inc., New York, and has taught design at The School of Visual Arts for thirty years.

ED GOLD (D. L. ODGE) is a professor at the University of Baltimore Publication Design Program, and author of *The Business of Graphic Design*.

STEVEN HELLER is the editor of the *AIGA Journal of Graphic Design* and author of over thirty books.

DK HOLLAND is a principal in The Holland Group, Inc., Design Issues Editor of *Communication Arts,* and Business Editor of the *AIGA Journal.*

KARRIE JACOBS is Critic-at-Large for *Metropolis,* and co-author of *Angry Graphics: Protest Posters of the Reagan Bush Era.*

TIBOR KALMAN is the founder of M&Co., New York, and Editor-In-Chief of *Colors* magazine.

JEFFERY KEEDY is acting director of the Program in Graphic Design at CalArts.

LEO LIONNI, a former art director, is the writer, designer, and illustrator of over thirty children's books.

ELLEN LUPTON is the Curator of Contemporary Design at the Cooper-Hewitt National Museum of Design.

KATHERINE MCCOY is co-chair of the design department at Cranbrook Academy of Art, Bloomfield Hills, Michigan.

JAMES MCMULLAN directs the High-Focus Drawing Program at The School of Visual Arts and is author of *Drawing From Life.*

PHILIP B. MEGGS teaches graphic design history at Virginia Commonwealth University and is author of *A History of Graphic Design.*

J. ABBOTT MILLER is the principal of Design Writing Research, New York and co-author of the *Bauhaus ABCs.*

MIKE MILLS is a graphic designer and contributor to the *AIGA Journal of Graphic Design* and *Eye* magazine.

SHARON HELMER POGGENPOHL teaches in the Institute of Design at the Illinois Institute of Technology and is editor of *Visible Language.*

RICK POYNOR is the founding editor of *Eye* magazine and the author of *The Graphic Edge* and *Typography Now: The Next Wave.*

PAUL RAND is a designer, painter, and author of *Paul Rand: A Designer's Art* and *Design, Form, and Chaos.*

JOHN RHEINFRANK III is Executive Vice President at Fitch Richardson Smith and director of its Exploratory Design Lab.

KEITH ROBERTSON lectures on Graphic Design Theory at Royal Melbourne Institute of Technology.

MICHAEL ROCK is an associate professor at the Yale School of Art, a contributing editor to *I.D.* magazine, and partner in Michael Rock/Susan Sellers in New York City.

GORDON SALCHOW is a professor of graphic design at the University of Cincinnati and a Vice President of the AIGA.

PAULA SCHER is a partner in the New York office of the international design consultancy Pentagram.

DUGALD STERMER is an illustrator and contributor to *Communication Arts* and the *AIGA Journal of Graphic Design*.

ANDREW SULLIVAN is the editor of *The New Republic*.

MARC TREIB is a professor of Architecture and Design at the University of California, Berkeley.

GERARD UNGER is a Professor of Typography at Reading University, Great Britain and has taught at Stanford University.

MASSIMO VIGNELLI is a principal of Vignelli Associates, New York.

KATE WELKER is a researcher and writer in Fitch Richardson Smith's Exploratory Design Lab.

LORRAINE WILD is on the faculty of the Program of Graphic Design at CalArts and a partner of ReVerb, Los Angeles.

DIETMAR WINKLER is a professor at the University of Massachusetts Dartmouth, and is on the editorial board of *Visible Language Journal*.

MARTHA WITTE is a designer at Allemann, Almquist & Jones, Philadelphia, and has taught design at Temple University.

INDEX

COLOPHON

LOOKING CLOSER: CRITICAL WRITINGS ON GRAPHIC DESIGN

Book design and cover by Michael Bierut, Pentagram Design

Typography by Esther Bridavsky, Pentagram Design
and Charlie Sharp, Sharp Designs

Set in Adobe Bembo

Design and typography done with Aldus PageMaker 5.0 software

Printed on 60 lb. Skyland Opaque Text Cream
and 12 pt. Kromekote C1 Side Covered Recycled stock
courtesy Champion International Corporation

Printed and bound at Capital City Press, Montpelier, Vermont

Graphic Design Books from Allworth Press

Electronic Design and Publishing: Business Practices, Second Edition
by Liane Sebastian

This book explains the rights and responsibilities of all the parties involved in the process of desktop publishing—including the client, designer, prepress house, and printer. This new edition contains the most recent changes and developments—including multimedia and interactivity. (176 pages, 6¾ × 10 inches, $19.95)

Graphic Designer's Basic Guide to the Macintosh
by Meyerowitz and Sanchez

For designers who contemplate the switch from traditional drawing techniques to computers. Easy-to-understand descriptions guide the reader through the electronic design process from concept to finished product. (144 pages, 8 × 10 inches, $19.95)

Careers by Design: A Headhunter's Secrets for Success and Survival in Graphic Design
by Roz Goldfarb

Written by the founder and president of a leading personnel agency, this book gives the inside secrets on how to build a successful career as a graphic designer. Former Pratt Institute President Warren Ilchman said, "… invaluable for the new student, the recent graduate and the established professional alike." (224 pages, 6¾ × 10 inches, $16.95)

Business and Legal Forms for Graphic Designers
by Tad Crawford and Eva Doman Bruck

Thirty-three business and legal forms, including sample contracts, needed to run a successful graphic design business. The book includes careful explanations and negotiation checklists. (208 pages, 8½ × 11 inches, $19.95) Computer disk in PageMaker for Mac or PC (forms only), $14.95

Licensing Art and Design
by Caryn R. Leland

A professional's guide for understanding and negotiating licenses and royalty agreements. Written in clear, everyday English. (112 pages, 6 × 9 inches, $12.95)

Legal Guide for the Visual Artist, Third Edition
by Tad Crawford

This acclaimed reference book about legal issues faced by visual artists has been completely revised for the first time since 1985. Written in an easy-to-understand style, it covers: copyrights, contracts (with collectors, galleries, agents, and publishers), taxation, estate planning, multimedia, and more. (256 pages, 8½ × 11 inches, $19.95)

Make It Legal
by Lee Wilson

A clear and precise guide to copyright, trademark and libel law, privacy and publicity rights, and false advertising law for graphic designers, advertising copywriters, art directors, commercial photographers, and illustrators. (272 pages, 6 × 9 inches, $18.95)

Please write to request our free catalog with a complete listing of our books. If you wish to order a book, send your check or money order to Allworth Press, 10 East 23rd Street, Suite 400, New York, NY 10010. To pay for shipping and handling, include $3.00 for the first book ordered and $1.00 for each additional book ($7 plus $2 if the order is from Canada). New York state residents must add sales tax.